AVIATION PROJECT MANAGEMENT

To Thalia, the bext project manager I know
Triant Flouris

Aviation Project Management

TRIANT FLOURIS
Daniel Webster College, USA

&

DENNIS LOCK

ASHGATE

Published by
Ashgate Publishing Limited
Gower House
Croft Road
Aldershot
Hampshire GU11 3HR
England

Ashgate Publishing Company
Suite 420
101 Cherry Street
Burlington, VT 05401-4405
USA

Ashgate website: http://www.ashgate.com

British Library Cataloguing in Publication Data
Flouris, Triant G.
   Aviation project management
   1. Airplanes – Design and construction 2. Airports – Design
   and construction 3. Aircraft industry – Management
   4. Airports – Management 5. Project management
   I. Title II. Lock, Dennis
   629.1'3'0068

   ISBN-13: 9780754673958

Library of Congress Cataloging-in-Publication
Flouris, Triant G.
   Aviation project management / by Triant Flouris and Dennis Lock.
       p. cm.
   Includes bibliographical references and index.
   ISBN-13: 978-0-7546-7395-8
   ISBN-10: 0-7546-7395-2
   1. Airplanes--Design and construction. 2. Airports--Design and construction. 3. Project
management. 4. Aircraft industry--Management. 5. Airports--Management. 6. Strategic planning.
I. Lock, Dennis. II. Title.

   TL724.F585 2008
   387.7068'4--dc22

                                                                          2008011371

Mixed Sources
Product group from well-managed
forests and other controlled sources
www.fsc.org Cert no. SGS-COC-2482
© 1996 Forest Stewardship Council
FSC

Printed and bound in Great Britain by
TJ International Ltd, Padstow, Cornwall.

Contents

List of Figures

Acknowledgements

Arlington Aguebor and Angela Wearing, both of York College, City University of New York.

Concordia University, Global Aviation MBA graduating class of 2008: Arturo Alvarado, Salvador Barrios, Razi Basbous, Andrey Chapochinikov, Virendra Chhikara, Sandra Estima, Marc Gervais, Bruce Liu, Tracy Medve, Jane Pan, Cesar Romero.

Simon Burtenshaw-Gunn.

John Cornish.

Alan Fowler.

Gower Publishing (for copyright permissions).

Isochron Limited.

Guy Loft and the production team at Ashgate Publishing.

Robert Milton.

Lisa Su and Paul O'Neil.

Foreword

After more than two decades in the airline industry about the only thing I am prepared to state categorically about management in this business is that no one could ever write a playbook that would cover every eventuality. In my own time at Air Canada, I found myself dealing with such diverse situations as Severe Acute Respiratory Syndrome, terrorist and media attacks, and the challenge of re-engineering a major corporation while balancing the interests of shareholders, employees, governments and the general public. Each of these challenges had to be confronted head-on, while at the same time there was the day-to-day requirement of running one of the world's great airlines.

Even at the best of times, ours is a business with narrow margins that leaves little room for error. Add to this the current high and unpredictable fuel prices and competitive pressures of global liberalization, and the importance of successful project management is evident. We have to provide an efficient, financially-sustainable and superior product in which delays and fuel consumption are minimized, environmental friendliness is maximized and, most importantly of all, safety and security are optimized.

While no one can anticipate every situation, prudent management demands that business people develop adaptable skills that will equip them to deal with any scenario that might come along. One of those core skills is the ability to effectively manage projects. Project management plays a vital role in ensuring that organizations use their resources most effectively whenever they embark on any kind of project, whether that is to expand existing facilities, introduce new products or services or even manage an unexpected event. Too many projects in our industry (often with a high public profile) have failed, and unfortunately will continue to fail, because their project management has been lacking.

Aviation projects are characterized by high capital costs and often also by the organizational complexities that arise whenever different groups or companies come together to combine their resources and skills in implementing a project. Modern project management practice came of age in the last half of the 20th Century and methods for planning, budgeting and controlling projects are well established. When correctly selected and used together these techniques comprise a methodology that can ensure a successful project outcome.

Clearly there is a need for more and better aviation project management training and education. This important new book will help to redress that deficiency with its clearly explained and well-illustrated account of the essential elements of the project management process, particularly as it applies to aviation projects.

Robert A. Milton
Chairman, President and CEO of ACE Aviation Holdings Inc.

Reviews for
Aviation Project Management

'Triant Flouris and Dennis Lock have made an important contribution to the literature with their new book, Aviation Project Management. The planners, designers and builders of many airport and other infrastructure megaprojects around the world would have benefitted enormously had it been available earlier, and billions of dollars of delays and cost overruns likely would have been avoided. The book will also be of interest to airframe and engine manufacturers, and airline executives, as well as students of aviation business and management, for it offers perceptive insights into strategic and tactical planning and decision making.'

Paul Stephen Dempsey, McGill University, Canada

'The challenge in the aviation business has always been to continually reinvent itself to meet competitive challenges. In order to do that, it takes change which must be managed at the project level. Aviation Project Management provides a cogent approach and definitive tools for the practitioner in aviation, providing the "how to", but most importantly, the "why" of change." It is a must read for every leader in aviation.'

Captain Dave Bushy, Chief Operating Officer of Cape Air/Nantucket Airlines and Former President of Aviation Accreditation Board International

'Triant Flouris and Dennis Lock offer sound advice for all project decision-makers; "Don't fly by the seat of your pants". Their book leads the reader through the essentials of sound project management, with plenty of emphasis on the wide variety of project types in the aviation industry. The differing worlds of equipment manufacturers, airports, airlines and infrastructure providers are all examined through examples and case studies. The authors do much more than merely address the basics of the subject. They particularly emphasise, for example, the importance of the risk assessment, cost management, the all-important human element and what they term the "greedy function" of purchasing. The book demystifies project management in a revealing manner and will undoubtedly come to be regarded as a standard, and highly accessible, work on the subject.'

Paul Clark, Director—IATA Training and Development Institute

'Aviation Project Management, which covers every aspect of project management from major stages of initiation, planning or development, production or execution, maintenance and controlling, and closing, will have enormous impact on adding value and bringing about beneficial change to airport capital plans by helping project managers achieve each project's goals and objectives while also confronting the many constraints on their attainment.'

Bill DeCota, Port Authority of New York and New Jersey, USA

Preface

The 'aviation industry' is really a collective term for a number of different industries, each of which has its own distinct qualities and management needs.

First there are the companies that design and make all kinds of aircraft, ranging from the smallest private planes to large wide-bodied passenger airliners. Projects and project management are essential to these companies, some of whom invest billions of dollars which they do not expect to recover for perhaps as long as 20 years.

Then there are the companies that operate the aircraft. These are the carriers of passengers and air cargo. They are a service industry. Service industries are not usually considered as a home for projects, but airlines and other companies that partake in the industry (such as corporate aviation) often have to invest in projects. When, for example, an airline sets out to rebrand a service or introduce a new passenger route, they would be unwise not to treat that venture as a project and manage it accordingly.

A third branch of the aviation industry is formed by the many airports and other aviation service providers (such as air navigation services, aviation product suppliers, and so on). Airports, for example, are a service industry without which the airlines could not operate, no large planes could fly, and no aircraft manufacturer would find a market. Airports, too, involve projects. Creating a new international airport requires all the project skills of civil engineering and construction companies as well as the high technology of the many companies that provide the avionics, air traffic control, and other systems necessary for the safe handling of both air and road traffic.

If we mention military aviation, another whole world of projects opens up. So the aviation industry is really a collection of associated industries, including both manufacturers and service providers, all of whom need project management if they are to become established and continue to operate efficiently and profitably.

Thus any of the many students who have chosen to study aviation must receive some grounding in project management because we contend that project management is a fundamental skill that leads to efficiency and competitive advantage.

There is much literature available and several new project management book titles emerge every week. However, very few of these deal specifically with aviation projects. We therefore perceived a need for an aviation project management text that would be of special benefit to students who are reading for a degree in aviation engineering or in one of the aviation service industries.

We decided to adopt the approach that aviation project management is a branch of project management that uses all the core project management techniques, but where the manager needs to understand the special nature of aviation and its projects. That led us to base this book on a well-established theoretical base to explain the traditional project management methodology, and then adapt and expand that so that we address more specifically the aviation industry.

Triant Flouris   and   Dennis Lock
Nashua, NH, USA   St Albans, UK

1

Introduction to Aviation Project Management

All projects share one common characteristic—the projection of ideas and activities into new endeavors. The ever-present element of risk and uncertainty means that the events and tasks leading to completion can never be accurately foretold. Examples abound of projects that have exceeded their costs by enormous amounts, finishing late or even being abandoned before completion. Such failures are far too common, seen in all kinds of projects in industry, commerce, and the public sector. The aviation industry (both at its core and throughout all its constituent industries) is by no means exempt. The consequences of such project failures can extend well beyond time and cost excesses, and can lead to expensive litigation, contractual penalties, and cancelled orders.

The purpose of project management is to predict, plan, organize, and control activities and resources so that projects are completed successfully in spite of all the difficulties and risks. This process should start before any resource is committed, and must continue until all work is finished. The primary aim of the project manager is for the result to satisfy the project sponsor or purchaser and all the other principal stakeholders, within the promised timescale and without using more money and other resources than those that were originally set aside or budgeted.

DIFFERENT TYPES OF PROJECTS

The principal characteristic of a project is its novelty. It is a step into the unknown, fraught with risk and uncertainty. No two projects are ever exactly alike: even a repeated project will differ from its predecessor in one or more commercial, administrative, or physical aspects. However, we find it convenient to identify four different types of projects.

Type 1 Projects: Civil Engineering And Construction

Projects in this category spring to mind whenever industrial projects are mentioned. One common feature is that work must be conducted on a site that is exposed to the elements, and usually remote from the contractor's head office. These projects are thus open to public gaze. They incur special risks and problems of organization. They may require massive capital investment, and they deserve rigorous management of progress, finance, and quality. Operations are often hazardous so that health and safety aspects demand special attention, particularly in work such as heavy construction, tunneling, and mining.

For very large industrial projects the funding and resources needed can be too great for one contractor to risk or even find. The organization and communications are therefore likely to be complicated by the participation of many different specialists and contractors, possibly with the main players acting together through a consortium or joint venture company established specifically for the project.

Type 2 Projects: Manufacturing

Manufacturing projects result in a piece of mechanical or electronic equipment, a machine, ship, aircraft, land vehicle, or some other product or item of specially designed hardware. The finished product might be purpose-built for a single customer but internal research and development projects for products to be sold in all market sectors also fall into this manufacturing category. Manufacturing projects are usually conducted in a laboratory, factory, shipyard, hangar, or other home-based environment, where the company should be able to exercise on-the-spot management and provide an optimum environment in which to do and manage the work.

Of course, these ideal conditions do not always apply. Some manufacturing projects involve work away from the home base, for example in installing and commissioning a machine or equipment on a customer's premises, flight testing an aircraft in different climates, customer training, and post-project service and maintenance.

International manufacturing projects are prone to higher risk and difficulties in control and coordination arising through organizational complexity, national rivalries, contracts, long-distance communications, multiple languages, and conflicting technical standards. Particularly difficult is the case of a complex product that is developed and manufactured by a number of collaborating organizations, sometimes with members based in different countries. An example is aircraft production, where the engines might be developed and manufactured in one country, the wings in another, and the final assembly taking place in a third country. The Airbus A380 project was a case in point, running 2 years late and well over budget. A contributory cause for the A380 problems was software incompatibility between different companies, so that when different sections of the aircraft were brought together for final assembly the wiring did not match and had to be reworked at great cost.

Type 3 Projects: IT Projects And Projects Associated With Management Change

This class of project proves the point that every company, whatever its size, can expect to need project management expertise at least once in its lifetime. These are the projects that arise when companies relocate their headquarters, develop and introduce a new computer system, launch a marketing campaign, prepare for a trade exhibition, produce a feasibility or other study report, restructure the organization, mount a stage show, or generally engage in any operation that involves the management and coordination of activities to produce an end result that is not identifiable principally as an item of hardware or construction.

Although management projects do not usually result in a visible, tangible creation such as a piece of hardware, much often depends on their successful outcome and they can require enormous investment. There are several well-known cases where, for instance, failure to implement a new computer system correctly has caused serious operational breakdown, exposing the managers responsible to public discredit. There have been several serious well-reported IT failures in air traffic control and air communications systems. Effective project management is clearly at least as important for these projects as it is for the largest aircraft design project.

Type 3 projects may be associated with, or even depend upon, Type 1 or Type 2 projects. For example, if a company decides to relocate to a new purpose-built office, the overall relocation project is itself a Type 3 management project but its success will depend also on the Type 1 project needed to construct the new building. Thus projects of different types may be associated with each other in a company's project programme or project portfolio.

Type 4 Projects: Projects For Pure Scientific Research

Pure scientific research projects (not to be confused with research and development projects) are a special case. They occasionally result in dramatically profitable discoveries. Conversely, they can consume vast amounts of money over many years, yet yield no practical or economic result.

These projects might be carried out for a company for its own eventual exploitation (such as the constant search for new drugs). However, successful pure research often has spin-offs in industries quite alien to those that sponsored the research. For example, the discovery of new materials with a high strength to weight ratio might originally have been sponsored by an automotive company, but the materials could be invaluable in new airframe design.

Research projects carry the highest risk because they attempt to extend the boundaries of human knowledge. The project objectives are usually difficult or impossible to define and there may be no awareness of the possible outcome. Therefore, pure research projects are not usually amenable to the project management methods that can be applied to industrial, manufacturing, or management projects.

Some form of control over pure research projects must, however, be attempted. Money and other resources cannot be spent without any form of monitoring or restraint. Budgets have to be set in line with available funding. A sensible method for controlling a pure scientific research project is to conduct regular management reviews and reassessments of the potential value of the project. At each review, a decision can be taken to stop the project (known colloquially as 'pulling the plug') or release new funding to allow it to continue at least until the next review. Although this can be unsettling for the scientists involved, the project sponsor is not expected to pour money forever into a vast hole. This procedure, where continued project funding is dependent upon regular reviews, is known as stage-gate control.

Although the research activities might themselves lie outside the scope of familiar project management methods, the provision of accommodation, communications, equipment, and research materials can constitute Type 1, 2, or 3 capital investment projects to which proper project management can and must be applied.

Project Types Within The Aviation Industry

Any one or any mix of the four above-named project types might be found within an aviation project. For example, a project to build a new runway, terminal building, or even an entire airport is primarily a Type 1 (construction) project, But that project will undoubtedly be associated with Type 2 (manufacturing) and Type 3 (IT and management change projects). The navigational system case example described at the end of this chapter is primarily a management change and IT project (Type 3) but it also has an important manufacturing element at the works of the principal equipment supplier.

PROJECT LIFE CYCLES AND LIFE HISTORIES

Most authorities and writers, when they talk about the life cycle of a project, refer to the period that begins with the authorization of work on the project (or signing of a customer-contractor contract) and ends with the handover of the desired product or service to the customer. Although that view can be too simplistic, it is the part of projects that is of most concern to project managers (and which is covered in this book). Figure 1.1 shows that the activities which take place during this period form a true cycle, because they begin and end with the customer.

Travelling clockwise round the cycle reveals a number of steps or *phases*. In practice, these phases often overlap each other, so that the boundaries between them are blurred. For example, some project purchasing and fulfilment work can usually start well before the design phase is complete.

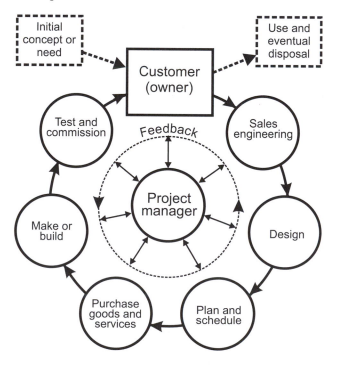

Figure 1.1   **The active part of a project life cycle**

The view of a project life cycle shown in Figure 1.1 is too simplistic for most projects because it ignores everything that happens before the start of actual work and takes no account of what happens to the project after its delivery to the customer. For a more complete picture we have to consider not only the project life cycle as seen by the project manager, but also the entire life history of the project from its initial conception to final death and disposal. Figure 1.2 shows this more complete view of a project life history.

Many writers limit their account of the project life cycle or life history to phases 6 to 13, because these are the phases that usually come under the control of the project manager. They constitute the most active period of the project life history (sometimes called the fulfilment period). This period corresponds in most respects to the life cycle in Figure 1.1. The chapters in this book are arranged as far as possible in this life cycle sequence.

FACTORS FOR ASSESSING PROJECT SUCCESS OR FAILURE

The success of the contractor and the project manager will usually be judged according to how well they achieve the three primary objectives, which are:

1. project completion within the cost budget;
2. the project delivered or handed over to the customer on time;
3. good performance, which requires that all aspects of the project are finished in accordance with the project specification.

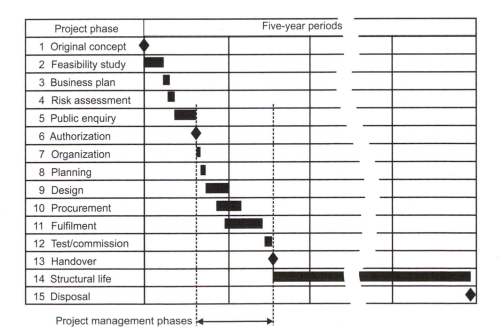

Figure 1.2   The project life cycle (life history) of a larger project

Factors necessary for achieving these three objectives include the following:

- good project definition and a sound business case;
- appropriate choice of project strategy;
- strong support for the project and its manager from higher management;
- availability of sufficient funds and other resources;
- firm control of changes to the authorized project;
- technical competence;
- a sound quality culture throughout the organization;
- a suitable organization structure;
- appropriate regard for the health and safety of everyone connected with the project;
- good project communications;
- well motivated staff;
- quick and fair resolution of conflict.

These issues are all important for good project management.

RELATIONSHIP BETWEEN THE THREE PRIMARY OBJECTIVES

It is occasionally necessary to identify one of the three primary objectives as being of special importance. This emphasis can affect the priority given to the allocation of scarce resources and the way in which management attention is concentrated. It can also influence the choice of project organization structure (discussed in Chapter 5).

A management decision to place greater emphasis on achieving one or two of these objectives must sometimes be made at the expense of the remaining objectives. The outcome of such a trade-off decision can be indicated by placing a spot or blob within a triangle which has one primary objective placed at each of its corners (shown in Figure 1.3).

For example, if cost is the greatest consideration, the blob will be placed in the cost corner of the triangle. Completing the project within budget or even at the lowest possible cost will become the main focus of management attention. A project for a charitable organization with limited funds would have to be controlled very much with budgets in mind, so that costs must be the project manager's chief concern. Cost is usually a very important factor in aviation projects and the aviation industry is well-known for working with 'razor-thin' profit margins.

If all the objectives are regarded as equal (balanced), the blob will be put in the middle of the triangle.

In our opinion, this balanced approach could work even in the case of low-cost carrier (LCC) airlines with limited funds, provided that the strategic objectives are pursued through financial optimization.

Industries such as nuclear power generation, aerospace, and aviation have to place such high emphasis on safety and reliability that performance to specification should be the overriding objective.

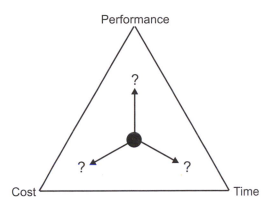

Figure 1.3   The triangle of objectives

Strict contractual terms can place a high emphasis on the time objective. A project to put on any event that has been announced to the public or to VIPs must deliver its promised performance at the appointed time. For example, an air show or flight demonstration (perhaps at a public display) is so dependent on meeting its pre-announced time and date that the time objective becomes extremely important. It might even be necessary to overspend on budgets to avoid missing the date.

The Quality/Cost Relationship

It is a mistake to believe that there can be a simple and acceptable trade-off between *quality* and cost. Those who promote total quality management argue, correctly, that quality can be achieved without extra cost. However, there is an even more fundamental reason why quality can not be downgraded or compromised to save money. This becomes clear when we accept the definition of quality as a service or product that is 'fit for the purpose for which it was intended'. No contractor or project manager should ever contemplate a result that is not 'fit for purpose'. Therefore downgrading quality is not an option. That is why 'performance' or 'level of specification' must be placed at the corner of the triangle of objectives instead of 'quality'.

This distinction between 'quality' and 'specification' is illustrated by the following example. Suppose that the initial estimates for a new flight training center building are too high and that construction costs must be reduced. One option might be to build on relatively simple foundations instead of using deep sunk piles, which could save thousands of dollars. But if the ground conditions demand piling for the building to be safe, that cost-saving option is ruled out on the grounds of reliability and safety. It would compromise quality and is not a viable option. The building would not be fit for its intended purpose.

However, suppose that the airline which has commissioned this training center building reviews the specification for interior finishes and finds that the proposed marble floor in the reception hall could be replaced with a carpeted floor at a substantial cost saving. The floor would still be serviceable and fit for purpose. Carpeting would, therefore, be an option that would not compromise quality. *Quality* has not been changed, but the *specification* has.

The Time/Cost Relationship

TIME IS MONEY!

(Benjamin Franklin, in *Advice to a Young Tradesman*, 1748).

There is usually a direct and very important relationship between time and money. If the planned timescale is exceeded, the original cost estimates are almost certain to be overspent. A project costs money during every day of its existence, working or non-working, weekday or weekend, from day one of the programme right through until the last payment has exchanged hands. These costs arise for a variety of reasons, some of which will now be explained.

The effect of project delays on direct costs The *variable* or *direct* costs of labor and materials are time-related in several ways. Cost inflation is one factor, so that a job started and finished later than planned might cost more that the original estimate because of price rises in materials and increases in wages, salaries, and other costs.

There are other less obvious causes where late working implies inefficient working, perhaps through lost time or waiting time (often the result of materials shortages, missing information, or poor planning, communications, and organization). If any project task takes longer to perform than its planned duration, it is probable that the budgeted labor-hours will be exceeded. This is true not only for a single task, but also for the project as a whole.

The effect of project delays on indirect (overhead) costs The *fixed* or *overhead* costs of management, administration, accommodation, services, and general facilities will be incurred day-by-day, every day, regardless of work done, until the project is finished. If the project runs late, these costs will have to be borne for a longer period than planned. They will then exceed their budget.

The effect of project delays on the costs of financing Another important time-related cost is financing. Where the contractor has an overdraft at the bank or relies on other loan financing, interest has to be paid on the loan. Even if the contractor finances the project from available funds, there is still a notional cost of financing, equivalent to the interest or dividends that the same funds could have earned had the contractor invested the money elsewhere (such as in a bank deposit account). If a project runs late, the financing period is extended, and the amount of interest or notional interest payable must increase correspondingly.

Much of the money for a large project is likely to be invested in work in progress as the project proceeds. This work in progress includes not only the tangible results of a project, such as construction or manufacture, but also intangible elements such as planning and engineering, or design. In many projects the contractor can only charge the customer for work that can be certified as finished. For example, in construction projects the amount of work completed usually has to be inspected and certified by an independent quality surveyor or engineer before it can be billed to the customer. The customer will not pay without the receipt of certified invoices to show that the work claimed has been done. Certified invoices are often linked to planned events or *milestones*. If a milestone has not been reached, a certified invoice cannot be issued. Payment of the contractor's revenue is then delayed, which means that the contractor must continue to finance the mounting costs of the project. The contractor could then suffer severe cash flow problems and even financial ruin.

Cost overruns in delayed aviation projects   It is clear from the above that if work can be managed so that it proceeds without disruption against a sensible, achievable plan, much of the battle to control costs will have been won. We decided to search the Internet for a recent case of an aircraft development project in which delays had caused significant overspending. Using the keywords 'aircraft', 'project', 'delay', and 'cost', Google produced 1 630 000 hits, leaving us somewhat spoilt for choice. However, Ian Stokes has compiled a well written and clearly argued account of misfortunes on the Airbus project, taking his information from a wide collection of sources (see http://www.management-projet. org/projet1/spip?article7). Stokes heads his article with the telling title 'Two Billion Euros of Hurt' and cites a 2-year delay in the €11 billion project as being partly responsible for a loss of €2 billion in profits.

Cost penalties   Some contracts contain a penalty clause which provides the customer with the sanction of a cost penalty against the contractor for each day or week by which the contractor fails to meet the contracted delivery obligation.

Aerospace manufacturing contracts fit into this category, especially with regard to new aircraft deliveries. If an aero manufacturer misses the scheduled delivery date of an aircraft to an airline client, a penalty is assessed that is commensurate with the length of the delay. The longer the client is kept waiting, the greater the penalty imposed on the manufacturer.

However, we need to be cautious when talking generally about contract penalties and premiums. For every rule there is an exception. Terms can vary considerably for individual contracts between different suppliers and clients. Further, the bargaining advantage between supplier and client can shift, depending on the prevailing market conditions or the so-called business cycle. For instance, the demand for new aircraft will fall if airlines defer fleet replacements owing to falling operating revenues.

PERCEPTIONS OF PROJECT SUCCESS OR FAILURE BEYOND THE THREE PRIMARY OBJECTIVES

Most project managers are expected to complete their projects so that they satisfy the three primary objectives of time, performance, and cost. These are usually the most important factors that drive the project contractor and they should align with the foremost expectations of the project owner. Most project management procedures (and this book) are directed towards achieving these goals, which could be summarized as delighting the customer while creating a commercial success for the contractor. In this context the contracting organization and the customer are both primary *stakeholders* in the project.

However, most projects have to satisfy more than two primary stakeholders. For example, a bank that has provided loan finance for a project will have a keen interest in whether the project succeeds or fails. There will always be people and organizations who, while not being principal stakeholders, nonetheless have an interest in how the outcome of a project might affect them. Subcontractors and suppliers are an example. Staff working on a project have a stake in the outcome because project success or failure can (apart from contributing to job satisfaction) have implications for their future employment and careers.

Identifying and ranking the stakeholders

Stakeholders are the people and organizations who affect, or will be affected by, the project. The principal stakeholders in most projects are as follows:

1. The customer or client.
2. The contractor that must perform all the project tasks, either directly or through suppliers and subcontractors.
3. The investor. For small projects the customer might be able to finance the project without external help but larger projects often need financing support from one or more banks, or from other sources such as shareholders.

In management projects and all other projects carried out internally within a company or group of companies, the company is the customer or client, and the internal department principally responsible for carrying out the work is effectively the contractor.

In some projects the initial customer purchases the project with the intention of selling it on to a third party. A common example is the property developer who commissions a new building from a contractor with the intention of selling it on (or leasing it) to occupiers. In that case the occupiers are sometimes known as the project end-users. Another example would be a customer that orders a batch of specially manufactured goods for selling on to retail customers. Those retail customers would also be end-users.

The range and nature of stakeholders will vary greatly from one project to another but the possible diversity and range of identifiable stakeholders can be illustrated by an example. Suppose that a project has been proposed to create a new international airport on a site that is mostly farming land but where there are one or two isolated dwellings. In addition to the airfield roads and runways, this involves hangars, maintenance sheds, markers, and beacons both within and outside the airport perimeter, the control tower with all its complex systems, a large terminal building, parking lots and approach roads, and many other installations.

The number of different stakeholder categories for this project would probably extend to hundreds. For example, there are the original landowners and residents who will be displaced and all the attorneys and realtors for whom they will create business. Several regulatory bodies, national and local, will take a keen or commanding interest at all stages of the project life cycle. When the airport becomes operational, end-users such as aircrews and passengers will appreciate the new airport. Those are all obvious stakeholders, but there will be many, many more.

Stakeholders can be categorized also according to the degree of interest that they have in the project (for example, through investment) or how their personal lives might be affected. Some stakeholders, although not directly working on the project, can have a considerable degree of influence through their statutory powers. Others can disrupt the project if, for instance, they belong to active pressure groups concerned with such things as greenhouse carbon emissions or wildlife conservation. Even one person who climbs a tree to prevent if from being felled can delay a project. Stakeholders can, therefore, be ranked according to their degree of interest or influence. The principal investors, statutory bodies, designers, and main contractors would all be in the first rank, and would be primary stakeholders. Below that rank there could be several more ranks until we reach the most junior employees and others who are on the fringes of the project.

We could use the remainder of this book to list and describe all these stakeholders and their interests and influences. So consider just one constituent (but important) part of this project, namely the terminal building. In the primary rank of its stakeholders we would find the project owner, the regulatory bodies responsible for enforcing building and fire regulations, the relevant civil aviation and/or airports authority, architects and designers, the main contractor, and the financial institutions and shareholders who provide the capital investment. Any one of these primary stakeholders could have a critical effect on this project.

The most important end-users, such as passengers and aircrews, are primary stakeholders, although they can have less influence on the success or failure of the initial construction project as measured by contractors' profits.

In the secondary rank for this terminal building, we would find all the subcontractors, suppliers of equipment and materials, aggressive local residents' associations, voluntary environmental agencies, and the law enforcement bodies such as police, customs, and immigration. And, what about other airports whose traffic might be reduced or increased when the new airport comes into operation and the route patterns change?

Now we come to the hundreds of other stakeholders in the lower ranks who, although they might not be able to influence the project, will have considerable interest in its success or failure. Here we find the officers who work in law enforcement, security, and the emergency services, companies supplying the duty free shops and those who serve in the shops, the caterers and their staff, cleaning contractors, and all the other people who will maintain and operate the new terminal facility. Even the families of those destined to work in the new building will become stakeholders, because their lifestyles will depend on the earned income. Users of the surrounding roads, local residents, hospitals, and the municipal authority will all be affected in some way by the new project, whether or not they actually use it as air travelers. Road and rail public transport organizations must consider how the airport development will affect their passenger numbers: some of their existing services might need to be changed to suit the new travel patterns (and take advantage of the new business generated).

Thus the owner of a large project and the project manager often have to look well beyond the boundaries of the project itself to consider many stakeholders. Professor Francis T Hartman declares that a 'project is successful if all the stakeholders are happy' (Hartman, 2000). Although Hartman's ideal may not always be achievable, it is best project management practice to try to identify all the stakeholders early and satisfy their aspirations as far as possible.

BENEFITS REALIZATION

In most industrial and manufacturing projects the project owner should start to realize the expected benefits immediately or shortly after the project is successfully finished and handed over (Phase 13 in Figure 1.2). A chemical plant, once successfully commissioned, should be capable of producing saleable product. A successful new office building should provide a pleasant working environment that can immediately improve staff satisfaction (and thus productivity). However, business change and IT projects can be different because their most significant benefits tend to be realized much later in the project life history, during the first months (or even years) of the period shown as Phase 14 in Figure 1.2.

Consider, for example, a large-scale project that is intended to replace and standardize the customer service and invoicing systems of an international airline. The execution phase of the project is finished when the IT designers have developed, documented, and tested the software. If the IT was contracted out, the IT specialist contractor might have had a successful project outcome, with all three primary objectives of cost, performance, and time satisfied at the time of handover to the user company. However, there is much more to the success of a management change project than the technical excellence and performance of the IT. It is only when the new system is up, running, and accepted by the managers and staff as well as the paying passengers that the project owner can begin to regard the project as a success. Implementing new systems and procedures can be very difficult in any organization where the staff resist change, have understandable concerns about possible redundancies, come from a rich mix of different cultures, or resent having to cope with all the teething problems that significant changes create.

In recent years these difficulties have led to new ways of assessing and managing the benefits realization of management change and IT projects. It is now recognized that the benefits realization process should start during early project definition by establishing benchmarks that can be put in place in the business plan. These benchmarks have some similarity with the milestones set in the project execution plans of all projects, but for management change and IT projects there are two important differences:

1. The most important benchmarks often occur some time after initial handover and commissioning of the project from the contractor to the customer (remembering that the contractor and owner can be in the same company).
2. Each benchmark must be *directly* associated with a cash inflow, cost saving, or other real benefit that can be tracked to a favorable entry in the company's accounts or management reports.

Benefits realization is appreciated among the more enlightened management fraternity as the most important driver in a management change or IT project, so that the intended long-term benefits are kept in the minds of the project manager and the other project stakeholders.

There is no reason why some of these new and specialized benefits realization management processes should not be applied or adapted for use in industrial and management projects.

CASE EXAMPLE: A SATELLITE NAVIGATION PROJECT

We conclude this chapter with an example of a project that failed. We analyze the reasons for failure and then suggest how the sensible application of project management methods would have produced the outcome intended by the project owner. The project is entirely a product of our imagination, as are the names of all the organizations, companies, and people, but the case is typical of real life and there is nothing imaginary about the moral of the story.

Project Description

Verulam Air Inc. is a small but expanding company that provides services between destinations within its national borders and is also expanding into some overseas markets.

The company owns a mixed fleet of approximately 20 aircraft, which it augments from time to time by leasing. This successful company always encourages its staff to make suggestions for improvements in efficiency and safety. One person suggested that there would be several advantages if the navigational methods could be changed to a satellite-based electronic system that could reduce or eliminate dependence on paper charts.

Before this project was undertaken, all Verulam Air flight navigation depended on printed charts. These were proving expensive to update and maintain and there was also a danger that some outdated charts could remain in use. Thus it was decided to explore a satellite navigation system that was developed and marketed by Never-Lost Systems Inc. The business plan for this project showed that for an initial outlay of $50 000, electronic equipment could be fitted to every plane in the fleet. Initial investigation by the Verulam Air's vice president of operations indicated that the Never-Lost system had received approval from the Civil Aviation Authority (CAA) and was accurate within acceptable tolerances.

Project objectives and outlook   The project was expected to repay its cost in 2 years, through savings in the replacement of paper maps and fewer navigational errors. The objectives were to be achieved in two stages:

1.   To make a saving through reduced reliance on paper charts.
2.   When fully implemented and CAA approved, to eliminate paper charts altogether and rely entirely on the Never-Lost technology.

The Never-Lost navigation system had been well received by other operators and there was every reason to assume that it would perform well and reliably for Verulam Air. In short, this project appeared to have everything going for it.

Project organization   Verulam Air did not make any conscious effort to set up an organization for this project. The project was sponsored by Verulam Air's vice president of operations, and he added responsibility for monitoring all aspects of the project to his busy personal schedule. The organigram in Figure 1.4 is our depiction of the project relationships that developed by default, overlaid on the existing line organization of Verulam Air Inc.

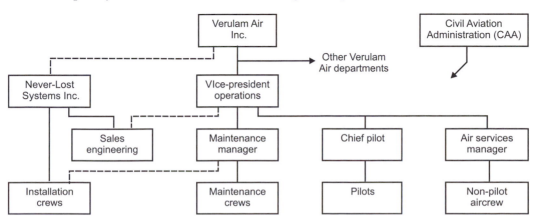

Figure 1.4   **Organigram of the failed Verulam Air satellite navigation project**

Planning and control   No special plans were drawn up for the progress of this project. However, there was an initial project meeting attended by all the senior managers of Verulam Air, at which target dates were agreed. No junior pilots were invited to this meeting. All those present entered the following dates in their diaries:

1. 5 January, 2009:   Discussion begins between Never-Lost Inc. and the vice president of operations.
2. 2 February, 2009:   A 'supply and install' contract to be signed with Never-Lost Inc.
3. 27 April, 2009:   The vice president of operations will announce the project by memorandum.
4. 6 May, 2009:   Equipment installation and pilot training begins.
5. 13 July, 2009:   All planes equipped.
6. 20 July, 2009:   Last group of pilots trained.
7. 20 July, 2009:   New navigation system put on trial, but with reliance still on paper charts.
8. 26 July, 2010:   CAA approval of paperless operation received.
9. 13 August, 2010:   All paper chart use now discontinued.

Project Results

The initial target dates were met, and the vice president of operations was able to issue a memorandum to all staff announcing the project, informing everyone that installation would start on 6 May, 2009. This came as a surprise to non-aircrew staff, but was more of a shock to the pilots group.

Many pilots resisted the change and failed to cooperate fully either with training or with the equipment trials. As a result, several small navigational errors resulted, along with apparent system malfunctions. No significant harm was done to flight paths because all pilots continued to rely principally on their familiar paper charts. What actually happened was that the pilots failed to achieve familiarity with the electronic system, so that mistakes in operating the equipment were largely the cause of the apparent malfunctions.

In an attempt to save the project, representatives from Never-Lost Inc., independent IT experts, a consulting group from the local university, and the chief pilot all became involved. Some causes, such as inadequate pilot training and software incompatibilities, were identified and attempts to go forward were made.

However, the pilots' principal reliance remained with the original paper charts. What little faith the pilots originally had in the project was lost and that became an impossible obstacle to overcome. In addition, in light of these events, the CAA (which had been monitoring every stage of the project) indicated that the originally planned 1-year approval period was no longer possible.

Failure to meet the original project objectives and zero pilots' faith in the electronics system was causing low morale and general discontent. This was threatening operational safety, and the project was abandoned in September 2009.

Analysis of Project Failure at Verulam Air

Other airlines had previously adopted the Never-Lost system successfully, with none of the difficulties described above. Further, although the original business plan and project definition were prepared without much thought and were not subjected to the amount of management appraisal that would usually be considered necessary, there was nothing intrinsically wrong with the project concept. Why, then, should Verulam Air have failed so badly in its attempt where other fleet owners had succeeded?

We have identified four major shortcomings that doomed this project from its beginning. These were:

1. inappropriate project organization;
2. inadequate planning using a flawed method;
3. no system of progress management;
4. disregard for people.

We end this case example by examining each of these four failings and by suggesting how the project should have been managed for success.

Project organization: how it should have been done   This project was not so much badly organized as not organized at all. No attempt was made by Verulam Air to set up an effective project management organization. The main responsibility for this failing lay fairly and squarely on the shoulders of the vice president of operations, who wrongly believed that he would have the personal time and mental capacity to manage this project single handed. That process is known generally, even outside the aviation industry, as trying to fly a project by the seat of the pants. There have been one or two remarkable military men and engineering geniuses in history who were capable of such feats and one or two might exist today, but they are very rare animals and they tend to die young from stress-related illnesses.

Project organizational structures will be discussed in some depth later (in Chapter 5) but we can make recommendations here for an organization structure that would have served this navigational project well. The principal players for this project can be identified as follows (not listed in order of seniority):

1. The vice president of operations: he was the first person at Verulam Air to recognize the value of the original staff suggestion. It was he who championed this project and attempted to drive it through to success. He was the senior manager who staked his own reputation on the success or failure of the project. He might be described as the project champion, or the project sponsor.
2. The project manager: a person not present in the actual project organization, but who should have been appointed. This man or woman should have the time and skills needed to concentrate entirely on the project and act as a focal point. Verulam Air was generally organized as a vertical line structure and one important function of any project manager is to give the organization structure the essential horizontal component that ensures good cross-departmental communication. The person appointed might not always have to perform this project management role full time, and could have been someone chosen from one of the operational departments of Verulam Air. Some initial training might have been needed in project management

methods. The project manager must be a person who can command the respect of both senior management and his or her peers.

3. A line pilot: chosen as a representative of all the pilots. He or she could have evaluated the Never-Lost system from the viewpoint of the end-users and acted as a channel for any of their misgivings.

4. A qualified IT representative: capable of finding the appropriate routes for solving technical problems.

5. A flight standards representative: who could confirm the positional accuracy of the navigational system.

6. The chief pilot of Verulam Air: one of whose important responsibilities would have been liaison with the CAA, though all stages of the project.

The organigram in Figure 1.5 outlines this organization. Reference to Chapter 5 will reveal that this organization structure is a coordinated matrix, which can often be ideal for a company that has a project overlaid upon its routine operations. Solid lines in the chart indicate lines of direct authority that drill down through the line management structures of both Verulam Air and Never-Lost. The dotted lines denote the vital paths of communication and liaison that were missing from the actual project.

A project manager is expected to plan the project in detail and ensure that all participants are aware at all times of their expected commitments. Although expected to chase up late performers, in a coordinated matrix the project manager apparently has no direct line authority. Thus in the solution that we propose for this particular project, the project manager would be expected to progress the work by persuasion rather than by command. However, although without line authority, the project manager would report directly to the vice president of operations, and so could call their wrath down upon any participant who refused unreasonably to conform to the project plan.

The end-user representative (number three in the above list) is located within the pilot group and is not shown separately in Figure 1.5.

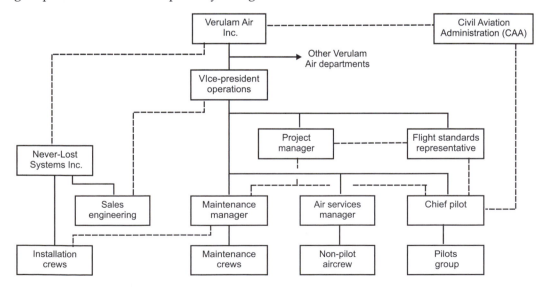

Figure 1.5   A more effective organization for the Verulam Air satellite navigation project

The air services manager and his group of non-pilot aircrew will not be directly affected by the new navigation system, and thus that department has no connection within the project matrix.

The position of the flight standards representative deserves mention, because that role has a quality management dimension. He or she must thus be allowed to work independently of any project management pressure, since quality must never be compromised by schedule urgency. However, this person must have well-defined communication links with the project organization.

The organization solution presented in Figure 1.5 is not the only possible one that could have been used successfully for this project. Chapter 5 examines other possible organization structures and discusses their relative advantages and disadvantages.

Planning method   In discussing planning, we pre-empt much that is to come in Chapter 7. The biggest failing in planning the Verulam Air navigational project was that insufficient consideration was given to identifying all the detailed tasks needed and the logical sequence in which they should be performed. What happened instead was that a few target dates were plucked out of the air at a meeting and entered in the diaries of those present. We call that inadequate method 'diary planning'. It works well for planning a small meeting but will always fail dismally when applied to any but the tiniest project.

Planning should have started by compiling a work breakdown structure (see Chapter 6). In the case of the relatively small Verulam air project, this could have been a simple task list such as that shown in Figure 1.6.

Task number and description	Estimated duration (weekdays)
1 Negotiate price and delivery with Never-Lost Inc.	25
2 Sign contract for supply and installation	1
3 Initial staff meeting to announce the project	1
4 Project authorization	1
5 Appoint the project manager	3
6 Inform the CAA	2
7 Establish the project organization	5
8 Never-Lost equipment lead time	20
9 Install system in first five aircraft during maintenance	5
10 Pilot training for the first trial group of pilots	1
11 Initial trials and debugging	40
12 First trial assessment and project review	5
13 Install system in all remaining aircraft	20
14 Train all pilots in small groups (as flying duties allow)	20
15 Full system trial	40
16 Second trial assessment and project review	5
17 Obtain CAA approval after extended trials	200
18 Abandon the use of paper charts	5

Figure 1.6   Task list for the Verulam Air satellite navigation project

Once most of the tasks have been identified they can be assembled in a chart showing their order of precedence and their timing. We generally prefer the critical path methods explained in Chapter 7, but a bar chart would have been effective for this project, especially if a software tool such as Microsoft Project had been used. We did indeed use Microsoft Project to plot Figure 1.7. That software will allow even someone with little or no previous experience of the critical path method to insert links between tasks to ensure that they are planned in a practical, logical sequence. Thus no task is shown as starting before its logical predecessors have been finished. We did specify those task links, but they have been omitted from the bar chart illustration for clarity. However, they are defined in the column headed 'predecessors', which, for every task, lists the immediately preceding tasks that must be finished before it can start.

Progress management   Once a plan has been made, the project manager has a tool that allows day-by-day monitoring of all the tasks that should be in progress to make sure that:

- tasks that should have started have in fact been started;
- tasks that are in progress are not running late when measured against the plan;
- when tasks are found to be running late, the causes of delay are investigated and measures are taken to put the tasks back in step with the plan;
- tasks that should be finished have in fact been finished.

The project manager must thus ensure that everyone works in accordance with the plan. However, that does demand that the details of the plan have been communicated to everyone involved. The project management job will be made much easier if everyone expected to perform project tasks was either directly involved in the initial planning, or at least was represented. Plans work best when all those expected to perform project tasks have agreed that the plan is feasible and have accepted personal commitment and responsibility to work to the plan.

We have said little so far about controlling the budget. Chapter 12 deals specifically with that subject but we can state two important generalizations here about how to control the costs of a project:

1. Bought-in materials, equipment, and services can account for as much as 80 per cent of the costs of some projects. Thus if all purchases are made using sensible procedures, recognizing that costs are committed when orders are placed and contracts are signed, much of the battle to control the budget will have been won. The purchasing process is described in Chapter 10.
2. Much is written and discussed about methods for controlling project costs, and particularly the costs of labor and subcontracts. However, remembering that a project which runs late is a project that will inevitably overrun its budget, the converse is true. If you can control progress and keep the project on plan, you will by default have done pretty well as much as you can to control the costs of labor and overheads.

Finally, we must recognize that plans will change and are dynamic. They may alter from day to day in the light of temporary problems and wrongly estimated job durations. They can also be modified as a result of changes to the project requirements (project changes are discussed in Chapter 11). A plan that is out of date is almost worse than no plan at all. Therefore the project manager must make sure that the project plan is always kept up to date.

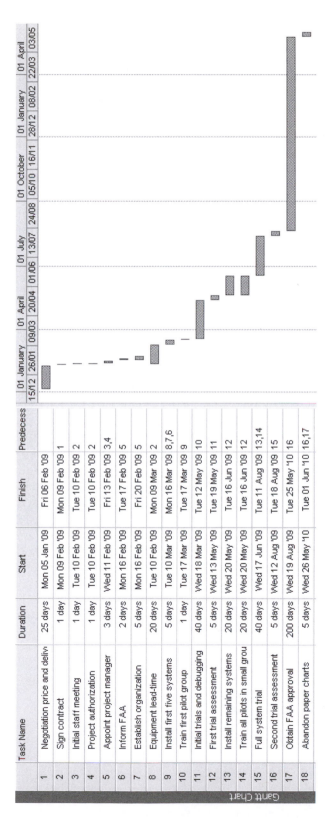

Figure 1.7   Bar chart plan for the Verulam Air navigation project (plotted by Microsoft Project)

People We have left the most important factor until last. No project can succeed unless all the people who work on the project are motivated towards achieving the project objectives. The Verulam Air project was principally a management change project. People in general do not like change. They prefer jobs and working practices that they can wear comfortably, like a pair of old carpet slippers. When they are told without warning that their jobs and working practices are about to undergo dramatic change, they will naturally be resentful and might resist the change, even to the extent of refusing to conform to the new regime.

The vice president of operations at Verulam Air made his first and biggest mistake when he failed to respect the feelings of all the people destined to work on his project. He simply issued a memorandum that announced the project and declared, in effect, 'this is what we are going to change and this is how you will be expected to work in the future'. This vice president was in fact a very pleasant individual who lived a contented life, had a lovely family, and gave regularly to charities. A pillar of the community, one might say, and a person who was generally liked and who commanded respect. But in simply announcing the introduction of the Never-Lost navigation system in an impersonal memorandum he unwittingly, unknowingly, but assuredly, displayed incredible arrogance.

What should have happened? As soon as the project proposal showed signs of becoming a viable project, the vice president of operations could have called a meeting of all the departmental managers and group heads to give them advance notice of the company's intentions.

One of the most important meetings of every project is its kick-off meeting, at which the project authorization is announced. This meeting describes the project and its advantages for the company. It sets the scene. It should certainly be attended by all relevant managers and supervisors and, if time and work pressures allow, all or most of the professional and other working people. Now is the time for the project sponsor to introduce the project, explain how it will improve the company's prosperity and thus benefit all its employees. The outline plan can be explained and the senior management can introduce the newly appointed project manager to everyone. This is the time to fire up enthusiasm and give people the incentive to face the coming changes. Everyone who leaves that meeting should be impatient to get started on their new project tasks.

When people are made to feel part of a new project or changed procedures, they will try to make them work. Even when a project has been badly planned and is poorly controlled, if all the people involved are motivated towards achieving success, they will strive for that success. They will even muddle through to finish a project that has been badly planned and organized. But the converse is true, as was proved at Verulam Air. No matter how good the planning and the project management systems, if you can't carry the people with you, the project cannot succeed and its benefits will never be realized.

REFERENCES

Hartman, F.T. (2000), *Don't Park Your Brain Outside*, Newtown Square, PA., Project Management Institute.

2

Defining the Project Task

Every aviation project should be defined as accurately and fully as possible before it is allowed to start, regardless of its type, size, complexity, or industrial setting. The investor must know how the money will be spent and what benefits can be expected in return. The contractor and others responsible for carrying out the project must know the extent of their commitments before any contract is agreed. Figure 2.1 illustrates that project definition is a continuous process which begins before a project can be authorized and ends only when the project has been completed and its final as-built state can be recorded.

PROJECTS WHICH ARE IMPOSSIBLE TO DEFINE ACCURATELY

Although this chapter is about defining projects, including aviation industry projects, it has to be admitted that some projects are so surrounded by uncertainty that they cannot be defined adequately before work starts. Such uncertainty is especially true in the context of a cyclical industry like aviation. Even when a costly research and development project has initially been successful, there might be no guarantee that the resulting product will sell, owing perhaps to a flawed business plan, to subsequent market changes, or legislative changes.

The world has been littered with defense, aerospace, and aircraft development projects that were cancelled, sometimes at a late design stage or even in some cases after an aircraft's successful test flights.

Among this category of high-risk projects are those where the investors are entrepreneurs in every sense of the word, funding their design engineers and manufacturers to develop their wares for markets that are either uncertain or which do not yet even exist. Very light jets (VLJs) are in this category at the time of writing (2008). The highly regarded Eclipse 500 from Eclipse Aviation is a low-cost, high-performance twin-engine plane in the VLJ range, but time will show how this will compete against its rivals and heavier aircraft. <http://en.wikipedia.org/wiki/Eclipse_500>.

Whether the VLJ concept proves to be a tremendous success (as some believe it will revolutionize air transportation in the air taxi and business segments) or evolves as one of the greatest disappointments ever in the aviation industry (due to the hype and economic infeasibility of large-scale air-taxi operations) the Eclipse was a 'first of its kind' concept. It paved the way for many more VLJs to be conceived and produced from established and other manufacturers such as Adam (A700 VLJ), Embraer (Phenom), and Cessna (Mustang). Eclipse, as a company and aircraft concept embodies the entrepreneurial spirit discussed above as it put forth the concept of a multifunctional VLJ first. Yet, it was the Cessna Mustang that delivered the first VLJ in November 2006.

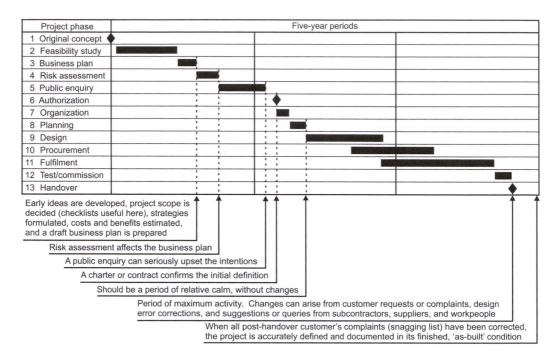

Figure 2.1   Definition of a large project from initial concept to completion

Another company embodying entrepreneurial spirit in a similar concept is Aerion Corporation. Aerion Corporation is home to the Aerion supersonic business jet (SBJ) concept. The target price is $80 million (in 2007 dollars), with development costs ranging from $1.2 to $1.4 billion. Entry into service is expected to be 2014 and if it is indeed produced it will allow non-stop travel from Europe to North America and back within one business day. <http://en.wikipedia.org/wiki/Aerion_SBJ>.

The practical testing outcome of the Aerion concept is further into the future than the VLJ subsonic concept, yet both are revolutionary concepts in their own right in the context of business and personal air transportation.

Limiting The Risk In Projects That Cannot Be Defined At Birth

If an investor still wishes to proceed with a new project that is surrounded by uncertainty, there are various safeguards that can limit the exposure to risk.

Stage-gating   Projects for pure scientific research are an extreme case of initial uncertainty. Chapter 1 mentioned how a step-by-step or 'stage-gating' approach can be used to authorize such projects, releasing resources in controlled amounts so that the risks can be kept within defined bounds. Each new tranche of investment depends on the satisfactory outcome of a periodical reassessment of the project. If the outlook is bleak, the plug can be pulled on the project and all further expenditure denied. It takes courage to abandon a project in mid-development, but that course is sometimes necessary to prevent sending good money after bad sunk costs.

Stage-gating is a valuable method for damage limitation of any project that cannot be defined with certainty in its early days. However, people working in a stage-gated project are unlikely to be well motivated because they work under the constant threat of sudden project closure. If the employer cannot guarantee equivalent alternative employment on other projects, some staff might decide to end the uncertainty by seeking safer employment elsewhere. The aerospace manufacturing industry, particularly in terms of aircraft development from concept to assembly, falls into this high-investment, high-risk category of projects—especially during times of economic cycle turns.

Avoidance of fixed-price contracts A commercial contractor whose role in a project has not been clearly defined can accept the order with some confidence if the payment arrangements, instead of being fixed price, guarantee reimbursement of all the contractor's costs plus reasonable fees or profit mark-ups. That should ensure that the customer or investor bears the financial risk. But even with the promise of full cost reimbursement, poor project definition can still be difficult for the contactor. It is always inconvenient to muster and commit resources to a project whose duration is unknown and which is liable to be cancelled at short notice. Again the complicated web of partners and contractors typical of aircraft development projects in the aerospace manufacturing industry fit this category.

Provisional cost items in fixed-price contracts Contractors are understandably reluctant to quote fixed prices for projects that cannot be well defined. But customers generally prefer to sign contracts against fixed-price quotations, so that they know their commitments and can set their investment budgets with confidence. Contractors (particularly for construction projects) deal with this difficulty by identifying and listing separately all parts of the project that cannot adequately be defined and which are beyond the contractor's control. Those features are often listed separately in the contractor's tender, outside the scope of work covered by the quoted fixed price, and they are known as provisional cost items (or pc sums).

Consider, for instance, a project to refurbish an old maintenance hangar or aircraft spare parts warehouse where part of the structure is hidden from view and is in uncertain condition. The fixed-price proposal might be conditional upon no structural defects being found when work starts. The contractor would then list a provisional cost item in the proposal, estimating the extra costs to be charged to the customer should additional work be necessary when work begins and structural decay or damage is revealed.

Feasibility studies to improve early project definition The investor or organization faced with a very uncertain outlook for a large project might start by commissioning a feasibility study from a consultant or consulting company, or even (where the capability exists) from within the organization itself to obtain more facts and expert advice. This approach is frequently used to examine and appraise the technical, logistical, environmental, commercial, and financial aspects of all kinds of projects that require a high level of investment. Banks and other institutions asked to finance or guarantee ill-defined projects may require a satisfactory feasibility study report before committing funds. Government departments often demand or commission feasibility study reports for projects which are of significant public or international importance. The Federal Aviation Administration engaged in this process with projects such as Next Gen (Next Generation Air Transport System).

A feasibility study for a big capital project can take years to prepare and cost large sums of money. Aviation is no exception in this respect. For example, a government wishing to develop new defense systems, or to replace its ageing fighter, bomber, or military transport fleet, will carry out studies involving not only technical experts and competing manufacturers, but also representatives of the relevant government defense departments and military chiefs.

Whatever the project, a good feasibility study report can do much to point a project in the right direction, recommend the most effective strategy, and define the risks and achievable objectives.

CHECKLISTS

Checklists are a good way of ensuring that no important task or cost item is forgotten whether a new project is being evaluated or a routine operation is taking place. Contractors who have amassed a great deal of experience in their particular field of project operation will learn the questions that must be asked to fill most of the information gaps and they can develop comprehensive checklists for use in future project cost estimates and proposals.

Checklist Examples

Routine sales One very simple application of a project definition checklist is seen when a sales engineer takes a customer's order for equipment that is standard, but which can be ordered with a range of options. The sales engineer might use a standard pro-forma (either on a pad or a computer screen), entering data in boxes and ticking off the options that the customer requires. People selling replacement windows use such methods. So do salesmen in automobile showrooms. Standard forms are convenient and help to ensure that no important detail is forgotten when the order is taken and passed back to the factory or warehouse for action. In this category are companies that sell aviation spare parts to airlines or to maintenance and repair organizations (MROs)—anything from aircraft windows to landing gear tires.

Construction projects Airports, as well other companies about to tender for large projects can make good use of checklists. One such list might be concerned with ensuring that all aspects of the building and performance of a new environmental management system are considered. Another case would be to ensure that the accommodation space and standards in a new terminal building can be properly specified. Local climatic and geological data at an intended airport construction site may have to be defined.

The designer or contractor of a construction project may not be aware of hazards such as high winds, earth tremors, or flooding. It is also necessary to check whether or not any special statutory regulations apply in the region, particularly in unfamiliar territory overseas. Other data might cover national working practices and the influence of local trade unions, the availability of suitable local labor, facilities to be provided for the contractor's expatriate staff, and so on. Many questions should be asked and answered. Checklists are ideal in these circumstances. The example in Figure 2.2 includes items that might feature in a checklist for a project that involves all the civil engineering and construction tasks in building a new airport at a foreign site.

Project site and other local conditions

Availability of utilities
- Electrical power
- Drinking water
- Other water
- Sewerage
- Other services

Transport
- Existing roads: Access difficulties (low bridges, weight limits, etc.)
- Nearest railpoint
- Nearest suitable seaport
- Nearest existing commercial airport
- Local airstrip
- Local transport and insurance arrangements

Physical conditions
- Seismic situation
- Temperature range
- Rainfall or other precipitation
- Humidity
- Wind force and direction
- Dust
- Barometric pressure
- Site plans and survey
- Soil investigation and foundation requirements

Local workshop and manufacturing facilities
Local sources of bulk materials
Local plant hire
Site safety and security
Local human resources available
- Professional
- Skilled
- Unskilled

Site accommodation arrangements for:
- Offices
- Secure stores

Site living accommodation for:
- Expatriate managers and engineers
- Workers
- Short stay visitors
- Married quarters (see separate checklist if these are required)

Figure 2.2   Part of a definition checklist for a new airport project

Aviation projects   Many aviation projects involve construction works, where much of the previous section will apply. Developers of new aircraft will of course need many checklists, not least of which is the one concerned with conditions that exist at airports where the new aircraft will be expected to ply their trade. For example, what local low-noise regulations must be satisfied, and will there be any short runways that could prevent access or limit maximum payloads?

Airline ground and aircrew are particularly familiar with checklists because pre-flight checks, in-flight checks, and post-flight checks must be performed before every take-off, during cruise, before and after each landing to ensure that there are no snags which might threaten the safe outcome of the flight. Similarly it is prudent for all project owners to use

Other site facilities
- First aid, medical, and hospital facilities
- Catering and messing arrangements
- Hotels or other accommodation for VIPs
- Local banking arrangements

Communications
- General mail and airmail service
- Special mail or courier service
- Telephone over public network
- Telephone over dedicated terrestial or satellite link
- Fax
- E-mail
- Other

Contractual and commercial conditions

How firm are the proposals?
What are the client's relative priorities for:
- Time?
- Cost?
- Quality?

What are the client's delivery requirements?
Do we know the client's budget levels?
Scope of work envisaged:
- Basic design only?
- Fully detailed design?
- Procurement responsibility: (ourselves, the client, or someone else?)
- Construction responsibility: (ourselves, the client, or a contractor?)
- Commissioning, training, operating, and maintenance manuals, etc.

How accurate are the existing cost estimates:
- Ball park?
- Comparative?
- Have all estimates been checked against the estimating manual checklists?

How is the project to be financed?
Is there to be a financial guarantor?
What do we know about the client's financial status and payment record?
Are contract penalty clauses expected?
Is the pricing to be firm or other?
What are the likely arrangements for stage or progress payments?
What retention payment will be imposed?
What insurances must we arrange?
What guarantees or warranties will the client expect?

Figure 2.2 *Concluded*

a checklist before allowing any project to take off, so that no hidden snags or forgotten tasks will prevent its safe passage to a successful finish.

Management change and IT projects   Internal management change projects can consume prodigious amounts of time, money, and other resources but cause considerable harm within and sometimes outside the organization if they fail. Inadequate project definition can be the root cause of such disasters and, here again, checklists are invaluable.

There is often a difficulty in compiling checklists for management change projects when compared with other projects. Organizations that embark on very large internal change projects will probably do so very infrequently, perhaps only once in 10 years or longer. Companies conducting multiple, repetitive industrial, aviation, or commercial projects can learn from their past experience (and mistakes). On the other hand, companies intending to make big changes to their internal organization procedures and IT do not have the experience of past projects that is essential for compiling checklists. Consultancy companies build up experience over time from their work with many different clients and are thus often able to give advice and help to define this kind of project. A checklist compiled by one UK consulting company (Isochron Limited) is shown in Figure 2.3.

010000	**Business analysis**	
010100	Business redesign	
010101	Major process procedures design	
010102	IS procedures design	
010103	Data model design (logical)	
010104	Report and management information design	
010105	Develop procedures documentation	
010200	Current state assessment	
010201	Information systems review	
010202	Use organization assessment	
010203	Process assessment	
010204	Reporting and MI assessment	
020000	**Business change**	
020100	Business user training	
020101	Identify communities to be trained	
020102	Conduct training needs analysis	
020103	Develop training plan	
020104	Develop training course material	
020105	Schedule training events	
020106	Administer training events	
020107	Deliver training courses	
020108	Monitor training feedback	
020200	Communications	
020201	Identify communication audiences	
020202	Develop communication strategy	
020203	Select communication media	
020204	Develop communication plan	
020205	Implement communication plan	
020206	Assess audience understanding of key message	
020207	Update communication plan	
020300	Project contract development	
020301	Identify objectives	
020302	Identify event milestones	
020303	Identify business values	
020304	Match flashpoints to value drivers	
020305	Quantify values	
020306	Determine project cost	
020307	Balance value against cost	
020308	Develop project contract	
020309	Obtain approval	

Figure 2.3   Initial task checklist for a management change project

020400	**Stakeholder management**
020401	Develop stakeholder management plan
020402	Implement stakeholder management plan
020403	Stakeholder analysis
020404	Develop stakeholder role transformation plan
020405	Implement stakeholder role transformation plan
020406	Manage stakeholder issues
020407	Integrate stakeholder mngmnt and communication plans
030000	**Project running costs**
030100	Facilities
030101	Accommodation charges
030102	IT charges
030103	Room hire
030104	Food and refreshments
030105	Printing and stationery
030200	Overhead allocations
030201	Other contributions to central funds
030300	Project administration
030301	Project accounting
030302	Resource management
030303	Project facilities management
030304	General administration
030400	Project management
030401	Project structuring
030402	Project planning
030403	Project control
030404	Project monitoring
030405	Issue management
030406	Change management
030407	Project reporting
030408	Travel
030409	Hotel
030410	Subsistence
040000	**Technology solution**
040100	Applications support
040101	Design support model
040102	User environment design
040103	IS environment design
040104	Procedures design
040105	Training design
040106	Implement support model
040107	Monitor support services

Figure 2.3   *Continued*

DEFINING THE PROJECT SCOPE

Before signing a contract it is extremely important that the contractor determines exactly what the customer expects to receive in return for money spent on the project. The customer's specification should set out all the requirements in unambiguous terms, so that they can be understood and similarly interpreted by customer and contractor alike.

040200	Custom development
040201	Application infrastructure development
040202	Business system design
040203	Testing design
040204	Data conversion application development
040205	Application software development
040206	System testing
040207	Implementation planning
040300	Hardware
040301	Servers
040302	Clients
040303	Connectivity
040304	Peripherals
040400	Implementation
040401	Data conversion
040402	Acceptance testing
040203	Installation of production system
040204	Refine production system
040205	Evolution planning
040300	Package integration and testing
040301	Installation and environment set-up
040302	Package integration design and pilot
040303	Package business system design
040304	Package application development
040304	Package integration testing design
040305	Data conversion application development
040306	System testing
040307	Implementation planning
040400	Package selection
040401	Package requirements analysis
040402	Vendor and package screening
040403	Package shortlist evaluation
040404	Final evaluation and selection
040405	Contracts and technology acquisition
040406	Development planning
040407	Licences

Figure 2.3   *Concluded*

Of particular importance is the way in which responsibility for the work is to be shared between the contractor, the customer, and others. The scope of work required from the contractor (the size of the contractor's contribution to the project) must be made clear. At its simplest, the scope of work required might be limited to making and delivering a piece of hardware in accordance with drawings supplied by the customer. At the other extreme, the scope of a large construction or process plant project could be defined so that the contractor handles the project entirely, and is responsible for all work until the purchaser is able to accept delivery or handover of a fully completed and proven project (known as a turnkey operation).

Whether the scope of work lies at one of these extremes or the other, there is almost always a range of ancillary items that have to be considered. Will the contractor be responsible for training customer's staff and, if so, how much (if any) of this training is to be included in the project contract and price? What about commissioning, or support during the first few weeks or months of the project's working life? What sort of warranty or guarantee is going to be expected? Are any operating or maintenance instructions to be provided? If so, how many and in what language?

Answers to all of these questions must be provided, as part of the project task definition before cost estimates, tenders, and binding contracts can be considered.

THE CONTRACTOR'S STRATEGY

When a project contractor evaluates a proposed new project, an important aspect of definition is the intended strategy for performing the work. Suppose that, after consideration of a customer's enquiry, a contractor decides to prepare a fixed-price tender. The contractor must develop and record an intended strategy for designing and carrying out the work. Without a good understanding of the project requirements and the intended strategy for meeting those requirements, estimating, budgeting, and pricing become very uncertain processes. Uncertainty in the general economic environment, as well as putting together multinational deals, can serve as further complicating factors. Availability and cost of capital can be an issue during the times of uncertainty in the macro economy whereas fluctuations in foreign exchange currency markets can complicate cross-border deals.

Without a documented internal project specification for design and strategy, there would be a danger that a project could be costed, priced, and sold against one design and strategic intention but executed using a different, more costly, approach. This risk increases when there is a long delay between submitting the tender to the potential customer and actually receiving the order.

Not Invented Here

It sometimes happens that engineers prefer to create a new design even though a perfectly adequate design already exists. They feel that they could do better themselves, or find fault unreasonably with the designs of others (even though those other engineers might enjoy a good reputation and their designs have been proved in successful earlier projects). This state of affairs is sometimes called the 'not invented here' syndrome. The results can be ugly. Two examples from our own experience follow (heavily disguised to protect the names of companies and people who were actually involved).

Case 1 A British company won an important export order to design, supply, and install expensive electronic control tower equipment to an overseas airport operator. Following an internal reorganization, the project's chief engineer resigned. His successor had different ideas and caused all design work completed or in progress to be scrapped and restarted. The design costs alone of that project eventually reached the same figure as the fixed price for which the whole project had originally been sold. That meant that the company had to write off the original design costs and bear all the considerable manufacturing and installation costs of the project itself.

Case 2 An American aircraft engine manufacturing company, with a very high reputation for product excellence, sent a set of engineering and manufacturing drawings to its new British subsidiary. This was a complete, finished design package for a large heavy engineering project. The intention was that it would provide the brand new machining and assembly shops with work during the start-up period when the local British design team was becoming established. The drawings produced in America required 'anglicizing', which meant that the British engineers had to check all the drawings and, with help from the new purchasing department, ensure that the standards specifications and lists of bought-out components would be compatible with purchases from British suppliers.

What actually happened was that the UK engineering design team poured scorn on the American design, and the whole project was redesigned (mostly unnecessarily) from scratch. The project was thus delayed by many months at an additional and avoidable cost of several million pounds. The British plant never recovered from its resulting cash flow problems and this, coupled with hitting the downturn slope in the cycle of its market sector, caused this high-tech company to become bankrupt and cease trading. That was a tragedy, because it disbanded a team of brilliant staff that had been recruited at high expense, who had all the advantages of working in a heavy manufacturing plant that was hailed at the time as the most modern in Europe.

Construction Specification

Construction projects offer another example of work that has to be defined by specification. All building contractors of any repute work from detailed specifications. The requirement to satisfy the statutory authorities is just one reason for documenting specifications of building location, layout, intended use, means of escape in case of fire, appearance, and many other factors.

There are, of course, many design aspects of a building which can greatly affect its costs, including for instance the style of interior decoration, the quality of the fittings and installed equipment, lighting, and air conditioning standards.

Disputes can be minimized, if not prevented altogether, when a contractor produces a detailed project specification and asks the customer to accept it before the contract is signed. Any changes subsequently requested by the customer can then be identified easily as changes from the agreed specification and charged as variations to the original order.

SPECIFICATIONS FOR INTERNALLY FUNDED DEVELOPMENT PROJECTS

Development programs aimed at introducing additions or changes to a company's product range are prone to overspending on cost budgets and late completion. One cause of this phenomenon is that chronic engineer's disease, which has been called 'creeping improvement sickness' or 'scope creep'. Management change and IT projects are also prone to unauthorized departures from the original intentions. The following short story illustrates this danger.

The Passenger Buggy Project

The managers of a small international airport had for a long time experienced difficulties with the movement of passengers between their terminal buildings and the pick-up and setting-down points for boarding buses. Some of the routes were over 200 yards long, and most were a combination of indoor passageways and open air sections. Disabled passengers were especially inconvenienced.

The narrow indoor passages ruled out any possibility of using gasoline-powered vehicles such as minibuses. There were too many curves and bends to allow traveling walkways. Wheelchairs were available, but these often caused difficulties and some unaccompanied disabled passengers required the services of airport porters or other staff to push them.

These difficulties were compounded by the existence of a holy shrine in the neighborhood with reputed healing properties. Many pilgrims who visited the shrine claimed to have received great spiritual comfort and there were accounts of miracle cures. Thus the airport had a higher than average proportion of disabled people passing through its terminals.

The airport's vice president of ground operations, Betty, was an enthusiastic and caring person with a fertile brain. She conceived the idea of transporting the disabled passengers using electric buggies. To avoid engaging additional staff to drive these vehicles, Betty imagined the buggies being automated, which she believed could be achieved using buried guide cables. Each boarding bus pick-up or setting-down point would have separate outward and return paths from its associated terminal building. Routes would be delineated on the surface by yellow lines painted over the buried cables. Betty knew that this technology was used in manufacturing plants to guide electric tow trucks transporting parts between work stations, and she also knew that they could be used for some domestic robot machines. So the technology was proved and should be no problem.

Betty approached a local company, Bunnies Betta Buggies (BBB), with her ideas. She knew BBB's marketing vice president socially, and friendly discussions followed. The idea was that BBB might be able to adapt golf buggies from its standard catalogue vehicles to track along the cables that the airport would bury. The airport would also provide parking bays where the buggies could be recharged, using chargers purchased from BBB.

One important safety requirement was that each buggy must be able to stop on a dime when it encountered an obstacle such as a pedestrian or another buggy. Betty proposed using automobile parking sensors as the core technology to solve that problem. The braking method was left to BBB's design engineers to specify.

Some supervision would be needed to ensure that stationary buggies were left in their parking bays and plugged into their recharging points, but the airport management considered that this could be covered using existing porters and attendants. An added advantage was that users of the buggies would have the mobility to visit the duty free shop and would be able to carry any goods purchased in their buggies' small baggage boxes. A fleet of 60 buggies was proposed, to cover all the pedestrian routes and all the terminal buildings.

These arrangements were agreed between the two vice presidents over a couple of convivial meals. A price of $5000 per buggy plus a one-off payment of $150 000 for the project development costs was agreed verbally. The technical details were not written into a formal specification, but the two vice president friends exchanged emails to outline the project requirements. The airport company issued a purchase order to BBB to confirm the agreement and create a binding contract.

The airport authorities hoped that the system would be up and running in time for a religious festival due to take place at the holy shrine in 9 months' time, when a high number of pilgrims could be expected to pass through its terminals.

The kick-off meeting at BBB   BBB's vice president of marketing informed his company's chief engineer (Henry) of the new airport buggy project and asked him to begin work immediately. He thrust a copy of the purchase order into Henry's hands. Henry was just about to depart for a long vacation, so he lost no time in inviting the key people who would work on the buggy project to a kick-off meeting in his office. Those present included managers from other interested departments, such as purchasing and manufacturing. One important member needed to establish the necessary quorum was, of course, the design engineer (George) who, with a small engineering group, was to be assigned to carry out the development and drawing work.

Discussion was focused on putting George on the right track to create the buggy envisioned by Betty at the airport. George was given a number of objectives but these were broadly based and were not written into a formal specification. George was simply asked to select the most suitable two-seater golf buggy from the company's existing catalogue and modify it so that:

- the steering tiller would be replaced with a servo-controlled automatic system that could follow buried cable;
- each buggy would travel at normal walking pace;
- car parking sensors fitted at the front would operate an electrical relay to temporarily disconnect the battery and engage a brake whenever an obstacle was detected in vehicle's forward path.

Whilst Henry was away on his extended vacation, George would be left to carry responsibility for this project alone, without supervision and with no possibility of resolving any doubts regarding the technical or operational requirements.

The design phase   George emerged from the kick-off meeting full of immediate ideas for modifying the buggies and grateful for being allowed the freedom of working without supervision. He made some initial notes and sketches and gained his own idea of possible modification solutions and the resulting production costs and buggy performance. Then George selected a suitable buggy from the BBB catalogue, requisitioned one of these from stock, and put his imagination and his design group to work.

George soon reached several conclusions. He knew that some of the airport routes were in the open air, so he decided to fit canopies to shield the passengers from inclement weather. These could not be flimsy affairs, so each canopy would add some weight to its buggy.

George thought that many passengers would want to carry heavy baggage in their buggies, so he decided to substantially increase the size of each baggage box. In this assumption George was mistaken because, once past the check-in desks, all passengers' hold baggage was taken from them and handled by airport staff. There would be cabin baggage and duty free purchases to put in the buggy boxes, but the original golf buggy boxes would have been adequate.

George realized that these modifications would add to the weight of each buggy, thus reducing the power to weight ratio. So George decided to fit more powerful electric motors. That modification would, in consequence, require fitting batteries with a higher ampere/hour rating. George also realized that he would need to extend and stiffen the chassis of each buggy, but he knew that a superior vehicle would result.

The problem of automatically-guided steering was solved by buying in the relevant electronic and mechanical components from a company that manufactured industrial robotic trucks.

For automatic emergency braking to prevent hitting obstructions, parking sensors were readily available for $200 a set from a local automobile spares dealer. By fitting a set of these at the front of each buggy, the proximity warning signal could be used to trigger the braking system and shut off power to the motor. Power would be restored automatically, and the brake would release as soon as the obstruction cleared out of the range of the sensors.

The standard buggy model chosen for this project had its motor coupled to the wheels through a train of reduction gears. In normal drive these gears gave the electric motor a mechanical advantage. When power was cut the converse was true and this produced a significant braking effect (similar to that obtained by engaging low gear in an automobile on a steep downhill gradient). However, George decided that solenoid-powered disc brakes would be needed on the buggy's front wheels to achieve the airport's 'stop on a dime' safety requirement.

George considered all these modifications to be necessary and worth the additional expense. He imagined his buggies traveling along their wires silently, smoothly, and effortlessly at the specified 'normal walking pace'. Being a fit young man, George's idea of normal walking pace was about 4 miles per hour.

Prototype production and testing   George's small design group produced the initial set of modified drawings in only 4 weeks, and George was then able to order components and manufacturing tooling. Rather than take buggies from stock and modify them, it was considered to be cheaper and more cost efficient to build the 60 special buggies from scratch, using a specially assembled set of production drawings. Thus each new buggy was to be built from a mix of standard stock parts and from other components that were specially modified or bought in. As these buggies were effectively a new design of vehicle, they were given a new catalogue number.

One new buggy was assembled first in BBB's model shop as a prototype. George arranged a simple test track by taping a guide cable along the surface of the company's parking lot. Weights were added to the prototype to simulate the load of two travelers and their heavy baggage. True to George's expectations, the prototype ran swiftly and accurately along the cable, at a fast rather than normal walking pace. It came to an impressive abrupt stop whenever obstructions were placed in its path. George was very satisfied with this performance. He then authorized permanent tooling and ordered the production batch of 60 buggies.

In the meantime, the airport managers buried guide cables along their chosen routes, designated and marked the buggy parking bays, installed battery chargers, prepared instruction signs for the passengers, and gave short training lessons to the parking attendants and porters.

Costs and delivery times for the first delivery batch   Although George was pleased with the outcome of his design, each modified buggy cost $5500 to produce, representing a loss of $500 for each unit sold at the contract price of $5000. Further, the costs of development and new tooling exceeded the agreed $150 000 purchase price. The modifications were so extensive that the full batch of 60 buggies were not delivered on time to the airport. Thus when the time for the religious festival arrived, only 40 buggies had been delivered and some disabled passengers still had to use wheelchairs.

Initial operating difficulties Now imagine the initial operation at the airport. Because there were insufficient buggies to deal with the total demand, a mix of buggies and wheelchairs traveled the routes. Thus the 40 buggies that were in operation occasionally encountered wheelchairs in their paths and accordingly stopped suddenly to avoid collisions.

On the first day of operation two of the buggies, each traveling at about 6 miles per hour, stopped so suddenly to avoid wheelchairs that their passengers were catapulted forwards to land on top of the wheelchair occupants and their pushers. It was very fortunate for all concerned that injuries were limited to minor cuts and bruises, and everyone knew that the consequences could have been far more serious. Use of the automatic buggies was therefore abandoned with immediate effect, whilst a safety review was carried out. All the wheelchairs were retrieved from the dispatch bay where they had been placed pending their disposal and once again wheelchairs and their pushers became a familiar sight.

The solution The airport managers instructed BBB to collect the 40 buggies and modify them by adding seat belts. More importantly, the running speed was to be reduced and governed at 2 miles per hour. The buggies eventually went back into use, but not until extensive safety tests had been carried out and a complete fleet of 60 modified buggies were in place at the airport. Wheelchairs were thenceforth banned from the automated routes.

Post mortem Now consider how the principal stakeholders of this project viewed the outcome. Eventually Betty and her airport colleagues viewed the project as a success. Disabled passengers now had a good practical solution to the mobility problem. These stakeholders viewed the eventual project outcome as a success.

The injured passengers had a different view, but they soon recovered from their slight injuries and were quickly and adequately compensated with gifts and money by the airport to hush the incidents up. The airport later recovered the costs of this compensation from BBB.

So it was the BBB company that felt the worst effects of the initial project failure owing to the high production and development costs and because they had to reimburse the airport for compensation paid to the slightly injured passengers.

BBB's financial losses and the personal injuries caused to passengers could all have been prevented if George had carried out the original intentions of Betty and BBB's vice president of marketing to the letter. But what exactly were those original intentions? George was given only vague guidelines at the start of this project and it was easy for him to choose and follow his own course of action.

'Normal walking pace' was wrongly construed by George as being 4 miles per hour. Even that speed would have been too high for safety but, in fact, his larger motors actually resulted in speeds nearer 6 miles per hour. If the original instructions had stated 2 miles per hour with a tolerance of plus zero and minus ten per cent, there could have been no confusion.

The original verbal instructions did not adequately define the payload to be expected for each buggy. Thus George could not really be blamed for seriously overestimating that requirement, which led directly to over-engineered buggies and inflated costs.

George did, in fact, design a very well-made product, but not the product that the airport management expected. He allowed his own ideas to intrude and lost sight of the original objectives. Although well built, these buggies were not fit for purpose because they were unsafe for persons with disabilities, the very people for whom they had been intended.

All of these problems could have been avoided if the following steps had been taken:

- The project should have been launched with a written specification in which all the buggy characteristics and operating parameters were quantified.
- A more effective check could have been kept on design and progress, which meant that the chief engineer (Henry) should have ensured that George would be given independent supervision throughout the project. Although Henry was away on vacation for most of the formative stages of this project, he should have made arrangements for a deputy to oversee design and development.

Thus George should have been kept within the intended project boundaries by the provision of a formal, precise, product specification. A simple project plan, such as a bar chart, would have helped to get all the buggies built and delivered on time.

Adding to this list of errors, there was no regular consultation with the customer during the project, so that Betty had no idea that she would take delivery of fewer buggies than expected, or that they would travel at a sprint instead of normal walking pace. She should have been kept informed of progress and she should have been invited to a demonstration of the prototype.

THE PROJECT SPECIFICATION AND VERSION CONTROL

Given the importance of specifying project requirements as accurately as possible, it is appropriate to give some thought to the preparation of a specification document.

Although customers might be clear from the very first about their needs, it is usual for dialogue to take place between a customer and one or more potential contractors before a contract for any project of significant size is signed. During these discussions, each competing contractor can be expected to make various preliminary proposals to the customer for executing the project. Some of those proposals might suggest changes to the customer's initial enquiry specification—changes intended to improve the project deliverables or otherwise work to the mutual benefit of both customer and contractor.

In some engineering companies this pre-project phase is aptly known as solution engineering. Each contractor's sales engineering group works to produce and recommend an engineering solution which they consider would best suit the customer (and win the order). Solution engineering might last a few days, several months, or even years. It can be an expensive undertaking, especially when the resulting tender fails to win the contract.

Although it is tempting to imagine the chosen contractor's sales engineers settling down contentedly to write a single, definitive project specification, the practice is likely to be quite different. The first draft descriptive text, written fairly early in the proceedings, will probably undergo various additions and amendments as the outline solution develops. It is likely to be revised and reissued more than once. The text will typically be associated with a pile of drawings, artists' impressions, flow sheets, schedules, or other documents appropriate to the type of project. Those documents, too, might suffer several changes and re-issues before the agreed solution is reached.

Projects of all types can undergo a process similar to the solution engineering process just described. For example, the requirements for a management change or IT project are likely to evolve as the various stakeholders make their views known, until a final consensus definition of the project task is reached.

A fundamental requirement when a contract is eventually signed, or a charter is approved for a management change project, is to be able to refer without ambiguity to the correct revision of the project specification. The correct version is that which defines the project according to the finally agreed intentions. This assurance is known as version control. Remember that the *latest* issue of any document might not be the *correct* issue.

The only safe way to identify any document is to label it with a unique serial or identifying number, and augment that with a revision number every time the document is re-issued with changes. If there are drawings and other documents that cannot be bound in with the specification document, these attachments must be listed on a contents sheet that *is* bound into the specification, and the list must give the correct serial and revision number of every such document.

Then everyone can be reasonably confident that the project has been defined.

CASE EXAMPLE: THE AIRLINE CHECK-IN DESKS REPLACEMENT PROJECT

The Airlines Involved

This imaginary case example took place in Chinesia, an Asian country with a long-established airline called Old Aire (a legacy carrier). The core business of this line was tourism, carrying mainly second class passengers on short- and long-haul flights to a number of national and international destinations. Much of this trade was linked to package holidays.

The higher organizational levels of Old Aire are shown in Figure 2.4, where it is apparent that the company operated three main departments. These were:

1. Finance, marketing, and company administration.
2. Flight operations (which included aircrews, stewarding, and catering).
3. Ground operations (which covered check-in desks, security, and aircraft maintenance).

These three departments tended to operate autonomously, with poor intercommunication between them.

In recent years a fast-growing fledgling carrier following the low-cost-carrier business model called New Aire Airways came into prominence in Chinesia. Although this smaller and newer company started taking some business from Old Aire, its specialty was carrying smaller groups of business class passengers for whom the company promised a 'superior travel experience' based on on-time performance and superior service for lower fares despite its one class cabin configuration. The original management structure for New Aire is also shown in Figure 2.4.

Contrasting the two organizations shown in this illustration shows that New Aire enjoyed good formal and informal communications between its different divisions and departments, contrasting with the rigid autonomous separation of Old Aire's three principal divisions.

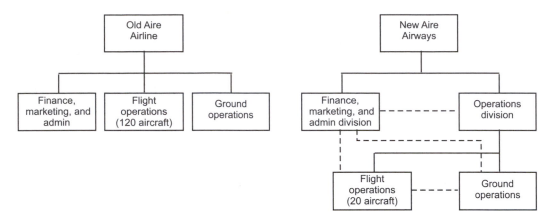

Figure 2.4   Chinesia's two airlines before their merger

Check-in Desk Difficulties For Old Aire

Many of Old Aire's facilities were either somewhat out-dated or approaching calamitous obsolescence. For example, passengers and check-in staff were complaining of their check-in throughput times. They pointed out that other airlines used bar-coded travel documents and labels, but the Old Aire check-in desks often had long queues, with passengers having to wait longer while their details were keyed into the old fashioned system. All of Old Aire's systems had been designed in-house, many years ago, using legacy software designed by their own IT staff.

The vice president of ground operations decided to put a project in hand to update all the check-in systems so that they would recognize bar codes and put an end to all the complaints. He saw no reason for discussing this project with any other manager from his company, since he was used to working autonomously and without consultation. The development costs of the new system would be very high, but the old system obviously had to be replaced. So the ground operations department engaged a small team of temporary IT staff to supplement its own resources and began to design a new check-in system.

Merger Negotiations

Old Aire's vice president of finance, marketing, and administration had been casting envious eyes at New Aire for some time and she began to conceive the idea of either a takeover or a merger. She felt that by combining their different strengths a world class airline could result. She approached the president of New Aire to sound him out on the idea. These two managers agreed that their company's joint interests would be best served if they could operate in partnership, and they began discussing the possible arrangements. Olde Aire's vice president obtained approval from her president, and then the two companies agreed to set up a joint working party to investigate the details. Each company was to provide its own project manager to serve on the working party.

The New Aire members of the working party were drawn from all parts of the company, and they were warned not to discuss their work outside the joint working party for prudent reasons of commercial confidentiality. But the Old Aire working party delegates were all taken from the finance, marketing, and administration department.

Lack of communication between the three different Old Aire departments meant that neither the flight operations crews nor the ground operations staff were made aware of the merger proposals.

A Project Saved By Common Sense And Checklists

Old Aire's project manager concerned himself with examining the different market opportunities that the proposed merger would create. He began formulating his business plans. However, he kept himself to himself and worked solely within his own department. He saw no need to discuss or check his strategies with members of the flight operations or ground operations departments. He had never had anything to do with those people directly in the past and saw no reason to change now.

New Aire's project manager came from a completely different company culture, in which openness and internal communications were encouraged and normal. Further, she had some previous project management experience. Thus she began compiling checklists on all aspects of the merger project so that she could identify, consider, and define all the tasks that would have to be done before the merger could be successfully completed. Her task was made easier because she was able to discuss all aspects of the project freely with managers in all New Aire's departments. She soon compiled quite detailed pre-project checklists.

One item on her checklist was 'examine check-in compatibility'. She had long been aware of Old Aire's reputation for having out-of-date technology at its check-in desks and she felt that something would need to be done about them before the two merged companies would be able to combine their check-in facilities. So she telephoned Old Aire's vice president of ground operations and began asking pertinent questions.

Old Aire's vice president of operations was astounded at hearing news for the first time of the proposed merger. He arranged to meet New Aire's project manager. When the subject of check-in technology was raised he soon realized that his appropriate course would be to abandon his expensive development project for new check-in desk installations. With the merger they would be unnecessary, because Old Aire would be able to use the superior existing New Aire desks where these were available, and the new merged company could simply install those in places where none previously existed. Thus an unnecessary project costing hundreds of thousands of dollars was stopped early in its tracks, and a great deal of money was saved.

In Chapter 1 we quoted from Professor Francis T Hartman's book in which he declared that a project is successful if all the stakeholders are happy (Hartman, 2000). He gave one section of that work the subtitle '[Bad] Communication—the only cause of failure' and wrote, 'Communication is at the heart of effective project management. It needs to be timely, complete, accurate and verified.' We endorse Hartman's statement without reservation and stress that its force takes effect right at the beginning of every project, when the tasks are first defined. We have demonstrated here that checklists are a valuable tool in the process.

REFERENCES

Hartman, F.T. (2000), *Don't Park Your Brain Outside,* Newtown Square, PA., Project Management Institute.

3

Estimating the Project Costs

The obvious reason for estimating costs is for pricing commercial and industrial projects. But good cost estimates are vital for every project that needs budgetary cost control—which for practical purposes means all projects.

COST ELEMENTS

Every cost or finance officer should have some knowledge of the terms used by cost accountants in general and of the project organization's cost accounting procedures practices in particular. Figure 3.1 shows the principal elements of a typical cost estimate. There are important distinctions between direct and indirect costs. Several definitions of direct and indirect costs breakdowns as they apply to the airline industry have been proposed by the authors of various books as they relate both to operational and non-operational costs. However, we give below a single generic definition, as conventionally used in project management textbooks.

- *Direct costs* can be directly and wholly attributed to the project and are the costs of labor and materials needed to perform the project tasks. Direct costs are also called variable costs, because they vary with the rate at which project work is performed. When no project work is done, no direct costs are incurred. Direct costs usually add value to the project. Examples of airline direct operating costs are fuel costs and airport charges, because these vary with the number of flights made and the distances traveled.
- *Indirect costs* are the overhead running costs of the business. They include heating, lighting, rent, council rates, and property maintenance. The salaries of management, accountants, salespeople, the HR department, and all other people in administration jobs are indirect costs. Most indirect costs continue relentlessly whether any project work is done or not, and tend not to vary from one day to the next. Thus indirect costs are also fixed costs. Indirect costs add costs to a project without adding value. Examples of airline indirect operating costs might include the renting of check-in counters and the salaries of counter staff because, within limits, these costs are fixed and must be absorbed by the business irrespective of the number of flights made.

Figure 3.1 also shows that project cost items can be either 'above-the-line' or 'below-the-line'. Above-the-line costs include the total estimated direct project costs plus an allowance for overheads. Below-the-line items are generally allowances intended to give some protection from risk and ensure that the project will be profitable

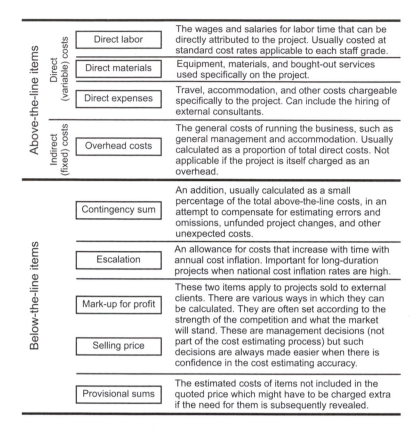

Above-the-line items	Direct (variable) costs	Direct labor	The wages and salaries for labor time that can be directly attributed to the project. Usually costed at standard cost rates applicable to each staff grade.
		Direct materials	Equipment, materials, and bought-out services used specifically on the project.
		Direct expenses	Travel, accommodation, and other costs chargeable specifically to the project. Can include the hiring of external consultants.
	Indirect (fixed) costs	Overhead costs	The general costs of running the business, such as general management and accommodation. Usually calculated as a proportion of total direct costs. Not applicable if the project is itself charged as an overhead.
Below-the-line items		Contingency sum	An addition, usually calculated as a small percentage of the total above-the-line costs, in an attempt to compensate for estimating errors and omissions, unfunded project changes, and other unexpected costs.
		Escalation	An allowance for costs that increase with time with annual cost inflation. Important for long-duration projects when national cost inflation rates are high.
		Mark-up for profit	These two items apply to projects sold to external clients. There are various ways in which they can be calculated. They are often set according to the strength of the competition and what the market will stand. These are management decisions (not part of the cost estimating process) but such decisions are always made easier when there is confidence in the cost estimating accuracy.
		Selling price	
		Provisional sums	The estimated costs of items not included in the quoted price which might have to be charged extra if the need for them is subsequently revealed.

Figure 3.1   Elements of a cost estimate for an aviation project

ACCURACY OF COST ESTIMATES

Good project definition should minimize cost estimating errors but these can never be eliminated. Thus initial cost estimates can never be perfectly accurate and most projects will produce unwelcome surprises that could lead to budget overspends (*variances*). The estimator's task is to use all the data and time available to produce the best estimate possible: that is, a carefully calculated judgement of what the project should cost if all goes according to plan.

Accurate estimates greatly assist those responsible for making competitive pricing decisions and improve the effectiveness of cost budgets and resource schedules.

Classification Of Estimates According To Confidence

Apart from the estimator's skill, accuracy depends on the project definition and the time allowed for preparing the estimates. Some companies classify cost estimates according to the degree of confidence that can be placed in them. Different organizations have their own methods, but the following categories are sometimes used:

- *Ballpark estimates* are made when only rough outline information exists or when there is no time to prepare a detailed estimate. A ballpark estimate might achieve an accuracy of ±25 per cent, given a generous amount of luck and good judgement.

- *Comparative estimates* are made by comparing work to be done on a new project with similar work done in the past. They can be attempted before detailed design and without final materials lists or work schedules but a project specification is essential. It should be possible to achieve ±15 per cent accuracy. Comparative estimates are often used when tendering for new work.
- *Feasibility estimates* need a significant amount of preliminary project design. In airport construction projects the building specification, site data, provisional layouts and drawings for services are all necessary. Quotations must be obtained from the potential suppliers of expensive project equipment or subcontracts. Material take-offs or other schedules should be available for estimating the costs of materials. Feasibility estimates should be accurate to better than ±10 per cent and they are often used for airport construction project tenders.
- *Definitive estimates* cannot be made until much of the work has been done. They are a combination of costs actually incurred plus an estimate of costs remaining to project completion. Estimates become definitive when accuracy improves to better than ±5 per cent.

Some organizations will assign wider accuracy limits. It is also possible to find asymmetric limits, so that a company might, for example, assume that its ballpark estimates are accurate to within plus 50 or minus 10 per cent.

STANDARD ESTIMATING TABLES

Standard tables, based on rates per quantities of work, exist to help the estimator in projects such as airport construction and in general civil engineering. Publishers such as the London publisher, Spon, produce books of such tables and update them annually. Companies can sometimes develop their own tables as they gain experience. However, for many projects cost estimating remains a matter of personal skill and judgement.

COMPILING THE TASK LIST

Cost estimating begins by making a 'shopping list' of all the tasks and materials that are going to cost money. Compilation of this list can be difficult but the omission of any significant item will result in an underestimate for the project. Checklists can be very useful. A work breakdown (described in Chapter 6) is a logical way of considering the total project and can reduce errors of omission. But at the outset of a project it is most likely that the work breakdown has to be compiled in fairly broad terms, because much of the detail will not be known until the project has advanced well into its design phase.

Software Tasks

Software is a familiar term in the context of computers, but most industrial and commercial projects have software in the form of schedules for inspection and testing, instruction and maintenance manuals, lists of recommended spares and consumables. These software tasks must usually be allowed for in the estimated costs by inclusion in the task list.

Forgotten Tasks

Tasks often forgotten for aerospace manufacturing projects include processes such as protective coatings, heat treatments, silk-screen printing, engraving, inspection, and testing. In some firms these may be included in overhead costs, but in many others they will not. For airport construction projects there can be many easily forgotten expenses, such as the provision of site huts, rubbish skips, and so on.

An expensive item sometimes neglected during cost estimating is the work of final commissioning, handover, and customer acceptance of the completed project. Contracts often demand that the contractor provides training facilities for some of the customer's operatives or technicians. Training sessions can involve the contractor's senior engineers in much hard work, both in the actual training and in preparing the training material beforehand.

DOCUMENTING THE COST ESTIMATES

Estimates should be set out according to a standard company procedure, itemized where possible by cost codes within the work breakdown structure. This will help to ensure that comparisons can readily be made later between the estimates and the cost accountant's records of the actual costs incurred, on a strict item-for-item basis. This is an essential part of cost control. As experience and data build up over a few years, it will also contribute to the accuracy of comparative estimates for new projects. If no work breakdown structure exists, the task list should still be sectioned and arranged as logically as possible.

Standard Estimate Formats

Calculations performed in odd corners of notebooks, on scraps of paper, and on the backs (or even fronts) of envelopes are prone to error and premature loss. Cost estimates should be tabulated and recorded in a logical and consistent manner, for which standard estimating formats can help considerably (either as hard copy or as forms on a computer screen).

Project estimating forms, in the form of spreadsheets, can be collated to fit the kind of work breakdown structures that are described in Chapter 6. One sheet can be allocated to each main project work package or group of tasks. Every row on the forms would be occupied by one task so that adding the costs along each row gives a task cost estimate. Totalling relevant columns provides a basis for compiling department budgets and coarse aggregated resource schedules.

Figure 3.2 shows an example of a multi-purpose estimating form. This version allows six different grades of labor to be shown and assumes that all labor-hours will be costed at the appropriate standard cost rates. The standard grade code and rate used should be entered in the space at the head of each labor column.

There is no need to complicate a general purpose estimating form by adding extra columns for such things as special tooling or heat treatments. These items can be

COST ESTIMATE									Project number or sales reference:			Estimate number: Case: Date:		
Estimate for:									Compiled by:			Page of		
1	2	3	4	5	6	7	8	9	10	11	12	13	14	15
Code	Item	Qty	Labor times and costs by department or standard grade						Total direct labor cost	Overhead cost at %	Materials			Total cost 10+11 +12+13
			Hrs	£ Hrs	£ Hrs	£ Hrs	£ Hrs	£ Hrs	£			Standard or net cost	Burden %	Longest delivery (weeks)	

Figure 3.2   A general purpose estimating form, particularly applicable to aviation manufacturing projects

accommodated by designating them as tasks, so that they can be written along rows in same way as any other task.

The column headed 'longest delivery (weeks)' in the materials section, although not connected directly with cost estimating, is convenient because the people who enter the material costs on the form are also the people most likely to be able to say what delivery times can be expected. Inclusion of task lead times will be useful later, when planning the project timescale.

COLLECTING DEPARTMENTAL ESTIMATES

Networked computers provide one method for gathering information from a number of different sources, which is of course a requirement in cost estimating. Some project management software, although designed originally for planning and control, allows system users to add estimating data to the project database. However, these methods are passive, and rely on the goodwill of people to provide the data.

Estimating requires people to make commitments and difficult judgements. Thus it is often regarded as a chore to be avoided if possible. A firm approach is sometimes needed to extract estimates from reluctant supervisors and managers. Personal canvassing is most likely to produce quick and dependable results. The process starts by preparing a complete set of estimating sheets for the project, with every known task listed and cost coded. The sheets should be arranged in logical subsets according to the work breakdown structure. The project manager or delegate can then tour all the departments involved, installing themselves purposefully at each relevant desk and remain firmly rooted there until all the desired data have been extracted.

Canvassing gives an opportunity to assess the estimating capabilities of the individuals concerned. Any estimate which appears unrealistic or outrageous can be questioned on the spot, and other details can be sorted out with the least possible fuss and delay. One type of question which must frequently be asked of the estimator takes the form: 'Here is a job said to require 4 labor-weeks; can four people do it in one week, or must the job be spread over 4 weeks with only one person able to work on it?' Answers to such questions are important for the subsequent scheduling of time and resources.

Cost Estimating Units

Generally speaking, whilst wages and their related standard cost rates change from year to year, the time needed to carry out any particular job by a given method will not. Labor-hours (once called man-hours) are therefore regarded as a more reliable constant basis for labor estimates. Comparative estimates for labor should be based on labor-hours, labor-weeks or other suitable time units, and then extended to cost using the current project cost rates.

THE ESTIMATING ABILITIES OF DIFFERENT PEOPLE

Project cost estimating, particularly for labor times, is not an exact science. If ten people were to be asked separately to judge the time needed for a particular project task, it is inconceivable that ten identical answers would be received. Repeat this exercise with the same group of people for a number of different project tasks, and it is likely that a pattern will emerge when the results are analyzed. Some of those people will tend always to estimate on the low side. Others might give answers that are consistently high. The person collecting project cost estimates needs to be aware of this problem. In fact, just as it is possible to classify estimates according to confidence in their accuracy, so it is possible to classify the estimators themselves.

Optimistic Estimators

It can be assumed that estimates will more frequently be understated than overstated. Many people seem to be blessed with an unquenchable spirit of optimism when asked to predict completion times for any specific task. 'I can polish off that little job in 3 days,' it is often claimed, but 3 weeks later the only things produced are excuses. Without such optimism the world might be a much duller place in which to live and work, but the project manager's lot would be far easier.

An interesting feature of optimistic estimators is the way in which they allow their cloud-cuckoo-land dreams to persist, even after seeing several jobs completed in double the time that they originally forecast. They continue to make estimates which are every bit as hopeful as the last, and appear quite unable to learn from previous experience. Engineers and designers are perhaps the chief offenders in this respect. Fortunately such estimates are at least consistent in their trend. Shrewd project managers will learn by experience just how pronounced this trend is in their own company. Better still, they will be able to apportion error factors to particular individuals. It is often necessary to add about 50 per cent to the original estimates to counteract the original optimism.

Pessimistic Estimators

Occasionally another kind of individual is encountered who, unlike more usual optimists, can be relied upon to overestimate most tasks. Pessimism is not particularly common and, when seen, it might pay to investigate the underlying cause. Possibly the estimator lacks experience or is incompetent, but that usually produces random results, and not a consistent error bias. The picture becomes clearer, if more unsavoury, when it is remembered that project estimates play a large part in determining total departmental budgets. High (pessimistic) estimates could produce bigger manpower budgets, leading to enlarged departments and thus higher status of the departmental heads. In these cases, therefore, 'E' stands not only for 'estimator' but also for 'empire builder'. Correction factors are possible, but action is more effective when it is aimed not at the estimates but at the estimators.

Inconsistent Estimators

The inconsistent estimator is the bane of the project manager's existence. Here we find a person who is seemingly incapable of estimating any job at all, giving answers that range over the whole spectrum from ridiculous pessimism to ludicrous optimism. The only characteristic consistently displayed is, in fact, inconsistency. Incompetence or inexperience suggest themselves as the most likely cause. Complacency could be another. People looking forward to retirement rather than promotion, and staff with a laissez-faire attitude can display these symptoms.

Unfortunately this category can manifest itself even at departmental head level, the very people most frequently asked to provide estimates. Only time can solve this one.

Accurate Estimators

There is a possibility of finding a person capable of providing estimates that prove to be consistently accurate. This possibility is so remote that it can almost be discounted. When this rare phenomenon does occur it can unsettle a work-hardened project manager who has, through long experience, learned that it pays to question every report received and never to take any estimate at its face value.

Correction Factors

Why not try to educate the estimators until they all produce accurate estimates and lose their characteristic errors? Prevention is, after all, better than cure. But the results of such a re-education programme must be unpredictable, with the effects varying from person to person, upsetting the previous steady state. In any case, all the estimators could be expected to slip back into their old ways eventually and, during the process, their estimating bias could lie anywhere on the scale between extreme optimism and pessimism. Arguing wastes time if nothing is achieved. Why not accept the situation as it exists and be grateful that it is at least predictable.

Here, then, is a picture of a project manager or proposals manager obtaining a set of estimates for a project, sitting down with a list of all the estimators who were involved, complete with the correction factor deemed appropriate for each individual, and then factoring the original estimates accordingly. Far fetched? This procedure has been proved in practice.

ESTIMATES FOR MATERIAL AND EQUIPMENT COSTS

The purchasing department should always be involved in estimating material and equipment costs and estimates for prices and delivery times must be obtained through their efforts whenever possible. If the purchasing organization is not allowed to partake in preparing the detailed estimates, a danger exists that when the time eventually comes to order the goods these will be obtained from the wrong suppliers at the wrong prices. It is far better if the big items of expense can be priced by quotations from the suppliers. The buyer can file all such quotations away in readiness for the time when the project becomes live. If the purchasing department is to be held down to a project materials budget, then it is only reasonable that it should play the leading role in producing the material estimates.

The responsibility for estimating the costs of materials and equipment therefore lies in two areas. The engineers or design representatives must specify what materials are going to be used, and the purchasing department will be expected to find out how much they will cost and how long they will take to obtain.

Expenditure on materials and bought-out services can exceed half the total cost of a typical industrial project and can be as high as 80 per cent, but materials and the purchasing function are not often given the importance that they deserve in project management. Materials need two types of estimate. These are:

1.   The total expected cost, including all delivery and other charges.
2.   The lead time, which is the elapsed time between placing the purchase order and receiving the goods at the point of use.

It might also be necessary to make estimates of other factors for operational purposes. For example, the volume or weight of materials that might be needed for storage, handling, or onward transport.

If no detailed design has been carried out, no parts lists, bills of materials, or other schedules will exist. In that case the engineers should be asked to prepare a provisional list of materials for each task. This may be impossible to carry out in exact detail, but the problem is not as difficult as it would first seem. In most work the engineers have a good idea of the more significant and most expensive items that will have to be purchased. There might be special components, instruments, control gear, bearings, heavy weldments, castings, all depending of course on the type of project. In airport construction projects outline assumptions can be made for the types and quantities of bulk materials needed.

Foreknowledge of the main items of expense reduces the unknown area and improves the estimating accuracy. If all the important items can be listed and priced, the remaining miscellaneous purchases can be estimated by intelligent guesswork. If, for example, the known main components are going to account for 50 per cent of the total material costs, an error of 10 per cent in estimating the cost of the other materials would amount to only 5 per cent of the total.

Any estimate for materials is not complete unless all the costs of packing, transport, insurance, port duties, taxes, and handling have been taken into account. The intending purchaser must be clear on what the price includes, and allowances must be made to take care of any services that are needed but not included in the quoted price.

Another cautionary word concerns the period of validity for quotations received from potential suppliers. Project cost estimates are often made many months—even years—before a contract is eventually awarded. Suppliers' quotations are typically valid for only 90 days or even less, so that there could be a problem with the materials cost budget or the availability of goods when the time eventually arrives for the purchase orders to be placed.

The general purpose estimating form shown in Figure 3.2 allows space for simple materials estimating requirements, like those needed for a small aerospace manufacturing project. For larger projects, especially those involving international movements, a format such as that shown in Figure 3.3 would be more appropriate.

ESTIMATING BELOW-THE-LINE COSTS

When all the basic costs have been estimated, and the overheads have been added, a line can be drawn under them and the total should amount to the estimated net cost of sales. However, there are usually other costs which have to be evaluated and entered below that line.

COST ESTIMATE FOR MATERIALS AND EQUIPMENT					Project number or sales reference:					Estimate number: Case: Date:				
Estimate for:					Compiled by:					Page of				
Cost code	Description	Specn. No (if known)	Proposed supplier	Unit	Unit cost F.O.B.	Quoted currency	Exchange rate used	Converted FOB cost	Qty	Project FOB cost	Ship mode	Freight cost	Taxes/ duties	Delivered cost
					Total delivered materials and equipment costs this page ⟶									

Figure 3.3   **Cost estimating form for purchased materials and equipment for a large aviation project**

Contingency Allowances

Additional costs are bound to arise as the result of design errors, production mistakes, material or component failures, and the like. The degree to which these contingencies are going to add to the project costs will depend on many factors, including the type of project, the general competency of the firm, the soundness (or otherwise) of the engineering concepts, and so on. Performance on previous projects should be a reliable pointer that can be used to decide just how much to allow on each new project to cover unforeseen circumstances. For a straightforward project, not entailing an inordinate degree of risk, an allowance set at 5 per cent of the above-the-line costs might be adequate.

The scope for adding an adequate contingency allowance will be restricted if there is high price competition from the market. If the perceived risk suggests the need for a high contingency allowance, the company might need to reconsider whether or not to undertake the project.

Cost Escalation

Every year wages and salaries increase, raw materials and bought-out components can cost more, transport becomes more expensive, and plant and buildings absorb more money. All these increases correspond to the familiar decrease in the real value of money which is termed 'inflation'. This decay appears to be inevitable, and the rate is usually fairly predictable in the short term. In a country where the rate of inflation is 10 per cent, a project that was accurately estimated in 2007 to cost $5m (say) might cost an extra million dollars if its start were to be delayed for 2 years.

Unfortunately, cost inflation rates are not easy to predict over the long term, because they are subject to political, environmental, and economic factors. However, a cost escalation allowance based on the best possible prediction should be made for any project whose duration is expected to exceed 2 years.

The rate chosen by the estimator for below-the-line cost escalation allowances might have to be negotiated and agreed with the customer (for example, in defense or other contracts to be carried out for a national government).

The conditions of contract may allow the contractor to claim a price increase in the event of specified cost escalation events that are beyond its control (the usual case being a national industry wage award), but that is a different case from including escalation in quoted rates and prices as a below-the-line allowance.

Provisional Sums

It often happens, particularly in airport construction contracts, that the contractor foresees the possibility of additional work that might arise if particular difficulties are encountered when work actually starts. For example, a client may specify that materials are to be salvaged from a building during demolition work, to be re-used in the new construction. The contractor might wish to reserve its position by including a provisional sum, to be added to the project price in the event that the salvaged materials prove unsuitable for re-use. It is not unusual for a project quotation to include more than one provisional sum, covering several quite different eventualities.

FOREIGN CURRENCIES

Most large projects involve transactions in currencies other than their own national currency. This can give rise to uncertainty and risk when the exchange rates vary. Some mitigation of this effect can be achieved if the contract includes safeguards, or if all quotations can be made and obtained in the home currency. Otherwise, it is a matter of skill, judgement, and foresight.

Common practice in project cost estimating is to nominate one currency as the control currency for the project, and then to convert all estimated costs into that currency using carefully chosen exchange rates. Although contractors would normally choose their home currency, projects may have to be quoted in foreign currencies if the terms of tendering so demand, and if the potential client insists.

Whether or not the contractor wishes to disclose the exchange rates used in reaching the final cost estimates, the rates used for all conversions must be shown clearly on the internally circulated estimating forms.

REVIEWING THE COST ESTIMATES

When the detailed estimates have been collected it should be possible to add them all up and declare a forecast of the whole project cost. However, it is never a bad plan to stand well back and view this picture from a different perspective. In particular, try converting the figures for labor times into labor-years. Suppose that the engineering design work needed for a project appears to need 8750 labor-hours. Taking 1750 labor-hours or 50 labor-weeks as being roughly equivalent to a labor-year, division of the estimate shows that 5 labor-years must be spent in order to complete the project design. Now assume that all the design is scheduled to be finished in the first 6 months of the programme. This could be viewed (simplistically) as a requirement of ten design engineers for 6 months.

The manager starting this project might receive a rude awakening on referring to records of past projects. These might well show that a project of similar size and complexity took not ten engineers for 6 months, but expenditure equivalent to ten engineers for a whole year. An apparent error of 5 labor-years exists somewhere. This is, in any language, a king-sized problem. Part of its cause could be the failure of estimators to allow for that part of engineering design which is sometimes called 'after-issue', which means making corrections, incorporating unfunded modifications, answering engineering queries from the workforce or the customer, writing reports, and putting records into archives.

It goes without saying that cost estimates for a project are extremely important. Any serious error could prove disastrous for the contractor—and for the customer if it leads the contractor into financial difficulties. Estimates should be checked as far as possible by a competent person who is independent of the original estimate compiler. Comparisons with actual cost totals for past projects (for all materials and labor—not just for the engineering design example given above) are valuable in checking that the new project cost estimate at least appears to be in the right league.

4

Risk

Everything we do from getting out of bed in the morning to returning there at night carries risk. Every journey carries some risk, whether it is by bicycle, car, train, ship, plane, or even walking. It is not surprising that projects, which metaphorically (and sometimes literally) break new ground, attract many risks. Project risks can be predictable or completely unforeseeable. They might be caused by the physical elements or they could be political, economic, commercial, technical, or operational in origin. Freak events have been known to disrupt important projects, such as the decision by a few family members of a rare protected species to establish their family home on ground that was just about to be trenched for an oil pipeline or the unexpected discovery of important archaeological remains under land destined to carry one of the main runways at a new airport.

The potential effects of risks range from trivial inconvenience to project disaster. Project risk management (and much of mainstream project management) is concerned with attempting to identify all the foreseeable risks, assessing the chance and severity of those risks, and then deciding what might be done to reduce their possible impact on the project or avoid them altogether.

In some industries risk management and its closely associated discipline of reliability engineering have to be taken particularly seriously because of the potential impact of project failure on public safety or the environment. Examples are projects for defense, nuclear power plants, petro-chemical plants, and all projects involving the transport of people by air or other modes of transport. High in this list of risk-sensitive projects are all those connected with aerospace and air transport, where a risk event might be anything from missing a flight connection to a catastrophic collision between two fully laden passenger aircraft over a densely populated city.

INTRODUCTION TO PROJECT RISK MANAGEMENT

Risks affecting project design and progress can occur at any stage in a project. Some are associated with particular tasks and others originate from outside the project and can manifest themselves without warning. Generally speaking, a risk event that occurs late in a project can be more costly in terms of time and money than a similar event nearer the start of the project. That is because as time passes there will be a greater value of work in progress and higher sunk costs at risk of loss or damage.

Some projects, because they are small or similar to projects that the contractor has undertaken in the past, might not need special attention to risk management other than considering some of the insurance issues discussed later in this chapter. However, for any project that breaks new ground or is complex and large, a risk management strategy must be developed, first to identify as many potential risks as possible and then to decide how to deal with them.

For very large projects it might be necessary to appoint a risk manager, who can devote all or most of their time to ensuring that a comprehensive risk strategy is put in place and then reviewed from time to time throughout the project to ensure that it remains valid. If a project support office exists, that is a logical place for the risk management function to reside.

Project risk management is a complex subject. Even the classification of risks is not straightforward and can be approached in different ways. There are several techniques for assessing and dealing with project risks, some of which are shared with other management disciplines (particularly with quality management and reliability engineering). This chapter will outline a few of the methods commonly used.

IDENTIFYING THE POSSIBLE RISKS

It is almost certain that some tasks will not be completed in line with their duration estimates and budgets. Some might exceed their estimates, whilst others could be finished early and cost less than expected. As explained in the previous chapter, statistical tools such as PERT (see Chapter 7) and Monte Carlo analysis can be used to attempt an assessment of the probability of the project finishing by its target completion date or of the intended return on investment being realized. However, those measures deal with uncertainty rather than with risk. Risks are unforeseen (and often unforeseeable) events that can result in a change of project plans or even total project failure.

Projects can incur risks from the 'accident waiting to happen' variety to the most unexpected and bizarre. Risks can materialize during project design and execution or after the project is finished and has been handed over to the customer.

Management change and IT projects seem to be particularly prone to risk of failure, with huge losses of money, delay in completion, or malfunctions. Projects in the aviation industry appear to have been vulnerable to failure through IT problems. We mentioned the Airbus 380 project in this context in Chapter 1 (where design faults in the wiring harnesses have been attributed to collaborating manufacturers using different versions of CAD software). There have been many reported instances of problems with both on-board and ground computer systems. For example, chaos can result if a flight reservation and ticketing system malfunctions. Air traffic control systems appear to have been vulnerable, with malfunctions causing widespread grounding of flights and with obvious potential to cause flight hazards. The frequently updated website <http://www.lessons-from-history. com> has a section labeled 'project success or failure' which has a rich fund of project failure stories, many of which are aviation based.

Checklists

We make no excuse for stressing the value of checklists at several places throughout this book, because each checklist is built on a fund of experience and can be a vital factor in preventing errors of omission in current and future projects and in operations.

In the project risk management context, checklists are important for suggesting or identifying project risks. Studying the history of similar projects from the past can highlight possible problems and help the project manager to learn from the experiences (and mistakes) of others. As experience is gained on each new project, the project manager and others working on the project will be able to improve and enrich the existing checklists from their new experiences. Experience can never itself be a substitute for a checklist that enshrines the experiences of many others: it should be regarded instead as an enabler for further checklist improvement and enrichment.

In this book we are discussing principally the project management aspects of checklists, but clearly checklists (along with instruction and operating manuals, training, and emergency exercises) play a vital part in maintaining the safety of ground and air operations.

Figure 4.1 is an example of a form that, although intended as an engineering project authorization document, is effectively also a checklist because it demands answers to a structured list of questions. This is an example of a procedure that is designed to reduce the risk of design errors and improve engineering reliability. This versatile form can be used in conjunction with a new engineering design, as part of the risk management process, as an authorization document for a small engineering project, or during the consideration of a proposed project engineering modification or change (changes are dealt with in Chapter 11).

Brainstorming

Brainstorming is an effective technique for identifying possible risks. The method relies particularly on the assertion that two heads are better than one, and its effectiveness depends on allowing all those who take part complete freedom of thought and imagination with no preconceived agenda. A brainstorming meeting of key staff is a particularly productive method for identifying all the possible project risks along with many of the improbable ones.

Much depends on how the brainstorming session is conducted. The leader or chairperson should encourage an atmosphere of 'anything goes'. Participants should be asked to think of all the possible things that might go wrong with the project, or as a result of the project. Participants must feel free to propose even the most bizarre risks without fear of ridicule. All suggestions, without exception, should initially be written on whiteboards or flipcharts.

When all creative imagination has been exhausted, the resulting lists can be examined critically, first to exclude the absolutely impossible entries and then to create an initial risk identification register.

RISK APPRAISAL AND ANALYSIS

Once identified and listed, risks can be ranked according to the probability of their occurrence and the severity of the impact if they should occur. This process will eliminate the most improbable risks arising from brainstorming, but it should bring to the fore those risk events that are most likely to happen and which would have the greatest impact on the project or on subsequent ground or flight operations. For this analysis it is necessary to consider the possible causes and effects of every risk.

Lock Airways **ENGINEERING PROJECT (EP)**		
Document ID:	Date issued:	Revision number:
Title:		
Document type:	Originator:	
Date received:	Assigned to:	
OPTIONS		
Attach to new EP:	EP title::	
Attach to existing EP:		
Detach from existing EP:		(employee number)
Fleet number:		
Units/aircraft affected (cross reference field, airframe, power plant, component, group year):		
Related documents (cross reference field, MD/AA/EPs):		
Miscellaneous references:		
Project description:		
Project scope:		

Engineer's name:	ID number:	Phone extension:	email address:

STATUS ➡ Open: ☐ In review: ☐ Closed: ☐ EP number:

ENGINEERING INVESTIGATION	
Reliability:	Planning:
EP Required by:	WARRANTY: ➡ Yes: ☐ No: ☐
Response:	

Respondent's name:	ID number:	Phone extension:	email address:

Figure 4.1   **A versatile international checklist/authorization document for small aviation engineering projects**

Risk analysis can be either qualitative or quantitative. Qualitative risk analysis involves considering each risk in a purely descriptive way, to imagine various characteristics of the risk and the effects that these could have on the project or subsequent operations. Qualitative risk analysis goes at least one stage further than qualitative analysis by attempting to quantify the outcome of a risk event or to attach a numerical score to the risk that ranks it according to its perceived claim for preventive or mitigating action.

Qualitative Cause And Effect Analysis

Fault-trees and fishbones   Fault-tree analysis (not described here) and Ishikawa fishbone diagrams are methods commonly used by reliability and safety engineers to analyze faults in design and construction. Project risk managers can adapt Ishikawa fishbone diagrams to examine risk cause and effect relationships. Figure 4.2, for instance, shows how an Ishikawa fishbone diagram might be compiled to analyze the numerous reasons why an engine might lose power or stop. Many items in this example could be expanded into greater detail, leading to quite a complex diagram, with many branches and sub-branches to the 'fish skeleton'.

Fishbone diagrams can also be used without adaptation to examine and analyze failures or poor performance in project organizations or communications. The fishbone process generally starts by thinking about the effect, and then looking back for the possible causes. However, project risk management is more often conducted from the opposite viewpoint, which means first listing all the possible causes (risks) first and then assessing their probable effects.

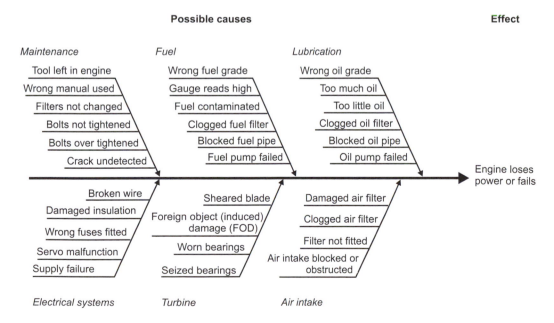

Figure 4.2   A simplified Ishikawa fishbone cause and effect diagram

Failure mode and effect analysis (FMEA)   Failure mode and effect analysis (FMEA) is another example of a method that has been imported into project risk management from reliability and quality engineering, This method is particularly helpful to aviation project managers because it starts by considering possible risk events (failure modes) and then attempts to predict all their possible effects.

Figure 4.3 shows a simple FMEA chart, which represents only a tiny portion of a total FMEA chart for a municipal airport construction project. A final column allows space for pre-emptive actions to be recommended that might mitigate or prevent damage from the risk. Only three items are shown in Figure 4.3 but there might be hundreds of items in a large, complex project. Another column is sometimes added to show when in the project life cycle the risk is most likely to occur.

FMEA charts are a qualitative process because, although the characteristics of each risk are considered, there is no attempt to give each risk a priority ranking number or to quantify the effects if the risk should occur.

Risk classification matrices   Figure 4.4 shows a risk classification matrix chart. Note that this matrix comprises nine sections. Although this is a simple classification method, an even simpler four-section matrix is often used, containing the following quadrants:

- high chance – high impact
- high chance – low impact
- low chance – high impact
- low chance – low impact.

As with FMEA, this again is a qualitative method, in which no attempt is made to evaluate any risk numerically. Each risk item is considered for its likelihood of occurrence (chance) and for the relative scale of the impact on the project should it occur.

	Item	Failure mode	Cause of failure	Effect	Recommended pre-emptive action
1	Pilot's automobile	Engine refuses to start	Poor maintenance	Pilot marooned at private hunting lodge with no other means of transport. Unable to get to airstrip at project site	Ensure good vehicle maintenance. Either keep back-up car at hunting lodge or don't go there
2	New maintenance hangar	Floor over basement collapses during first aircraft engine exchange	Errors in floor loading calculations when hangar was built	Personal injuries. Damage to engines. Damage to aircraft. Schedules disrupted	Triple check vital structural calculations
3		Floor over basement collapses during first aircraft engine exchange	Floor slabs incorrectly poured	Personal injuries Damage to engines Damage to aircraft Schedules disrupted	Ensure operatives get good training and instruction. Employ competent site engineering manager

Figure 4.3   Tiny part of a failure mode and effect matrix (FMEA) for a new municipal airport project

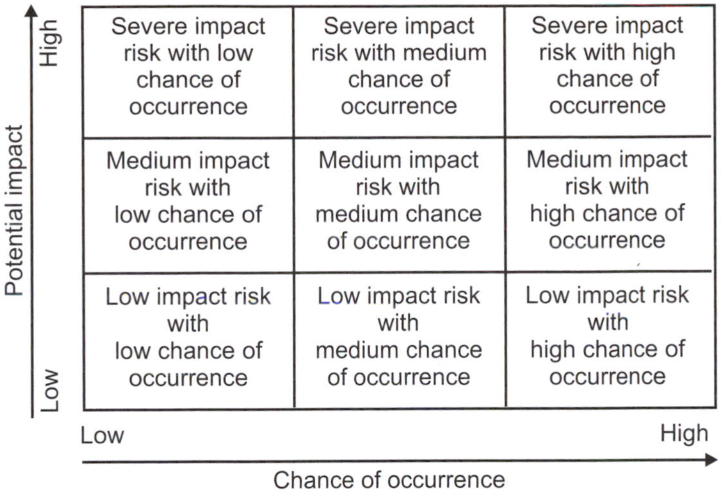

Figure 4.4   A matrix for qualitative risk classification

Suppose, for instance, that a project is being planned to move a large airline company headquarters from a central city location to a purpose-built office building that is close to London Heathrow airport. The following are a few of the many risk events that might be visualized and assessed:

- Some office equipment could be damaged or stolen in transit. The risk of that happening might be high, but the impact could be considered medium because most equipment is easily replaceable.
- Some key staff might decide not to relocate with the company. That could be thought to have a medium chance, and the effect would have a medium impact on the company's performance when starting up in the new location
- The collapse of the new premises just before occupation date through an earthquake in that part of the UK would be very low chance, but the impact would unquestionably be devastatingly high.
- The chance of moving day being made thoroughly miserable for all concerned through rain would be high, but with low practical impact.

Figure 4.5 is a simple qualitative risk assessment matrix showing how the principles illustrated in Figure 4.4 might be applied in practice. This exercise is not complete, because as yet no thought has been given about what to do if any risk event should occur.

Quantitative Analysis

Quantitative analysis methods attempt to assign numerical values to risks and their possible effects. They often examine the probable impact on project time and costs. Alternatively, the evaluation process can produce a ranking number for every identified risk. Ranking numbers denote the priority that a risk should claim for management attention and expenditure on preventative measures.

Risk event	Chance of happening	Potential severity	Difficulty of detection	Comment
Action by environmentalists	High	High	Low	We shall be building in a nature reserve
Strikes or other industrial action	Low	High	Low	Loyal workforce with no previous problems
Project manager struck by lightning	Low	High	Low	But she is a keen golfer
Hairline cracks in structural steel	Low	High	High	Suppliers have high quality reputation
Software bugs	Medium	High	High	Process safety depends on computer controls
Exchange rate changes	Medium	Medium	Low	Not difficult to detect but impossible to predict
Materials shortages	Medium	Medium	Low	

Figure 4.5   A qualitative risk assessment matrix

Although all quantitative methods produce 'actual' numbers they can give a false sense of precision. We should remember that the results are based on estimates, assumptions, and human judgement. Those contributing assessments might be fundamentally flawed, mistaken, or simply too difficult for any person to make with any degree of certainty.

Failure, mode and effect criticality analysis (FMECA)   The qualitative failure, mode and effect analysis method illustrated in Figure 4.3 can be adapted and extended to attempt risk quantification. The method then becomes failure mode effect and criticality analysis (FMECA). Figure 4.6 shows one version. In this example, three assessment columns are provided, in each of which the risk analyst is expected to enter a number expressing the degree of significance. Every item is ranked on a scale of one to five (others use one to three or one to ten), with the highest numbers indicating the greatest degree of significance. The entries might be those of the risk analyst or, preferably, the collective opinions of a risk committee or brainstorming group. In some procedures the column headed 'Detection difficulty' is replaced by one headed 'Prediction difficulty'.

Item 2 in Figure 4.6 for example, considers the possibility and potential seriousness of a structural failure in a new hangar. This is for a building created as part of an airport project, and the collapse in question might happen during heavy maintenance operations, such as the exchange of a large aircraft engine. If the floor has been incorrectly designed, and has pits or a basement below, it might not be sufficiently strong to carry the weight of two engines and the associated lifting rigs. The assessor clearly thinks this is unlikely to happen because they have ranked chance at the bottom end of the one to five scale. There is no doubt, however, that if this event did occur it would be extremely serious, so the severity has been marked as five.

Detection difficulty means the expected difficulty of noticing the cause of this risk (design error in this case) in time to prevent the risk event. Here there is a considerable element of judgement, but the assessor thinks that although the chance of a design error

	Item	Failure mode	Cause of failure	Effect	Chance	Severity	Detection difficulty	Total ranking
1	Pilot's automobile	Engine refuses to start	Poor maintenance	Pilot marooned at private hunting lodge with no other means of transport. Unable to get to airstrip at project site	2	1	3	6
2	New maintenance hangar	Floor over basement collapses during first aircraft engine exchange	Errors in floor loading calculations when hangar was built	Personal injuries Damage to engines Damage to aircraft Schedules disrupted	1	5	3	15
3		Floor over basement collapses during first aircraft engine exchange	Floor slabs incorrectly poured	Personal injuries Damage to engines Damage to aircraft Schedules disrupted	1	5	2	10

Figure 4.6   **Tiny part of a failure, mode, effect criticality matrix (FMECA) for a new municipal airport project**

is very low, the difficulty of spotting a mistake if it did occur would be higher (three on the scale of one to five).

The product of these three parameters, 1 x 5 x 3 gives a total ranking number of 15. Theoretically, when this calculation has been performed on every item in the list, the list can be sorted in descending sequence of these ranking numbers, so that risks with the highest priority for management attention come at the top of the list.

Some assessors use weighted parameters. For example, it might be considered that the severity of the risk should play a higher part in deciding ranking priority. So the severity column could be marked on a higher scale, say from one to ten. Item 2 in Figure 4.5 might then be marked nine on this extended scale, which would increase the ranking factor for this item from 15 to 27.

Although not usual practice, a case might be argued for allowing zero scores in the 'Chance' and 'Severity' columns. That would, of course, result in a total ranking factor of zero. That would be one way, but not the most direct way, in which to dispose of some of the more outlandish risk events identified during an 'anything goes' brainstorming session.

RISK REGISTER

When all the known risks have been listed, assessed, and ranked it is time to consider what might be done about them. That process requires that all potential risks in aviation projects be listed in a risk register (or risk log). A fairly typical example of a risk register page is shown in Figure 4.7 and it should be apparent that this is modeled closely upon the FMECA method demonstrated in Figure 4.6. However, the risk register has the following noticeable additions:

- an ID number for each risk listed;
- space for writing in the proposed action that would be taken should the risk event materialize;
- a column headed 'Action by' in which the name of the person or manager responsible for taking action for each risk can be entered. That person might sometimes be referred to as the risk owner.

Risk ID	Date registered	Risk description and consequences	Probability P = 1-3	Impact (severity) S = 1- 3	Detection difficulty D = 1-3	Ranking P x S x D	Mitigating or avoiding action	Action by:

Figure 4.7   Example of a format for a risk register (or risk log) for an aviation project

The risk register should be reviewed and updated regularly throughout the life of the project. It is advisable to use the computer to sort the risks according to their ranking, with the highest-ranked risks placed at the top.

METHODS FOR DEALING WITH RISKS

When all the known risks have been identified, assessed, ranked, and registered it is time to consider what might be done about them. These are the decisions that must be entered in the two columns at the right hand of the risk register. The project manager usually has a range of options:

1. **Avoid the risk**: The only way to avoid a risk is to abandon the possible causes, which could even mean deciding not to undertake a project at all.
2. **Take precautions to prevent or mitigate risk impact**: This is a most important part of risk management, requiring the active participation of all managers and staff. It needs high-level risk prevention strategy combined with executive determination to ensure that all preventive measures are always followed throughout all parts of the organization. It requires the creation of a risk prevention culture, covering all aspects of project tasks, health and safety, and consideration for the environment. Here are a few examples of the many possible practical measures, listed in random sequence:

   - provision of marquees for VIPs at an airport in case of rain during the inaugural celebrations for a new or rebranded airline;
   - regular inspection and testing of electrical equipment to ensure safe operation;
   - double-checking to detect errors in design calculations for vital project components or structures;
   - provision of backup electrical power supplies for vital operations, essential services, and computers (very important in all aspects of ground and flight operations);
   - frequent backup and secure offline storage of business data;
   - avoidance of trailing electric cables in offices;
   - ensuring that means of escape routes in buildings are always clear of obstructions and that smoke screen doors are kept closed;
   - regular fire drills, testing of fire alarms, and emergency lighting;
   - ongoing safety and emergency training for all flight operations and ground operations staff;
   - on the job training of backup or seasonal staff to understudy key roles in the organization;
   - regular inspection and maintenance of vehicles such as push-back trucks and baggage trailers
   - provision of safety clothing and equipment to protect workers and crew members, and enforcement of their use;
   - restricted access to hazardous areas;
   - provision of clear safety markings on all aircraft;
   - adequate and ongoing training, above the minimum regulatory standards, for all those operating potentially hazardous equipment for ground or flight operations;
   - regular financial audits and the installation of procedures to identify or deter fraud;
   - and so on, and so on: this list could be very long.

3. **Accept the risk**: Rain might make the day chosen for office relocation miserable for all concerned but the risk would have to be accepted. There are numerous small things than can go wrong during the course of any project, and most of these risks can be accepted in the knowledge that their effect is not likely to be serious, and that they can be overcome by corrective measures or replanning. For example, an airline launching an inaugural service might have to accept a risk of short-term teething problems at an international destination arising from the employment of third-party service providers that are not accustomed to the airline's practices and standards.

4. **Share the risk**: If a project, or a substantial part of it, appears to carry very high risk, the contractor might seek one or more partners to undertake the work as a joint venture. Then the impact of any failure would be shared among the partners. Sharing a risk big enough to ruin one company might reduce its impact to little more than a temporary inconvenience. Risk sharing of this nature is common in aerospace manufacturing projects. Boeing and Airbus, for example, rely on a multitude of suppliers located around the world in the realization of their various projects. Hence, suppliers, depending on their position in a specific project share in the risk of project delay or failure. For example, Airbus places 46 per cent of its aircraft-related procurement with suppliers across the US and Canada, <http://www.airbus.com/en/worldwide/north_america/us_indus_partners> (accessed 20 January, 2008).

5. **Limit the risk**: There are occasions when project risks should only be accepted with safeguards in place to limit their potential effect. A good example is an internal project, perhaps for pure research, that cannot be adequately defined at the outset. No one can tell how much the project will eventually cost or what its outcome might be. Yet the opportunities are too great to consider avoiding the risk altogether.

    The usual solution to starting an ill-defined project is to limit the risk by authorizing work step-by-step. It may be possible to divide the project into a number of stages for this purpose: indeed the process is sometimes called stage-gating. The stages might be determined by:

    - the occurrence of significant events in the project that can easily be recognized when they happen;
    - the imposition of a time limit for each stage;
    - a budgetary limit for each stage; or
    - a combination of any two or all of these.

Funding or authorization of expenditure on each new stage of the project would depend on a critical review of the work carried out up to the review date, coupled with a fresh appraisal of the value of continuing with the project. This approach has the advantage of limiting the committed risk. Although it is not possible to define the entire project in advance, it should be possible to look the short way ahead necessary to define each new step. Each limited step so defined may then be amenable to the project management procedures that cannot be used for the whole project.

In the step-by-step or stage-gate approach it always has to be borne in mind that it might become necessary to abandon the project at any stage and write-off the expenditure already incurred. The aviation and defense industries have a long history of abandoned projects. A spectacular example worth mentioning here (although it happened 50 years ago) is that of the Bristol Brabazon in the UK. This very large and heavy turboprop aircraft was impressive for its time and won public praise, but the project was abandoned for commercial reasons after a successful maiden flight that was watched by a large crowd of enthusiastic spectators. Another British project abandoned after several test flights was the very advanced and promising TRS2 strike aircraft, on which the plug was pulled largely for political reasons.

6. **Transfer the risk**: Some risks, or substantial parts of them, can be transferred to another party on payment of a fee or premium. This leads to the important subject of insurance, which is discussed in the next section.

INSURANCE

The Basic Principles Of Insurance

The fundamental principle of all forms of insurance is that premiums paid by the many will pay for losses incurred by the unfortunate few who suffer a loss. A portion of the premiums paid will cover the cost of running the insurer's business, expenses, and commissions and, together with any investment income, provide a profit and return on the capital employed.

The financial impact of many risks can be offset by insuring against them. The client pays the insurance company a premium for this service and the insurer might itself choose to spread the risk by sharing it with one or more other insurance companies. Figure 4.8 shows that managers do not enjoy complete freedom of choice when deciding which risks should be included in their insurance portfolio.

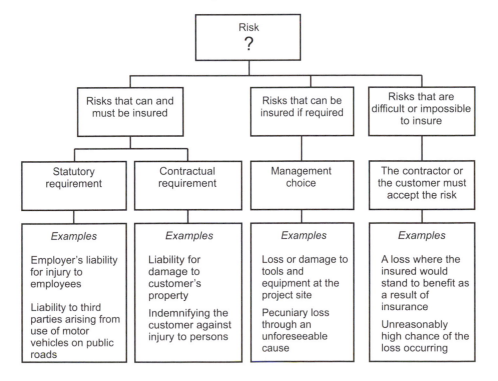

Figure 4.8   Risk and insurance in project management

Insurance customers are either retail or commercial. A retail customer is a 'natural person' (policyholder or potential policyholder) acting outside their normal trade or profession. A commercial insurance customer is someone acting within their normal profession, for example, an airline.

An example of a retail customer would be an individual (a 'natural person') who is not connected with the construction trade and who project-manages the construction of a small hangar on their own private airstrip or helipad. Greater protection and more information are provided to a retail customer than to a commercial customer because the commercial customer is deemed to have greater knowledge or to have access to a professional insurance intermediary.

The policyholder (or potential policyholder) should be given all the necessary information before the inception of insurance cover, to assist them to arrive at an informed decision. In addition, the actual policy wording, terms and conditions must be available and agreed before inception to achieve 'contract certainty'. In plain English, that means that the intending policyholder must know exactly what will, or will be not, covered by the insurance, together with details of the cost.

Categories Of Insurance

There are four main classes of insurance:

1. Legal liabilities (payments to others as a result of statutory, contractual, or professional commitments, compensation awarded by the courts, legal expenses, (but not fines imposed by the courts).
2. Protection against loss or damage to property, including temporary works and work in progress, owned construction plant, hired-in plant, and employees' effects.
3. Cover relating to personnel.
4. Pecuniary loss.

A policy may combine cover for two or more of the above classes of risk.

Obligatory Insurances

Legal requirements oblige companies to obtain adequate insurance cover against some risks. These obligations arise either from various government laws and regulations or from conditions contained in a binding commercial contract.

Statutory requirements   At the top of the insurance shopping list are those items which must be insured in order to comply with laws and regulations. Third-party insurance for motor vehicles used on public roads is a familiar example. Employers are obliged to insure their employees against injury or illness arising from their employment (Employers' Liability Insurance) and every employer has to display a valid certificate on its noticeboards to show that such insurance exists.

Statutory regulations of particular interest to the manager of construction and engineering projects cover the periodic inspection and certification of lifting equipment, pressure systems, and local-exhaust ventilation plant. No project which includes the installation of such equipment should be handed over to a client without the relevant written (or other) scheme of examination and the accompanying inspection certificates. If the correct documentation is not supplied, the client will not legally be able to operate the equipment.

In the UK these statutory regulations form part of the Health and Safety at Work Act 1974. Much of this legislation resulted from European Directives and similar legislation has been enacted in other EU member countries. The principal European regulations are:

- Lifting Operations and Lifting Equipment Regulations 1998 (LOLER)
- Provision and Use of Work Equipment 1998 (PUWER)
- The Management of Health and Safety at Work Regulations 1999
- The Pressure Systems Safety Regulations 2000 (PSSR)
- Control of Substances Hazardous to Health Regulations 1998 (COSHH)
- Electricity at Work Act 1988 (E@W)

Similarly, in the United States, the Occupational Safety and Health Administration (OSHA) which came into being in 1971, aims to ensure employee safety and health. US Congress created OSHA through the Occupational Safety and Health Act of 1970.

Inspection work is usually performed by engineer-surveyors employed by an engineering insurance company. The insurance company is sometimes engaged by the contract principal, but more usually by the main contractor. The larger of these insurance companies, with many years' experience of such work, are able to advise on compliance with national and local legislation covering equipment and construction materials.

The project manager of an airport construction or expansion project must check that inspection certificates required by the regulations are current and valid for plant hired for use on the airport. This will help to protect the project manager's organization from any liability that might arise from the use of a plant hire fleet that has been poorly managed by the plant hire company. Failure to comply with these, and other, regulations may have an adverse effect on the insurance cover. In addition, non-compliance could render the parties liable to prosecution.

Contractual requirements and other legal liabilities In commercial and industrial projects, whether for airport construction or aviation manufacturing, it is certain that some onus will be placed upon the parties (usually the contractor) to insure against several risks. All the model terms of contract for engineering, civil, and construction contracts embody such requirements. The project contractor will also wish to make certain that subcontractors are bound, in turn, by similar conditions.

Liability insurances are most likely to feature prominently in project contracts. The project purchaser will want to know, for example, that the contractor has adequate cover for legal liability in the event of personal injury, illness, or death caused to anyone as a result of the project.

In summary, liability insurances may be required for:

- compensation to persons for bodily harm (employees of either party, others working on site, visitors, and members of the public);
- property loss or damage, including work in progress;
- financial loss;
- infringement of property rights;
- accidents;

- product liability (arising from use of a product);
- professional negligence;
- nuisance caused by the works;
- environmental damage.

Every organization or professional person with project responsibility (including architects, consultants, surveyors, designers, and project management organizations) must make certain that they have adequate professional liability insurance to cover any liability that they might incur in the course of their work.

Other Risks That Can Be Covered By Insurance

In addition to the statutory and contractual requirements, there is a range of other risks against which a contractor might be required to insure, or for which a contractor might decide that insurance is prudent. Some of these are listed below.

Contractors' all risks insurance for construction and engineering projects All risks insurance cover provides protection during the works, until the project is complete and handed over to the customer. Thereafter, insurance becomes the customer's responsibility.

All risks policies typically protect work in progress and temporary works against fire, storm damage, theft, and malicious damage but any new policy proposal should be studied with care, as it is likely to list exceptions. In addition to work in progress, the cover should include loss or damage to:

- construction plant and machinery;
- hired plant;
- construction materials in transit to site;
- temporary buildings and site huts;
- employees' tools and effects.

In addition there will be other, minor, extensions of cover built into the policy for little or no extra cost.

Reinstatement costs after an accident will also be covered, including the costs of removing debris and the fees of architects, surveyors, and consulting engineers. The insurer might also agree to pay additional expenses (such as overtime costs and express carriage rates) incurred as a result of expediting reinstatement work.

Contract all risks (CAR) policies usually apply to civil engineering and construction projects, while the less common engineering all risks (EAR) policies are for contracts that relate specifically to the construction and installation of machinery.

Exclusions and conditions in the policy, and in the policy schedule, should be examined carefully and understood before the insurance is entered into.

Decennial (latent defects) insurance Decennial insurance, which can cover a period of up to 10 years, is designed to insure against damage to premises caused specifically by an inherent defect in the design, materials, or construction of a project. In the event of a successful claim, decennial insurance removes the need for the project owner to suffer the expense of taking legal action for recompense against the contractor.

Accident and sickness insurance   Provisions for personal accident, sickness, and medical expenses insurance will need particular consideration when employees are required to travel, whether at home or abroad. Those working on projects in foreign countries will expect to be adequately covered for the higher risks involved, and such cover will have to be extended to spouses and children if they are also allowed to travel.

Key person insurance   Key person insurance offers various kinds of protection to an employer against expenses or loss of profits which result when illness, injury, or death prevents one or more named key persons from performing the duties expected of them. Arrangements are flexible and policies can be tailored to suit particular circumstances.

Pecuniary insurance   Pecuniary insurances are designed to protect a company against financial losses from a variety of causes. Risks that can be covered include embezzlement, loss through interruption of business, and legal expenses. Advance profits insurance may be possible in some limited circumstances to provide cover for delay in receiving planned return on project investment caused by late completion of the project.

Of particular interest to contractors where business with foreign customers is involved is export credit insurance. In the UK, the Government's Export Credits Guarantee Department (ECGD) provides guarantees that can provide security against bank loans for large capital goods and long-term projects. The Export-Import Bank of the United States provides a similar service in the US, whilst most other industrialized companies have similar schemes. The contractor will be expected to bear some of the risk, although its proportion will usually be small. The security offered by credit insurance can be an important factor in obtaining finance for a project.

Risks Which Cannot Be Covered By Insurance

There are risks which an underwriter will either refuse to insure, or for which the premium demanded would be prohibitive. Such cases arise in the following circumstances:

- where the chances against a loss occurring are too high or, in other words, where the risk is seen as more of a certainty than reasonable chance. Examples are losses made through speculative trading or because of disadvantageous changes in foreign exchange rates;
- where the insurer is not able to spread its risk over a sufficient number of similar risks;
- where the insurer does not have access to sufficient data from the past to be able quantify the future risk;
- where the insured would stand to gain as a result of a claim. Except in some forms of personal insurance, the principle of insurance is to attempt to reinstate the insured's position to that which existed before the loss event. A person cannot, for example, expect to benefit personally from a claim for loss or damage to property not belonging to them (property in which they have no *insurable interest*).

These items must, therefore, be excluded from the insurance portfolio. In some cases other commercial remedies might exist for offsetting the risks.

UNIQUE PROPERTIES OF AVIATION INSURANCE

Aviation insurance was already an incredibly complex and dynamic field before it was impacted by the terrorist atrocities in the US on 11 September, 2001 (now usually referred to simply as 9/11). In the 1990s, some major airline risks were insured and reinsured with the involvement of hundreds or even thousands of insurers and reinsurers taking a share. But, currently the trend is for market consolidation, so that the number of participants has fallen significantly, although there would still probably be over a hundred participating insurers for any major airline's specific risk.

Several features of aviation insurance set it apart from other classes of insurance. Three significant features are:

1.   the limited number of risks available to insure;
2.   its small size;
3.   its potential exposure to catastrophic events.

Size And Scope Of Aviation Insurance

The main complication for aviation insurers is the relatively few risks available to insure. This is especially so if just airlines are considered. Airclaims (2004a) records that at the end of 2003 there were only 765 airlines worldwide, and they operated about 16 400 western-built jet airliners. Airclaims (2004b) states that this number increases to 2207 airlines operating about 26 000 aircraft, if all airlines operating jet or turboprop powered aircraft of 15 seats or more are included. However, the actual number of individual risks is significantly fewer, because several airline groups consolidate their insurance and purchase on behalf of all the members of the group. In addition, the exposure, in terms of fleet value (or indeed size of fleet) is dominated by a few very large airlines or groups of airlines, with the 20 largest accounting for well over 50 per cent of the total value at risk. The 100 largest airlines probably account for 90 per cent of the exposure (measured either by value or the passengers carried).

The aviation insurance market is relatively small compared with many of the other classes of non-life insurance. It has been estimated that the total gross annual premium for all aviation insurance business is currently about $7500 million and according to Viccars (2001), 'Aviation premiums represent approximately 0.1 per cent of the worldwide insurance market.' Viccars (ibid) reports, 'It was said that the annual premiums for the [aviation] class were less than the annual plate glass insurance premium for the state of New York.' The aviation industry premium level is probably considerably smaller than, for instance, the annual premium for automobile insurance in a reasonably sized country.

However, 'While aviation as a class has one of the smallest premium bases in the insurance industry, it has some of the highest potential catastrophe exposure.' (Viccars, ibid, p.xvi).

Particular Exposure To High Risk And Potential Catastrophe In Aviation Insurance Claims

Some new Boeing 747s are insured for over $250 million and many wide-bodied jets will be insured for more than $100 million each. Coupled with that, cover for passengers and for third-party liabilities will be bought, with combined single limits (CSLs) of $1500m or

$2000m. The total annual gross premiums income for airline business can easily exceed $3000m, but clearly there is the potential for a single loss of a fully-laden wide-bodied passenger aircraft to account for perhaps as much as two-thirds of those total premiums.

Worse still, there is always the chance of a collision between two large passenger aircraft. In Tenerife, Spain on 27 March, 1977 two Boeing 747 airliners collided at Los Rodeos (TCI) airport with 583 fatalities. To date, the Tenerife accident has produced the highest number of lives lost (excluding ground fatalities) of any single accident in aviation history. The aircraft involved were Pan American World Airways Flight 1736 and KLM Royal Dutch Airlines Flight 4805. KLM 4805, taking off on the only runway of the airport, crashed into the Pan Am aircraft which was taxiing in the opposite direction on the same runway.

In 1996, the Lloyd's insurance syndicate introduced a number of Realistic Disaster Scenarios (RDS). Lloyd's Syndicates have to demonstrate their capability to meet all their commitments, which might arise from these prescribed scenarios, if they are to continue to do business in Lloyds. There is currently only one RDS which specifically addresses aviation risks. This RDS, titled 'Aviation Collision' initially ran as follows:

> 'Assume a collision between 747s of the syndicate's two highest airline exposures occurring over a major US city; Assume liability loss of US$1 billion per airline'

> (Lloyds, 1997)

This assumed 'liability loss' has more recently been increased to a total of $4 billion, along with other changes (Lloyds, 2004). An actual occurrence of this scenario would produce a loss equivalent to more than 130 per cent of the 2003 gross premium income from all airline business worldwide.

With the exception of 9/11 (where the incurred loss falling on aviation policies exceeded $4.3 billion) there has been no aviation loss at the time of writing which has approached these levels. Nevertheless, in any one year, while there are relatively few total losses and/ or fatal accidents, there is always the potential for a 'catastrophe'. With a small premium base and occasional catastrophic losses, the airline insurance market can be very volatile.

OBTAINING PROJECT INSURANCE

Insurance can be sought directly from an underwriter, or through a broker; preferably one with a good reputation and experienced in the insured's type of project activity. The insurer will need to be supplied with sufficient information for the risk to be adequately defined, and the contractor will be expected to inform the insurer of any change of circumstances likely to affect the risks insured. The insurer may wish to make investigations or even follow up the project work using its own experts.

Professional advice from insurers can often be of great benefit in reducing risks, especially in the areas of health and safety and crime prevention.

Two events in 2001 had a severe impact on insurers and will affect reinsurance and capacity for many years to come. One of these events was the insolvency and collapse of Independent Insurance plc, a company that insured a large number of contractors and construction trade clients for very low premiums. This caused every insurance company and broker to conduct internal audits, critically re-examining the risks to their own businesses. The other 2001 event was, of course, the 9/11 terrorist atrocities in the US which we have already mentioned, and which highlighted to insurance and reinsurance companies the potential for such enormous claims to be repeated in the future, whether from terrorist attacks or other causes. Insurers have since sought to limit their exposure to such risks and they have instituted a regime of stricter underwriting controls and lower risk-acceptance thresholds.

Liability insurance is becoming expensive. Employer's liability cover, even though a legal requirement, is becoming difficult to obtain. Some insurance companies have had to close because they are unable to effect such insurance.

It is, therefore, now more important than ever for a project manager to involve an insurance specialist at a very early planning stage, lest they should find that no insurance cover is available at short notice.

PLANNING FOR CRISES AND EMERGENCIES

Some risk events can have such a potential impact on a project that special crisis management contingency plans must be made. Such contingency plans can extend to projects that would need to be set up specially and rapidly to deal with a sudden crisis, for example, in areas that are particularly liable to epidemic diseases, famine, flooding, hurricanes, earthquakes, or other natural disasters. Crisis contingency plans should also be put in place by process industries and other companies that carry out operations which, if they should go wrong, could be hazardous for people and the environment beyond the factory gates. Aviation is clearly an industry in which crisis and emergency training has to be taken very seriously and regularly implemented. One cannot always say when or where a disaster will strike, but at least plans can be put in reserve to be implemented immediately when the need arises.

Organization

Once the possibility of a crisis has been established, the first step in devising a contingency plan is to identify the key people who will take charge should the event occur. These people will constitute a sleeping organization, ready to awake at a moment's notice in case of need. The core organization might include senior representatives of local and national government, the emergency services, particular charities and relief organizations, and so on. Each person should have the authority to instruct others within their home organization and the permission to identify the relevant resources that could be made available should the crisis happen. A team leader or steering committee must be appointed that will manage the project should it become live. This group of key people might be called the crisis action committee.

Contingency Planning

Once the key people have been elected or selected to serve on the action committee, they must meet to design appropriate contingency plans, and then meet again at regular intervals to ensure that the plans are kept up to date. The committee might have to arrange for emergency funds, stores, and special equipment to be stockpiled or at least located against the time when they might suddenly be needed. Lists of secondary organizations and other helpers must be established, which although not part of the action committee, could be called upon to give urgent and immediate assistance. These secondary associations might include, for example, specialist engineering or chemical contractors, explosives or decontamination experts, building and demolition contractors, caterers, and a wide range of charitable organizations that could offer relief services. There might also be a need to plan for immediate advertising in the appropriate media to make public appeals for funds.

Tabletop And Other Exercises

One thing that the action committee will need to do as early as possible is to assess what might happen should the crisis arise. The committee will need to use their collective imagination to consider and be prepared in advance for as many of the problems as possible.

A tabletop exercise can contribute to this process, where the members of the action committee carry out a role-playing exercise to consider as exactly as possible what might happen and what they themselves and their subordinates might do should the crisis happen.

Many crisis contingency plans can be tested by field exercises, in which some or all of the services act out their parts as if the crisis had actually happened. Field exercises can reveal shortcomings in the contingency plans and test vital aspects such as mobility, response speeds, and how to communicate and coordinate the various participants under emergency conditions, when power, water, and telephones might all be out of action.

When the plans have been made and tested they must be documented, incorporating all the lessons learned from tabletop and field exercises so that they are ready to put into action effectively and with minimum delay. This is, in effect, creating a project handbook or project manual for a project that might never happen. When a crisis does cross from imagination to reality, however, contingency planning can save time and many lives.

Training of air and ground crews to ensure their effective response to a range of possible emergencies is routine in all well-managed airlines and airports. To give an example, all crews of passenger aircraft will receive training in the safe and rapid evacuation of passengers when an emergency occurs on take-off or landing. That training must be backed up by exercises in simulated emergency conditions, such as the existence of smoke in the cabin, or a reduction in the number of escape doors/emergency chutes owing to fire or crash damage. The training must be refreshed at regularly intervals (perhaps every 6 months) so that crews will always be ready and trained to respond to a crisis. We cite just two of many examples to demonstrate how such training can save lives.

British Airways flight BA038 from Beijing (a Boeing 777) had on board 136 passengers and 16 crew when, as reported by the media, both engines lost power late into final approach at London Heathrow in January, 2008. The co-pilot (who was the handling pilot at the time) glided the aircraft for 2 miles to clear residential housing, a busy motorway, and (by only 20 feet) the airport perimeter fence. That remarkable skill had been enhanced through regularly training for just such emergencies on a flight simulator. In the actual event, the aircraft came to rest at the front edge of the runway after skidding for thousands of feet on grass. With the undercarriage torn away, wings badly damaged, and fuel spilling out, the cabin crew used well-rehearsed procedures to evacuate all the passengers without serious injury. Equally well-rehearsed ground fire crews were quickly on hand to spray foam over spilt fuel and the hot engines to prevent fire.

At Toronto in 2005 there was an even more dramatic case where disaster was prevented by the crew of an Air France Airbus A340. This aircraft attempted to land during a severe thunderstorm, with torrential rain reducing visibility and impairing braking efficiency. The approach was too high and touchdown occurred 3800 feet down the drenched runway. The aircraft was traveling at 80 knots when it ran out of runway and skidded to rest in a ravine, where it caught fire. Yet, although there were some serious injuries, the Air France crew of 12 evacuated all 297 passengers without loss of life. That kind of escape from disaster can only be achieved through high professionalism which, in turn, depends on regular and well-organized crisis or emergency training exercises.

In many industrial and management projects risk management is regarded as an important yet academic aspect of project management that some do not take seriously. In aviation projects, risk management is at the heart of projects and safe operations.

REFERENCES

Airclaims (2004a), *Jet Operating Statistics*, Issue One, Hounslow, Airclaims Ltd (now Ascend World-wide Ltd).

Airclaims (2004b), *Turbine Airliner Fleet Survey*, Spring 2004, Hounslow, Airclaims Ltd (now Ascend Worldwide Ltd).

Lloyds (1997), *Regulatory Bulletin Annexe 1*, February, London, Lloyds of London.

Lloyds (2004), *Realistic Disaster Scenarios*, April, London, Lloyds of London.

Viccars, P. (2001), *Aviation Insurance: A PlaneMan's Guide*, London, Witherby.

5

Organizing the Project

An effective organization will ensure that clear lines of authority exist, and that all members of the project know and willingly accept what they have to do to make the project a success. This is part of the management communication framework, essential for motivating all the staff employed. A well-motivated group can be a pleasure to work with. A badly informed group, with vague responsibilities and ambiguous levels of status and authority, is likely to be poorly motivated, slow to achieve results, costly to run, and frustrating to manage.

Good management communications include adequate feedback paths through and across the organization. These allow progress to be monitored, difficulties to be reported back to executive management, and expert specialist advice on technical or commercial problems to be sought and given.

Every business has its own ideas about how to organize itself and its work. It is highly probable that if three businesses doing similar work could be compared, three different organization structures would be found. Further, all three businesses might be successful, implying that it is not always possible to declare firmly that there is one best organization solution. This chapter cannot, therefore, dictate exactly how every project should be organized. Instead, it describes the advantages and disadvantages of possible organization options, so that the reader can judge which might be appropriate for a particular project.

For many people these arguments are academic, because most project managers are appointed to an organization that already exists and have no authority to change it. Power to create organizational change is owned by more senior management, so perhaps it is they who should be reading this chapter.

MATRIX ORGANIZATIONS

Case Example: A Coordinated Matrix Organization At Lox Airparts Inc.

Execjetair Inc., (known as EJA), the manufacturer of a successful small twin jet executive aircraft, received a customer's order to design, make, and deliver a fleet of six aircraft to a slightly modified design that would increase the operating range at the expense of reduced payload (including a reduction from eight to six passenger seats). EJA immediately recognized one requirement, which was the addition of the two auxiliary fuel tanks, each to supplement one of the two existing tanks. All fuel tanks were enclosed within the wings. The new auxiliary tanks were to be mounted in space newly created within each wing, and the port and starboard tanks would be designed as mirror images of each other.

Thus, for the fleet of six aircraft, the minimum initial requirement was for six port tanks and six starboard tanks.

EJA issued a simple invitation to tender for the design and manufacture of these 12 fuel tank assemblies, each comprising a double-skinned aluminium tank with internal baffle plates. The tanks were to be supplied fitted with mounting lugs and fuel pipe connections, and holes had to be drilled to take instruments. EJA issued a general arrangement sketch of each wing, cut away to show the exact shape, mounting position, and all connection requirements for the port and the starboard tanks.

By far the lowest bid was received from Lox Airparts Inc., (LAP) a company with a good reputation for supplying routinely manufactured small precision aircraft components and replacement spare parts as subcontractors to several aircraft manufacturing and maintenance companies. LAP ordinarily carried out practically no creative design work itself but worked from drawings and manufacturing instructions provided by their customers.

LAP were delighted to win the contract for these 12 tanks, but they had made this contract with EJA at a selling price set below the estimated design and manufacturing costs. LAP's business strategy in this case was to deliberately accept a loss as a means for buying into a new area of the components market, thus expanding capability and product range.

The existing line and function organization at Lox Airparts Inc.   Figure 5.1 shows the organization of LAP just before the contract with EJA was signed. Many businesses that carry out routine commercial and manufacturing functions are organized in this fashion, which is known as a line and function organization. Senior managers occupy the top positions, and specialists (such as operations managers, accountants, and marketing managers) report to them. Other staff occupy the lower layers. The whole is like a family tree, following hierarchical management patterns that were laid down many thousands of years ago in the army and the church.

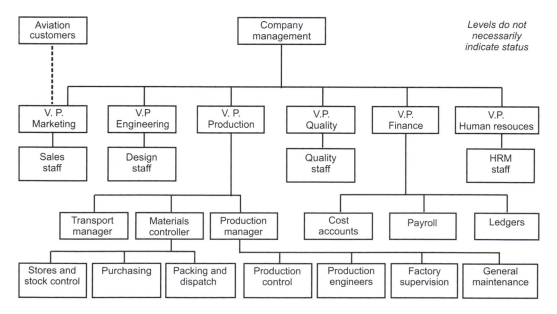

Figure 5.1   Outline organization of Lox Airparts Inc. before the EJA fuel tanks project

This line and function organization is also known as a vertical organization, because the lines of command (and their corresponding upward reporting lines) are predominately vertical. Although ad hoc horizontal lines of communication will inevitably develop between the various functions and the staff, no formal provision is made for these in the organization structure.

A coordinated functional matrix at Lox Airparts Inc. Planning and coordination difficulties arise when a company with a line and function organization encounters its first project. Senior company managers are accustomed to looking down their own lines of command into departments that perform routine functions. But a new project is a cross-functional operation that demands horizontal as well as vertical commands and communications. No person in this existing line and function organization has the time, the skills, and the assigned duty needed to plan a project as a whole entity and follow that entire venture through all the stages of its life cycle from design to packing and dispatch.

Fortunately LAP senior managers were aware of this shortcoming in their organization. They overcame the difficulty by appointing a temporary project manager with specific responsibility for planning and coordinating the EJA fuel tank project. The new organizational arrangement is shown in Figure 5.2.

The new arrangement is an example of a coordinated matrix organization. The project manager must have the necessary skills to plan a project, issue schedules, and then monitor all tasks to ensure that they are carried out within the required timescale and, as far as possible, within their cost budgets. This is a temporary organization that will revert back to the former line and function structure unless, of course, LAP receive further orders for projects.

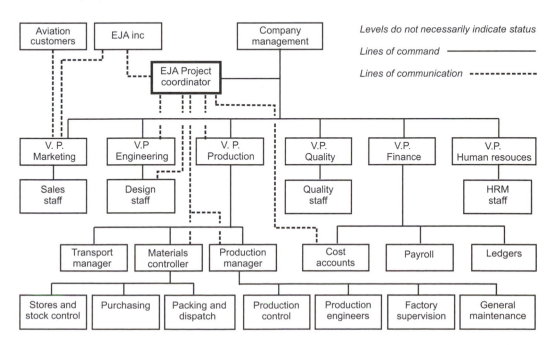

Figure 5.2   Outline organization of Lox Airparts Inc. during the EJA fuel tanks project

In this coordinated matrix the project manager has no line authority. This person is a planner and coordinator and can only request that project tasks are carried out according to the schedules that they produce. Thus the job title 'project coordinator' more accurately describes this role and is often used in preference to project manager. Organizational theorists would call this a staff position in a line and staff organization. If functional managers ignore the project manager or argue among themselves, the project coordinator's obvious remedy is to appeal to senior line management for help or arbitration. The position has some similarity with that of the secretary (or PA) to a senior executive. The secretary has no personal power or authority, but other personnel usually have the common sense to respect the secretary because failure to do so would call down the wrath of the relevant senior executive.

A coordinated matrix has the big advantage that it is very easy to establish and calls for no change in the existing company organization. It is not disruptive. When the lone project is over, the company simply carries on as before (except that it must decide what will happen to the project coordinator, who will then be without a project and without a job).

The duties of this project coordinator can be listed as follows:

- assimilate all project requirements by studying the EJA specification for the port and starboard tanks and the purchase contract;
- establish liaison with EJA, and thenceforth become LAP's principal point of contact for this project. This should help to create good communications between the two companies;
- plan the fuel tanks project, using critical path network analysis, and obtaining the input and agreement of all key project personnel within LAP;
- with the same key personnel who assisted with planning, estimate the project costs and establish project budgets for the individual tasks and for the functional departments;
- using suitable software, convert the network plan into work-to lists, one list for each functional manager involved in the project. If considered necessary, carry out resource scheduling at this stage. Each work-to list should be filtered so that it contains only tasks that are the responsibility of its particular functional manager;
- monitor the progress of every active task through all stages from initial work instruction to completion;
- attempt to replan or otherwise contain any time slippages, especially on critical tasks;
- report immediately to higher management any slippage that is in danger of delaying project completion and delivery of the fuel tanks;
- by collaboration with the cost accountant, monitor task costs again relevant budgets;
- ensure, using a suitable procedure, that any request for a design modification is critically examined and considered by key project staff before it is allowed (there is more on this important subject of managing changes in Chapter 11).

Matrix Solutions For Multiple Projects

When a company handles several projects simultaneously, it can appoint a coordinator or project manager for each project. If the individual projects are small, one coordinator can often be assigned to look after a group of projects. If there are regularly many projects in progress, the company might appoint a projects director to oversee the coordinators. Sometimes a project support office is set up that includes planner and cost control engineers, who will then form part of a projects support office.

The matrix arrangements for a main contractor that regularly undertakes civil engineering or construction projects (which could include airport construction or enlargement) will be different from those of a manufacturing company. One important difference for construction and civil engineering companies (together with their associated professions such as architects) is that practically all their work is to do with projects and no new order is a routine repetition of past work.

Figure 5.3 shows a notional multiple project matrix structure for a construction company (which might include some aviation construction projects within its work portfolio). This kind of matrix is also seen in companies engaged in petrochemical, mining, or other large capital projects.

Different Matrix Strengths

By no means is every matrix organization a coordinated matrix in which the project manager (or project managers) act merely as coordinators without line authority. The way in which power is apportioned between project managers and the various departmental managers can vary considerably from one company to another. Organization charts cannot show all the subtle nuances of power, and Figure 5.3 does not show how power is distributed between the project managers and the functional managers. Thus the chart in Figure 5.3 remains valid for all the variations of the matrix that will now be described.

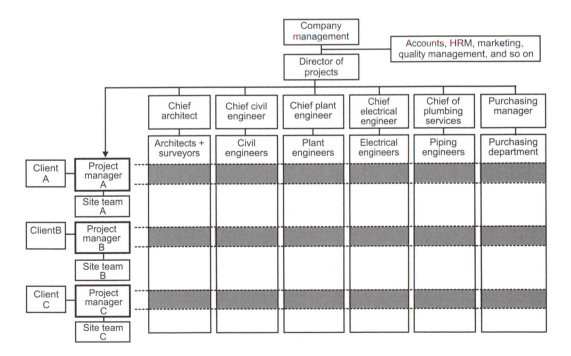

Figure 5.3   **Outline of a matrix organization for a large contractor engaged in civil engineering and construction projects (including airport facilities and buildings)**

Weak matrix   A weak matrix describes any form of matrix organization in which the project manager's power is very low compared with managers of the specialist functions. Thus a coordinated matrix is an example of a weak matrix.

Balanced matrix   The balanced matrix provides for a balance of power and authority between the project managers and the functional department managers. All managers are expected to work together harmoniously and make joint decisions (for example on the allocation of resources). This is a common form of matrix and is elegant in theory. However, it depends on universal goodwill, which does not exist in all companies, and is thus not an ideal solution for every project case.

Strong matrix   In a strong matrix the authority of the project managers is greater than that of the functional managers, at least as far as work allocation and progressing is concerned. The intention is that the functional managers nominate members of their departments to work for the project managers on specified projects. The people assigned report principally to the project managers (although they might remain physically located in their home departments).

The very strongest matrix form is the secondment matrix, where functional managers must release nominated members of their staff completely to work for project managers for as long as they are needed (which might involve temporary physical relocation of the staff concerned).

PROJECT TEAM ORGANIZATIONS

It is, of course, possible to arrange things differently from the matrix options described above. A complete work group or team can be created for each project as a self-contained unit with the project manager placed at its head. The project manager is given direct line authority over the team.

The example shown in Figure 5.4 is a project team organization that might be set up for the main contractor of large construction project (which could include an airport development project). The project manager is in direct command, with complete authority over the team members.

Communications across the various technical and professional disciplines are easier and faster in a team when compared to a matrix. All members of the team identify with the project and can (at least in the short term) be strongly motivated towards achieving the project goals.

The key members of the team should preferably be located near each other, in the same building if possible. Ideally, an office should be provided for use as a 'project war room', where team members can meet formally or informally whenever they wish. Drawings, charts, and plans can be displayed on tables and walls. War rooms should also be equipped with appropriate means for communicating with computer and communication networks.

Project Task Forces

A task force is an extreme form of a project team. It demands total dedication to the project, sometimes almost with fanaticism. A task force can generate the highest levels of

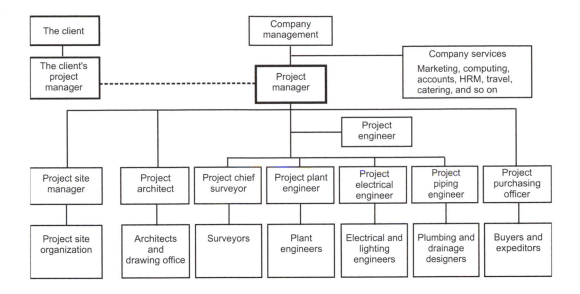

Figure 5.4   A possible project team organization for a construction project contractor

motivation and appreciation of urgency. It is the ideal arrangement for rescuing a project that is in danger of running late.

The task force leader must possess very strong determination and drive. They should also be experienced in the project management arts: if not, it might be prudent to engage an external project management consultant, either to lead the task force or to provide urgent on-the-job training and guidance.

The task force members will work more effectively if they can be located together, away from their normal working locations, with an office that can be used as their project war room.

Task forces in aerospace manufacturing projects   A self-contained project team might seem to be impracticable in a manufacturing company owing to the capital invested in the general manufacturing facilities. Expensive plant cannot usually be allocated for task force use and set aside full time for the project, no matter how urgent the work is.

This problem can be solved by including in the task force managers (or their senior delegates) from all the departments involved in executing the project. When the project demands the urgent use of scarce or expensive common resources, the relevant task force member will have the authority to instruct their home department to carry out the work.

Task forces in management change projects   Most management change projects begin with studies that have to be kept confidential, to avoid creating unfounded but damaging rumors. This is especially important where the project might lead to company reorganization or relocation and redundancies. When a relocation project is being considered, it is inevitable that several different locations will be considered and it is important to keep these possibilities confidential if staff rumors are to be avoided. For example, before Boeing moved its corporate headquarters from the original Seattle site (established in 1916), three cities in widely different parts of the US were short listed. Dallas and Denver featured in the shortlist before Chicago was chosen.

The time for openness and consultation with staff in management change projects must come, but not until the results of a completed study have suggested one or more preferred solutions or business plans and removed much of the doubt.

A task force comprising senior delegates from all company departments that would be affected by the management change project can be set to work in a secure office, allowing the study work to be carried out in secrecy. When external consultants are engaged to lead the study, the presence on the task force of people who know their departments' operations intimately can prevent expensive and damaging errors and omissions in the proposed solutions.

TEAM OR MATRIX: WHICH ORGANIZATION IS BEST?

Team Pros And Cons

Project teams have the advantage that they can each be directed to the successful completion of one project. A team can be completely autonomous. It is provided with and relies on its own resources. There is no clash of priorities resulting from a clamor of different project managers in competition for scarce, shared resources.

An important aspect of motivation is the generation of a team spirit, in which all members of the team strive to meet common goals. It is easier to establish a team spirit when a project team actually exists (as opposed to the case where the people are dispersed over a matrix organization that has to deal with many projects).

If the work is being conducted for a government defense contract, or for any other project that requires a secret or confidential environment, the establishment of a project team greatly helps the organizers to contain all the work and its information within secure boundaries.

However, unless the project is very large, the individual specialist subgroups within the team will be too small to allow optimum flexibility of labor and other resources. For example, where a specialist department in the organization employs 100 people on a project, the absence of a few workers through sickness might result in some rescheduling but would be unlikely to cause disaster. If, on the other hand, a project team had been set up to include its own independent specialist group, perhaps justifying the employment of only six people, the infection of three of these with influenza could set the project back by 3 weeks.

There is a danger that professional people working alone in small project teams are deprived of the benefits of working in a department with colleagues of their own specialist discipline. It is less easy for them to discuss technical problems with their peers or have access to the valuable fund of technical and professional data (historic and current) that such specialist functional groups accumulate.

Even if a project is of sufficient size to justify its own exclusive team, not all the problems of project coordination will necessarily be overcome. Very often it might be found impossible to house all the participants under one roof, or even in the same locality. Although team organization might be logical and ideal for the project, a general lack of coordination between the functions is still a possible risk.

A big problem with project team organization is realized when the project end is in sight. Team members will have concern about their future work, or indeed whether or not there will be any future work for them at all. That concern is a powerful demotivator and can lead to a slowing down of work in an attempt to delay project completion and put off the evil day.

Another possible danger with a team is that something could go seriously wrong with the project after its supposed completion, with expert attention required from the team's engineers to satisfy the customer and put matters right. If the team no longer exists, and the engineers who designed the project have been dispersed, events could take an embarrassing, even ugly, turn.

Matrix Pros And Cons

The matrix option allows the establishment of specialist functional groups which have 'eternal life', independent of the duration of individual projects. This continuity of work promotes the gradual build-up of expertise and experience. Specialist skills are concentrated. Pooling of skills provides for flexibility in deploying resources.

Each member of every specialist group enjoys a reasonably stable basis for employment (provided the order book is full). There is a clear promotion path within the discipline up to at least chief engineer level, and each person in the group is able to compete against their colleagues for more senior positions within the group as vacancies arise in the long term.

Performance assessment of each individual, and any recommendation for promotion, improved salary, or other benefits, is carried out by a chief engineer or other manager of the same engineering discipline within the stable group. This is more likely to result in a fair assessment and employee satisfaction. These possibilities are not readily available to the specialist engineer working alone in a multidisciplined project team.

The matrix organization has its own characteristic disadvantages. Not least of these is the split responsibility that each group member faces between their functional line manager and the project manager in a balanced matrix. Employees are expected to serve two managers. Personal stress and conflict will arise if an individual receives conflicting instructions from the project and functional managers. That violates the long-established principle of unity of command.

Summary

So, team or matrix? The arguments will no doubt continue as to which is the better of the two organizations. Some of the pros and cons are summarized in Figure 5.5. As a general guide, large projects of long duration will probably benefit from the formation of project teams. Matrix organizations are indicated for companies that handle a number of small projects in which neither the amount of resources nor the timescale needed for each project is great.

On a more personal note, think of yourself for a moment as being a member of the project organization, and imagine how each of the different possible organizations would affect your own motivation and job satisfaction. If you have the power to choose the project organization structure, that imaginative experience might lead you to make the correct choice.

Characteristic	Organization indicated	
	Team	Matrix
Maximum authority for the project manager	●	
Freedom from duplicated or ambiguous lines of command	●	
Maximum motivation of staff to meet difficult targets	●	
High security of information: by enclosing work in secure areas	●	
High security of information: by restricting the number of staff who need to know about the work	●	
Most flexible deployment of resources		●
Most effective use across the company of those with rare specialist skills or knowledge		●
Large project, employing many people for a long duration	●	
Several small simultaneous projects, each needing a few people for a short time		●
Career motivation of individuals: opportunities for promotion within a person's specialist discipline		●
Career motivation of individuals: through long-term continuity and relative stability of the organization		●
Post-design support to construction or commissioning staff		●
Efficient post-project services to the customer		●
Establishment of 'retained engineering' information banks from which future projects can benefit		●

Figure 5.5   Project team versus a balanced matrix

HYBRID ORGANIZATIONS

Sometimes companies adopt a hybrid organization, operating a matrix organization in general, but with teams set up for certain projects when the need arises.

An example of such a hybrid organization is shown in Figure 5.6. This shows the same contracting company that was illustrated in Figure 5.3. That company was organized originally as a matrix. However, now it has just signed contracts for two new projects, each of which will require only one of the specialist functions from the whole matrix.

Project D is for the repair of Runway 27 at XYZ airport. This runway has suffered cracking and surface deterioration and is in urgent need of repairs. However, it is the main runway at the airport and works can only be carried out at night. A task force is the ideal organization for seeing this project through to completion as soon as possible, and the obvious home for that task force in the contractor's organization is in the civil engineering group.

Project E is to replace the runway lighting, some of the cabling, and the control tower switchgear at ABC airport. To keep the airport operational, the project manager will arrange for the lights to be replaced six at a time, during non-operational night hours. This will

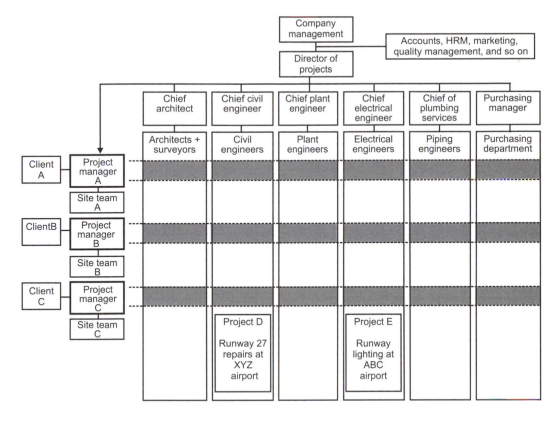

Figure 5.6   **Outline of a hybrid organization for a large contractor engaged in civil engineering and construction projects (including airport facilities and buildings)**

continue until eventually all the lights have been renewed. The switchgear changeover can be made during daylight hours, picking a day when there is bright sunshine. This project has no particular urgency, but it must be carefully planned to avoid operational disruption. Clearly this project can be organized as a team contained entirely within the electrical group.

So this contractor's matrix organization has now become a hybrid, in which the original matrix organization has been supplemented by two specialist, custom-made project teams.

CONTRACT MATRIX ORGANIZATIONS

In large aviation construction projects the customer/supplier chains can form a contract matrix. In the example shown in Figure 5.7, the project owner (the customer or client) has engaged a managing contractor to design the project, carry out purchasing, hire subcontractors, and generally manage all the activities at the airport site.

The organization chart shows that many of the companies involved in the project will have their own project managers, in addition to the principal project manager employed by the main contractor.

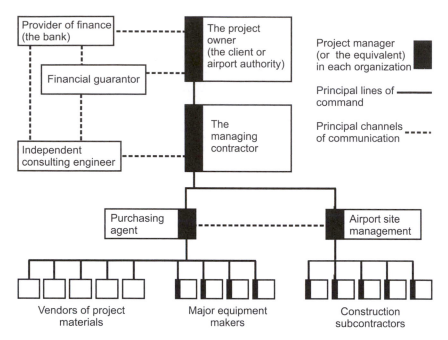

Figure 5.7   A contract matrix organization for an airport construction project

This project is being funded by a bank, which has lent funds on condition that the project owner finds a guarantor who is willing to underwrite a substantial part of the lending risk. In the UK, for example, the Export Credits Guarantee Department (ECGD) acts as guarantor for some projects carried out for overseas clients, whilst the Export-Import Bank (Ex-Im) fulfils a similar role in the US.

Both the bank and the guarantor need expert independent advice. This has been provided in the example of Figure 5.7 by a professional engineering organization. This organization, sometime known simply as 'the engineer', can inspect progress and certify all significant claims for payments so that monies are only paid against work that has actually been performed correctly and in the quantities listed on the contractor's invoices.

JOINT VENTURE PROJECTS

For very large projects several companies might agree to combine their resources and share the technical problems, expense, and risk by forming a consortium or joint venture company. This approach will add yet another complication to the organization and at least one more project manager.

Many aviation projects, such as the design of large passenger aircraft or sophisticated military and naval aircraft involve such a wide range of different technologies and such vast investment (and risk) that a joint venture or consortium organization has virtually become the norm. These organizations span not only several different companies, but also international borders, with all the difficulties of language differences and cross-border engineering standards compatibility. However, for aerospace manufacturing companies such as Airbus and more specifically with the A-330F project most recently, a joint venture structure seems to provide an integrated base from which to reach for longer-term strategic goals. Early in 2008 Airbus announced a commitment to establish an A330 Freighter aircraft final assembly line in Mobile, Alabama if Northrop Grumman (supported by Airbus's parent company, EADS-European Aeronautic Defence and Space Company) received the order to build aerial refuelling tankers from the United States Air Force.

An example of a joint venture organization is given, in outline, in Figure 5.8.

For any complex project, apart from the obvious need to define responsibilities and all the contractual details, it is vital that the lines of communication between all the parties are clearly established and specified. It is not unusual to find projects where the participants are separated by thousands of miles, working in countries with different engineering standards. The project manager will have to plan for details such as working with companies that have different national working practices, workdays, and holidays. The volume of information for a large project, whether in the form of drawings, other technical documents, commercial correspondence, queries, and even hotel and travel arrangements can be mind-boggling.

THE PROJECT MANAGER

If the objectives of project management could be condensed into responsibility for ensuring work completion within time and cost restrictions, these goals could be achieved by a variety of approaches. One project manager might operate successfully by inducing fear and trepidation in subordinates, so that their every word is seen as a command to be instantly obeyed. Another might achieve the same results through gentle but firm persuasion. The essential element here is the ability to motivate people, by whatever means: the seasoned expert will be able to vary their management style according to the response of the individual being managed.

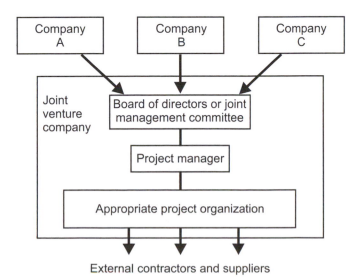

Figure 5.8   One form of a joint venture organization

The skilled and successful project manager will strive to understand the needs and culture of those in the project organization as early as possible and, then adapt the management style accordingly. This approach stands far more chance of gaining the respect and support of staff than the alternative, more arrogant, method of attempting to impose a 'one size fits all' style of management and expect that all employees conform to this approach. Some employees may be more prone to 'gentle persuasion' and others to 'authoritarian means.' Employees have varied skills, backgrounds, and motivation levels to be treated in a monolithic fashion during projects.

The average project participant will appreciate being led by a project manager who displays competence, makes clear decisions, gives precise, achievable instructions, delegates well, listens to and accepts sound advice, is enthusiastic and confident, and thus generally commands respect by example and qualities of leadership.

Perceptiveness And The Use Of Project Information

Other essential characteristics of the project manager can be grouped under the heading of perceptiveness. Project managers must be able to extract the salient facts from a set of data or a particular set of circumstances. They must then be able to use these facts to best effect by taking action themselves or, where that is not possible, by reporting important exceptions to executive management (with unimportant and irrelevant material filtered out).

Most project managers will become accustomed to being presented with information that is incomplete, unduly optimistic, inaccurate, deliberately misleading, or completely wrong. Project managers will learn to check much of the information that they receive, particularly by knowing what questions to ask to probe its validity. As they gain experience of a particular organization they should become capable of assessing the reliability of individuals or departments, so that they can apply 'confidence factors' to the data which those individuals or departments submit and the stories that they tell.

The Project Manager As A Hunter/Gatherer Of Information

All project managers know the frustration caused not simply by receiving inaccurate information, but by receiving no information at all. Data deficiencies can take the form of delayed instructions or approvals from the customer, late information from subcontractors and vendors, and tardy release of design and other information within the project manager's own company. It can be difficult to obtain reliable and regular reports of cost and progress from far-flung project outposts, particularly where the individuals responsible feel themselves to be remote and outside the project manager's immediate authority or are educated to standards below those of the fully developed nations.

The ability to gather and assess relevant data is, therefore, another essential property for project management. It is no good expecting to obtain the complete picture and manage a project simply by sitting fixed behind a desk for the duration of the project. The project manager must take (and be seen to take) an active interest. They should visit personally and regularly those parts of the organization on which the project is dependent (a process sometimes known as 'management by walkabout'). It might be necessary for the project manager to visit vendors, subcontractors, the customer, and a remote construction site at suitable intervals in order to gather facts, resolve local disputes, generate enthusiasm, or simply to witness progress at first hand.

General Knowledge And Current Awareness

Project managers in the age of technology could be described as specialists. Their background may be in one of the specialist engineering or other professional disciplines and they will certainly need to be trained in one or more of the current special project management techniques if they are to operate effectively. Nevertheless the term 'specialist' can be misleading, since much of the project manager's time will be taken up with coordinating the activities of project participants from a wide variety of administrative, professional, technical, and craft backgrounds. This work, far from requiring specialization, demands a sufficient general understanding of the work carried out by those participants for the project manager to be able to discuss the work sensibly, understand all the commercial and technical data received, and appreciate (or question) any reported problems.

The project manager should understand the administrative procedures that will be applied throughout the project organization. If a person is asked to handle a flow of project data between different departments, they should be able to use their understanding of the administration and its procedures to arrange for the information to be presented in the form most likely to be helpful to the various recipients. In the jargon of computer technology, the project manager may be asked to solve interface problems, the solutions to which need some understanding of how the peripheral units operate.

There is little doubt that project management tools, techniques, and philosophy will continue to undergo development and change. The project manager must be prepared to keep abreast of this development, undergoing training or retraining whenever necessary, and passing this training on to other members of the organization where appropriate. Some new developments will advance the practice of project management in general and others will not.

Some practices and techniques will be more useful to a particular project situation than others. The project manager must be able to choose, use, or adapt the most appropriate management methods for the particular project. Temptation to impose unsuitable methods on an organization for the sole reason that they represent the height of current fashion must be resisted.

Technical Awareness Of The Project Manager

Although there are many projects in commerce and industry where the project manager can be successful even though they have not been trained in the core technical discipline of the business, aviation projects do demand that technical skill. It is important that aviation project managers have either technical expertise or at least a high degree of appreciation of the industry.

Aviation as a field is a complex aggregation of technical knowledge and skill sets. Further, most of its projects and operations are subject to scrutiny and approval from national or international regulating authorities. This is not an environment for the beginner, and the project manager who comes in as a complete outsider would have significant difficulty in coming to terms with the industry-specific jargon and the regulatory background.

Support, Cooperation And Training For The Project Manager

No matter how experienced, competent, enthusiastic, and intelligent the person chosen for the job of project manager, they cannot expect to operate effectively alone, without adequate support and cooperation. This obviously includes the willing cooperation of all staff engaged on the project, whether they report to the project manager in the line organization or not. But it also includes support from higher management in the organization, who must at least ensure the provision of essential finance, accommodation, facilities, equipment, manpower, and other resources when they are needed and the availability of suitable clerical or other supporting staff. Just as those working on the project need to be properly motivated, so does the project manager, and supportive higher management who show constructive and helpful interest in the project can go a long way to achieve this. They can also help in the longer term by providing opportunities for training as new techniques or management systems are developed.

A person who is responsible for the overall allocation and progressing of project tasks will inevitably be called upon to decide priorities or criticize progress. The project manager must often arrange for the issue of work instructions knowing that they have no direct authority over all the departments involved. In a matrix organization, departmental managers alone are responsible for the performance, day-to-day management, and work allocation within their own departments. I have even known cases where departmental managers have told project managers to keep out of their departments. In such circumstances the project manager's influence can only be exerted as reflected authority from higher management, without whose full backing the project manager will be ineffective.

The main show of authority which the project manager can wield stems from their own personality and ability to persuade or motivate others. In these enlightened times discipline no longer implies the imposition of rigid authoritarian regimes or management by fear through the constant threat of dismissal or other punitive action. Mutual cooperation and established job satisfaction are the more likely elements of an effective approach, especially in the long term. There will, however, be occasions when firm discipline has to be exercised; when, in the last resort, the full backing and support of higher management must be available as a reserve force which the project manager can call upon in any hour of need.

The project manager should keep abreast of new developments in project management. Various training establishments arrange project management seminars where, in addition to the formal training given, delegates from different companies are able to meet and discuss mutual problems and solutions, and exchange views and experiences generally. The effectiveness of these individuals and of the profession as a whole must benefit from this type of exchange.

Just as important as the project manager's own training is the creation of an enlightened and informed attitude to modern project management methods among all those in the project organization. Ideally, when the objectives of a particular project are outlined, the project manager should ensure that participating managers, engineers, and line supervisors have at least been given an elementary grounding in the appreciation of scheduling, principles of cost and progress control, and the interpretation of associated computer reports. This should all be with specific relevance to the procedures chosen for use on the actual project. Training or instructions should be given in the use of the various forms and other documents to be used and (where appropriate) in the active use of relevant computer systems. There is a danger that people who are suddenly asked to work with unfamiliar techniques and procedures, without sufficient training or explanation, will fail to cooperate. People neglected in this respect cannot be expected to provide the necessary feedback and other responses. If participating staff understand the procedures and the reasons for them, their cooperation is far more likely to be forthcoming and effective.

PROJECT SUPPORT GROUPS

Unless the organization is too small to support the additional expense, it makes sense to set up a central project management support or project services group. This is staffed with people (not too many!) who are capable of the day-to-day chores of planning; resource scheduling, cost estimating, work progressing, cost and progress reporting, and general supervision of the company's project management computer systems.

A project support group can be used in most kinds of project organization. The group can be a functional department within a pure project team, where it will serve and report directly to the project manager. If the organization is a multi-project matrix or a hybrid organization, the support group can be established as one of the departmental functions (an arrangement illustrated by the project services group in Figure 5.6).

A project support group concentrates a company's expertise in the techniques of project management, just as any functional grouping can enhance a particular professional discipline. Centralization helps to standardize project administration procedures across all projects in a company. A project services group can be the logical place from which to coordinate all parts of the project cycle, from authorization to closedown. It can administer procedures such as project registration and change control.

Some powerful project management computer systems, especially those handling multi-project scheduling, are best placed under the supervision of specially trained experts. Those experts must have a good working knowledge of all the organization's projects and combine that with special training in using the system and safeguarding the integrity of its database and back-up files. A central project services group is an excellent place in which to place that responsibility.

6

Compiling the Work Breakdown Structure

This chapter describes the work breakdown process. This means breaking the project down into manageable chunks from which work can be allocated to departmental managers and other members of the project organization.

THE WORK BREAKDOWN STRUCTURE (WBS) CONCEPT

A WBS is a logical, hierarchical tree of all the tasks needed to complete a project. The top of the tree is the project itself. The next layer or level down contains the main *work packages*. Levels below that progressively get more detailed until the bottom level is reached that shows all the smallest day-to-day tasks or project components. Anyone familiar with the arrangement of folders and files in a computer memory, or who has researched their ancestral family tree, should be familiar with this idea.

The work breakdown concept is also seen in the 'goes into charts' that engineers and designers use when organizing their drawings, bills of materials, and parts lists into a logical pattern. So, the first example of a WBS in this chapter is for a manufacturing project. Figure 6.1 is a summarized version of the top WBS levels for an imaginary project to design and develop a small prototype aircraft. All aerospace engineers will recognize how this WBS arrangement corresponds closely to the upper levels of a 'goes into' chart. Apart from its relationship to the major components of the airplane, one can see how this breakdown might also dictate the allocation of various senior aerospace engineers or design managers to different parts of this design and development project.

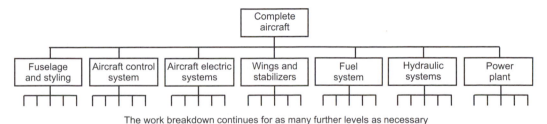

The work breakdown continues for as many further levels as necessary

Figure 6.1   **Simplified upper level WBS for an aircraft project**

Importance Of A Project WBS

Every project must have a work breakdown if it is to be managed successfully, although for the very tiniest of projects that work breakdown can be a simple task list. No one puts the case for the WBS better or more eloquently than Stephen Devaux, who wrote:

'If I could wish but one thing for every project, it would be a comprehensive and detailed WBS. The lack of a good WBS probably results in more inefficiency, schedule slippage, and cost overruns on projects than any other single cause. When a consultant is brought in to perform the role of "project doctor", invariably there has been no WBS developed. No one knows what work has been done, nor what work remains to be done. The first thing to do is assemble the planning team and teach them how to create a WBS.'

(Devaux, 1999)

Logical Interfacing And Completeness

In addition to regarding the work breakdown as a family tree, it is also possible to visualize it as a jigsaw puzzle, with every piece put in its right place and with no piece missing. This concept is useful on two counts:

1. It is important that when the work breakdown is produced every piece of the puzzle is included, with no piece missing to spoil the total picture. This objective is sometimes difficult to achieve, but the risks of omission can be reduced by the use of suitable checklists. Brainstorming can be useful for projects with no similar predecessors.
2. A method must be found that clearly and simply identifies each piece of the puzzle and denotes its position in relation to all the other pieces. This objective can be achieved by giving each piece an identification number which, through the use of a carefully devised, logical coding system, acts as a locator or address. Coding systems are introduced later in this chapter.

SOME WBS EXAMPLES

A few people find difficulty in constructing work breakdown charts and we have both seen students' coursework in which work breakdown charts have been confused with organization charts. Thus this chapter contains a sprinkling of WBS examples that represent various kinds of projects.

Project For A National Charity Fundraising Week

For our first WBS example we have chosen a familiar everyday kind of project with which all people come into contact in their ordinary lives. We refer to projects conducted by national charities in which various means are employed to persuade us to donate money. Members of the public are not alone in receiving charitable requests. Most corporate bodies are asked to contribute to a number of charities, either anonymously or occasionally in return for publicity (when the donations can become sponsorship payments). Of course companies in the aviation industry will receive such approaches, and responsible managers with social conscience will usually be willing to sanction payments for cancer research or other charities that present a good case.

Childaire is a (fictitious) children's charity, set up with the particular specialization of assisting parents or guardians to provide essential air travel for their children (done in partnership with a specific airline). Childaire would assist, for example, in cases where a child had to be flown urgently to a distant specialist hospital for expert medical care. Children sometimes become separated from one or both parents in times of natural disaster, through family break-ups, or other reasons. In all such cases Childaire would consider paying for air travel so that adults and children could be reunited. The charity occasionally also pays for small parties of deprived children to travel for short holidays that their parents could not otherwise afford. The partner airline to the charity provides discounted airfares as well as assisting with the fundraising activities.

Much of the work carried out by any charity must be devoted to collecting as much money as possible. Without such strenuous mercenary efforts a charity would not be able to render its humanitarian services.

The Childaire charity managers need more funds, and are about to stage a 1-week event to raise $2 million. Sensibly, Childaire has decided to treat this as a project, and one of the first things that they must do is to appoint a project manager. One of the project manager's first tasks is to draw a WBS. The result is shown in Figure 6.2.

This WBS is seen to have four main elements or principal work packages, and one can easily imagine that a different senior manager should be made responsible for each of these.

One manager will organize all public relations activities nationwide that tell the public about this special week and the work of Childaire. Thus the second level WBS breakdown for this public relations work package might include newspaper advertising, television commercials, posters, billboards, mailshots, and so on.

Someone else can be put in charge of 'local events'. These will be arranged through a network of volunteers, and might include coffee mornings, students' rags, village fetes, sponsored walks, and so on. As this is a children's charity, many of the activities will be centered on schools as far as possible.

No fundraising week would be complete without its flag day, in which volunteers make their presence felt in the streets of towns and cities throughout the land, carrying tin cans with slots in their tops for the receipt of donations. Optimists might even be seen carrying buckets for this work. Someone must organize the purchase of cans and their labels, find the volunteers, and make sure that all the filled cans are promptly and safely returned to headquarters or other designated secure collecting point (such as a participating bank).

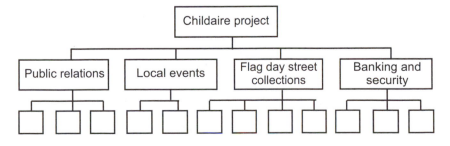

Figure 6.2   WBS for Childaire's national fundraising week

If the fundraising week is successful, hundreds of thousands of pounds might be collected. In all events where money is concerned there is scope for fraud and theft, so Childaire has been wise enough to include a task for overseeing the handling of all the money collected, to try to ensure that it ends up in the charity's bank and not in the pockets of fraudsters and thieves.

An Airport Development Project

A large city has long been ashamed of its lack of a suitable airport, and at last has reached agreement for a new airport development with the relevant aviation authority, the local government agencies, and the neighborhood residents and businesses. The site is scrubland that has to be leveled and landscaped before any construction work can take place. The region is poorly served by public roads or rail transport, but these facilities are to be treated as separate projects and we are concerned here only with roads in the immediate environs of the airport.

Figure 6.3 shows a small part of the large WBS that would be needed for this airport project, from initial site preparation to opening day.

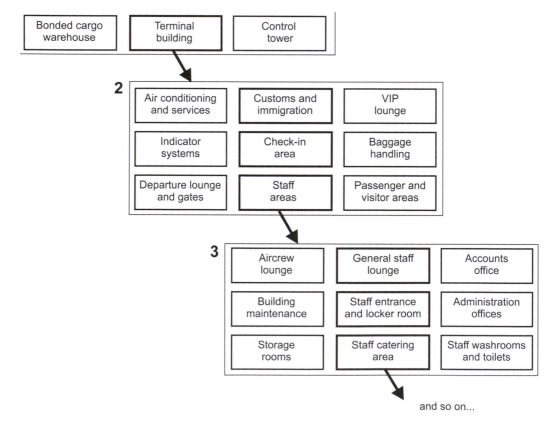

Figure 6.3   Simplified upper levels of a WBS for a new airport development project

Each of the main work packages at level one is concerned with a significant part of the whole airport project, and entities big enough to be called subprojects that warrant their own subproject managers.

Level two of this WBS expands each of the work packages from level one. There is space in our illustration to show only one of these breakdowns, and we have chosen the overseas passenger terminal (which will handle both arrivals and departures). Our illustration is not complete, but it does show many of the principal aspects of the overseas terminal subproject.

Level three breaks each second level item down further still, and again we show just one of these breakdowns for simplicity. This time we have selected the staff areas, which will be grouped together in one part of the terminal building. These staff areas are not accessible by the traveling public. They include lounges for terminal staff and for aircrew, for airline ground staff, and so on. Also in this part of the building will be changing and locker rooms, administration offices, staff canteens, possibly a staff crèche, together with utility rooms and administration offices.

And so this WBS must be continued until, eventually, the lowest levels are reached in which all the tiniest components of the new airport and its immediate environs are listed. Thus this WBS can be drawn only at the upper levels when the project starts, and the lowest levels will not be known until much of the design concept has been completed.

A Large Public Event Project: The Inaugural Celebration Ceremonies For An International Airport

This is an example of a management project. When judged against the scale of many modern projects, organizing a celebration might seem to be a trivial affair. However, suppose that you were asked to manage a large public celebration. There are going to be guests coming from many parts of the world, lavish displays of flowers, music and entertainment, sightseers, media representatives, and many other things to plan and manage. You would need a lot of help, which would involve delegating parts of the project to various experts. How would you go about breaking this project down into manageable chunks?

The WBS design for this airport inauguration project is not quite as straightforward as might first be thought and there is more than one possible solution, any of which might be workable. Two of these solutions are shown in part in Figure 6.4. In both cases only the first level of breakdown is shown, and some work packages have been left out through lack of space. However, the diagrams in Figure 6.4 are adequate for the purposes of illustration. Remember that the aim of the WBS is to break the project down into bits that can be assigned to different managers or other people in a logical way.

In the upper WBS of Figure 6.4 it is assumed that a different manager will be engaged for each specialist function. For example, a music and entertainments organizer will be expected to choose the music for the ceremony, which includes everything from the piped music for the open air spectators to a small orchestra playing in the foyer of the new terminal building. The person organizing the floral displays will be expected to provide these inside the main terminal building, and at several external locations.

One important role is the security manager and they will have responsibility for both security and routine policing at all venues connected with this event.

Now consider the lower of the two WBS patterns given in Figure 6.4. Here the major work packages have been determined primarily by the location of the tasks involved.

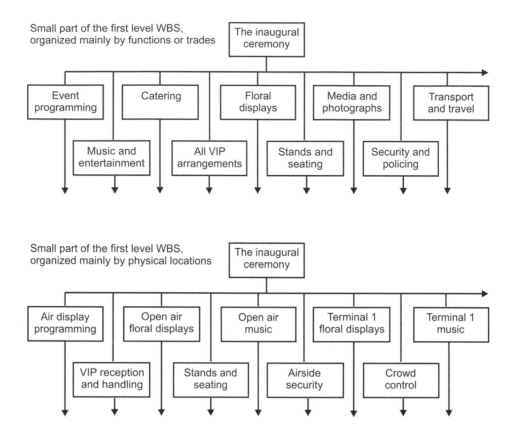

**Figure 6.4   Different possible WBS patterns for an airport inauguration
ceremony**

Thus, for example, organizing the floral displays in the open air is seen as a different
task from organizing floral displays within the terminal building, so that two different
managers and different florists might be appointed to these tasks.

The functional solution shown in the upper Figure 6.4 diagram is probably more cost
effective and tends to place top-level tasks in the hands of fewer managers and, moreover,
managers who should have the essential technical or operational skills. However, some
might prefer the WBS in the bottom half of Figure 6.4, which shows that there are projects
where more than one acceptable pattern of the WBS can be found

CODING SYSTEMS

General

Every project task will need to be given a name or descriptive title, but such names
must always be augmented by a specific code. Names usually describe the nature of
the task (for example, secure license, procure aircraft, sign vendor contract) but they do
not usually indicate where the task lies with respect to the work breakdown or, indeed,
within the physical layout of the finished project. Moreover, names are often abbreviated

in schedules, so that 'test customer billing system' might be reduced to 'test cust bill' where column space is limited in a schedule or report. It is essential that every task be given some short tag that identifies it uniquely and, at the same time, indicates its exact position in the WBS hierarchy.

A code may be a sequence of alphabetic characters, a set of numerical digits, or some mix of these two (an alpha-numeric code). Coding systems should be designed so that the maximum amount of information about each item is conveyed by the minimum possible number of characters.

Everyday examples of product codes used by manufacturers include the familiar type numbers used by some automobile manufacturers. German companies in particular use codes rather than stylistic names for their cars, so that the purchaser knows (for example) that a BMW 3 series refers to a range with smaller bodies that their BMW 5 series.

Examples abound in the aviation industry. Airbus model numbers are of the form A3nn, with example being A300, A310 (<http://www.aerospaceweb.org/question/planes/q0276a.shtml>). Another very familiar case is the Boeing commercial airliner system.

Boeing codes take the form 7n7-xxx. Here the outer two 7s of the first three digits proclaim that the aircraft is a commercial airliner. For example, a 747 is a four-engined large wide-body aircraft, whilst a 767 is another commercial airliner, but with a twin-engined narrow-body design. Boeing then add a further three digits of the form y00, to identify a particular design variant. Thus a 767-300 is a particular variant of the Boeing 767. Boeing further developed this system so that two digits replace the last two zeros to identify a particular customer. Using this coding system, a Boeing 767-200 delivered to Air Canada would be coded 767-233 (<http://en.wikipedia.org/wiki/Boeing_Commercial_Airplanes>).

Compatibility Of Codes With Other Systems

The designer of a project management coding system must always bear in mind that it should not be developed in isolation from other management and engineering information systems in the same organization. There are many advantages to applying a common coding system over all projects and other activities in a company. Suitable design will enable the same system to be used for all departments, so that codes relate to costs, budgets, document numbers, and the physical components of projects.

Functions Of Code

A code is a short and precise method for conveying essential data about an item. For project management purposes an item might be anything from the whole project to the smallest part of it, physical or abstract. It could be a component, a drawing, a job, a manufacturing operation, a piece of construction work, an engineering design activity, part of a computer program—anything, in fact, which is necessary for the project. One thing that most of these items have in common is that they are associated with cost. Each item (either by itself or grouped with others) has costs that must be estimated, budgeted, spent, measured, reported, assessed, and (where appropriate) recovered.

There are many reasons for allocating codes to items, rather than simply describing them in words. For example, codes can be designed to be precise and unambiguous. They also have the advantage, essential in computer systems, of facilitating filing, analysis, editing, and sorting for reporting and control.

The code for a particular item will perform the first of the following functions and possibly one or both of the others listed below:

- a code must act as a unique name that *identifies* the item to which it refers;
- the identifying code, either by itself or by the addition of subcodes, can be arranged so that it categorizes, qualifies, or in some other way, *describes* the item to which it relates;
- a code can act as an address. Postal zip codes are an obvious example. Bin numbers used in stores and warehouses are another.

The best coding systems are those which manage to combine these functions as simply as possible in numbers that can be used throughout a company's management information system.

Examples follow that show the kind of information that can be contained within the code for any item. The systems used as examples here and illustrated in Figures 6.5, 6.6, 6.7, and 6.8 are taken from light and heavy engineering and from mining, but the general principles are interchangeable between these and all other types of projects.

Coded WBS For An Avionics Project

Figure 6.5 is a WBS for a small avionics project, to which codes have been added, as follows:

- **Project identifier**: The project identification number for the breakdown shown in Figure 6.5 is 110-0000. This number is sufficient to identify the project for all accounting, engineering, and manufacturing purposes. Such project numbers are typically allocated from a register. Some companies might call them contract numbers or works order numbers instead. It is possible to design the project numbering method in a way that allows each number to signify certain key information about its project, in addition to acting as a simple identifier. Examples of this also occur in Figures 6.7 and 6.8.
- **Item identifier**: Each number, provided it is unique within the system, is an unambiguous way of naming any item. It is easy, however, to transpose digits or make other errors when entering numbers on forms or keyboards. It is wise, therefore, to bracket a concise description with the number whenever possible as a simple precaution against undiscovered numerical errors. Thus it is usually better to refer to an item as 'Transformer 110-2210' in documents such as purchase requisitions rather than just '110-2210'.
- **Relationship within the project**: Further examination of Figure 6.5 shows that the code numbers have been designed to correspond with the work breakdown (or family tree) hierarchy. Examples are given for components of the Transformer 110-2210 and set out more clearly in Figure 6.6. The numbers denote that all numbers starting with the string 110 are used on Project 110-0000 and, further that numbers starting 110-221 are used on Transformer 110-2210.
- **Operation identifier**: The task of winding the purpose-built transformer 110-2210 might be given a related cost code, such as 110-2210C, where the C suffix

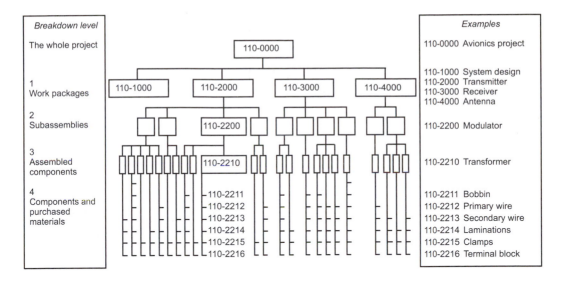

Figure 6.5   Part of the WBS and coding structure for a small avionics project

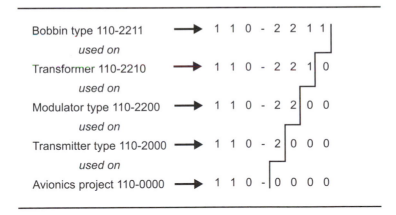

Figure 6.6   Detail from the avionics project WBS

denotes the coil winding operation. A two-digit suffix is more likely to be used than a single letter, allowing greater scope for detailed breakdown into several individual operations.

- **Identifiers for department, discipline or trade and labor grade**: A one- or two-digit subcode is often incorporated to show which department is responsible for a particular task or cost item. More digits can be added to denote the trade or engineering discipline involved. Consider, for instance, the activity of designing Transformer 110-2210. The cost code might be 110-2210-153 with the three-digit subcode 153 in this case showing that the engineering department (1) is responsible for the task, the engineering discipline is electrical (coded 5), and the last digit (3) indicates the standard cost grade of person (for example senior engineer, engineer or designer) normally expected to carry out the task of designing this transformer.

Two Examples Of Coding Systems For Larger Projects

Figure 6.7 shows the codes used by a heavy engineering company for the WBS of all its highly capital-intensive projects. This example proved very practicable in all respects for many years. Figure 6.8 shows a WBS coding system that might have been developed for the airport construction project, the WBS for which was shown in Figure 6.3.

BENEFITS OF A LOGICAL CODING SYSTEM

Without coded information in a database, something akin to chaos would reign in all but the smallest project because of the multiple flows of data. Coding facilitates database collection and redistribution of data throughout a project organization. These states of order and chaos are illustrated in Figure 6.9.

Although the primary purpose of a coding system might be to identify parts or to allocate costs, there are many benefits available to the company which is able to maintain a logical coding system in which all the codes and subcodes have common significance throughout the company's management information systems. These benefits increase with time and the accrual of records, provided that the system is used consistently without unauthorized adaptations or additions.

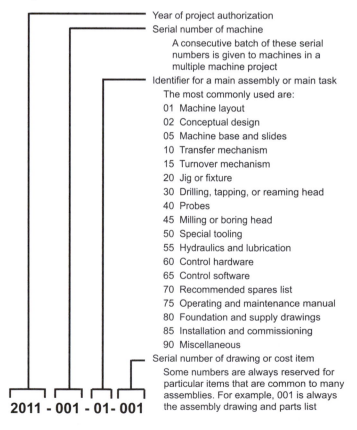

Figure 6.7   Codes used by a heavy engineering company

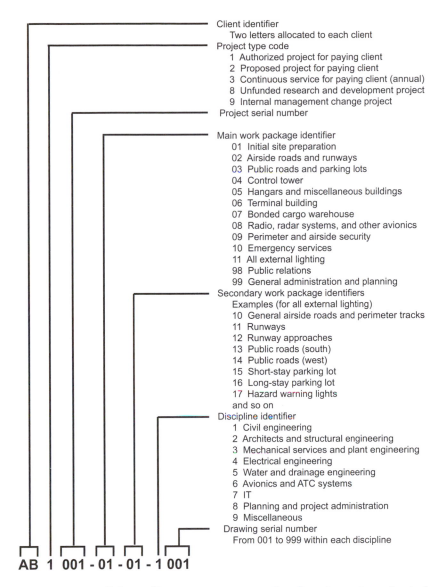

Client identifier
    Two letters allocated to each client
Project type code
    1 Authorized project for paying client
    2 Proposed project for paying client
    3 Continuous service for paying client (annual)
    8 Unfunded research and development project
    9 Internal management change project
Project serial number

Main work package identifier
    01 Initial site preparation
    02 Airside roads and runways
    03 Public roads and parking lots
    04 Control tower
    05 Hangars and miscellaneous buildings
    06 Terminal building
    07 Bonded cargo warehouse
    08 Radio, radar systems, and other avionics
    09 Perimeter and airside security
    10 Emergency services
    11 All external lighting
    98 Public relations
    99 General administration and planning
Secondary work package identifiers
    Examples (for all external lighting)
    10 General airside roads and perimeter tracks
    11 Runways
    12 Runway approaches
    13 Public roads (south)
    14 Public roads (west)
    15 Short-stay parking lot
    16 Long-stay parking lot
    17 Hazard warning lights
    and so on
Discipline identifier
    1 Civil engineering
    2 Architects and structural engineering
    3 Mechanical services and plant engineering
    4 Electrical engineering
    5 Water and drainage engineering
    6 Avionics and ATC systems
    7 IT
    8 Planning and project administration
    9 Miscellaneous
Drawing serial number
    From 001 to 999 within each discipline

AB 1 001 - 01 - 01 - 1 001

Figure 6.8   A possible coding arrangement for the airport project shown in Figure 6.3

The benefits depend on being able to retrieve and process the data effectively, which invariably requires the use of a computer system. If a coding system is designed logically (taking account of hierarchical structure and families) and is well managed, some or all of the following benefits can be expected:

- easy retrieval of items from records of past projects which correspond to or are similar to items expected in new projects, essential as a basis for making comparative cost estimates.
- easy search and retrieval of design information (especially flowsheets, calculations, and drawings) for processes, assemblies, or components used on

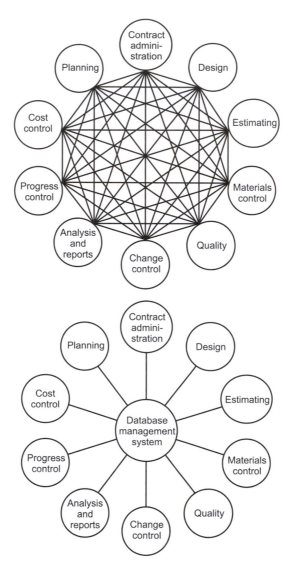

Figure 6.9   Coded data in a database brings order from chaos

past projects which are relevant to a current project. This 'retained engineering' can save considerable engineering design work, time, and costs if all or part of the previous design can be reused or adapted. Not only does such design retrieval avoid the unnecessary costs of designing everything afresh, but it also allows the new project to incorporate designs that have already been proven or debugged, so that the scope for errors is reduced.

- rapid identification of purchase requisitions and specifications from previous projects for equipment which corresponds to new equipment requirements. One application of this is to speed the preparation of new purchase specifications, particularly when much or all of the previous text can be used again.
- grouping of components into families according to their basic shapes and sizes. This is particularly necessary for manufacturing operations where the plant is arranged in cells for group technology.

- if it is possible to use a common system, then the cost estimates, budgets, recorded costs, drawing schedules, many other documents, and tasks on the project plan can all be related in a database for project administration, management reports, and control.
- the ability to carry out statistical analyses on cost records and other documents from past projects for a variety of reasons, including monitoring performance trends.

The consistent use of a logical coding system in an engineering company from our past experience yielded many benefits. The following examples illustrate only two of the many possibilities for exploiting properly coded records:

- the averaging of recorded costs for commonly recurring work packages in a range of categories from many past projects. This led to the preparation of project estimating tables (expressed in labor-hours and updated materials costs). These tables proved very useful for planning and resource scheduling new projects and for making global checks on detailed estimates for new project proposals.
- analysis in detail of past shipping records enabled a table to be compiled that listed all the main components commonly produced in the company's very heavy engineering projects. For each item it was possible to forecast the most likely average and the maximum weight of each part of the project after it had been broken down into parts of 20 tonnes or less for shipping. Cost estimates were added with the help of a shipping company. The result was given to the materials control manager as a 'ready-reckoner'. With occasional updating, this table was used successfully for estimating future project shipping costs to all parts of the world.

CHOOSING A CODING SYSTEM

Once a coding system has become well established it is difficult and unwise to make any fundamental change. Any comprehensive system has, therefore, to be designed with a great deal of care, so that it will serve the organization well into the future. Suppose that a company has been operating for many years with a comprehensive arrangement of codes that are recognized by all its management information systems. Suppose, further, that this arrangement of codes is common to many applications and procedures. As an example, the number for the drawing of a manufactured component would also be used as (or would be a recognizable constituent of) related manufacturing job numbers, job cost records, and the stock and part number of the component itself. If this company were to make a change to the numbering system, so that numbers which previously had one meaning would denote something entirely different in the future, some of the following problems might arise:

- drawings filed under two different systems;
- similar inconvenience caused to long-standing customers who maintain their own files of project drawings;
- no easy way of identifying similar previous jobs for the purpose of comparative cost estimating;
- difficulty in retrieving earlier designs. The opportunity to use retained engineering from past work to reduce future design effort might be lost;

- staff must live with two different systems instead of one universal set of numbers;
- problems for storekeepers and stock controllers, with more than one part numbering method—parts common to earlier projects may have to be renumbered for newer projects, so that there is a possibility of having identical common parts stored in two places with different part numbers;
- mayhem created in any attempt to use a relational database that relies on code numbering.

The Need For Simplicity

This is the place to insert a word of warning. It is tempting to be too ambitious and try to make numbers include too much information. The result can be codes that contain 14, 15, or more characters. It is easy to fall into such a trap, especially when the system is designed by a committee, each of whose members contributes their own idea of what the numbers might be expected to denote. Beware of phrases such as, 'Wouldn't it be nice if…'

The designer of a system that depends on exceptionally long codes may feel very proud of their system's capability. Computer systems are well able to accept and process huge numbers, but please remember the human element—the 'people interface'. People will have to work with these numbers, entering them in written or electronic records. We remember an attempt to introduce a very complex coding system on a mine development project in a remote area of Australia. The system designer was a highly qualified and well-respected member of the London head office management staff. Supervisors, professional people, and artisans at the mine were all expected to read and write 18-digit job codes on documents without making mistakes while exposed to unpleasant and hazardous conditions both above and below ground. The people at the mine never even attempted to use the codes. Even if they had used them, the depth of information that the codes contained was far in excess of that needed for management information. Simple codes use less effort and result in fewer errors. Remember the sensible slogan KISS: **K**eep **i**t **S**imple, **S**tupid.

WHAT HAPPENS WHEN THE CUSTOMER SAYS 'YOU SHALL USE MY CODING SYSTEM!'?

Not infrequently, an irritating problem arises when customers insist that their own numbering system is used, rather than the project organization's own long-established and proven arrangement. This happens, for example, when a project owner is to be presented with a complete set of project drawings as part of the contract and wants to be able to file these along with all the other drawings in the owner's head office system. This, unfortunately, is a case where 'the customer is always right'.

This problem of having to use customers' codes is not always restricted to drawings. In some projects it can apply to equipment numbers or part numbers. It also occurs, and is a great nuisance, in the cost codes used for work packages or large purchases for major projects. The customer and contractor sometimes work together to plan, authorize, and arrange the release of funds (either from the customer's own resources or from an external financing organization). In such cases the customer might insist that all estimates, budgets, and subsequent cost reports for the project are broken down against the customer's own capital appropriation or other cost codes.

Three Options

There are three possible options when the customer asks the contractor to use a 'foreign' coding system.

Option 1: Say 'No! to the customer   The person who adopts this course is either courageous or foolhardy. It might even be impossible under the terms of contract. In any case, it would be a short cut to achieving bad customer relations or losing the customer altogether.

Option 2: Change over completely to the customer's system   With this option, the contractor calls the project a 'special case', abandons the in-house system, asks the customer for a set of their own procedures, and uses those for the project. This option cannot be recommended for the following reasons:

* the information management benefits of the in-house system would be lost for all data for the project;
* it will soon be discovered that every project is a 'special case'. The contractor might soon find that must deal with as many coding systems as there are customers.

Option 3: Use both systems simultaneously   This option, the sensible compromise course, offers the only proper solution. Every drawing and other affected item must be numbered twice, once for each system.

Everything must, of course, be diligently cross-referenced between the two systems. This is tedious, time consuming, and means that staff have to learn more than one system. Some time ago it would have caused enough extra work to provide a weak argument for trying to obtain extra reimbursement from the customer. Fortunately, computer systems greatly reduce the effort needed for cross-referencing, sorting, and retrieving data numbered under duplicate systems.

REFERENCES

Devaux, S.A. (1999), *Total Project Control: A Manager's Guide to Integrated Project Planning, Measuring and Tracking*, New York, Wiley.

7

Planning the Aviation Project Timescale

An optimist would say that a glass is half full. A pessimist will say that the same glass is half empty. But a project manager will declare that the glass is twice as big as it needs to be.

INTRODUCTION TO PROJECT PLANNING

Whenever any job has to be accomplished according to a time or date deadline, it is advisable to have some idea of the relationship between the time allowed and the time needed. This is true for any project, whether a dinner is being prepared or an airplane built. In the first case one would be ill advised to tell guests 'Dinner is at 7pm—but the potatoes will not be ready until 7.30pm'. Similarly, there would be little point in having an eminent person arrive to fly on the inaugural flight of a new airplane only to be told that though the aircraft is almost assembled and ready to go, its engines will be installed in 2 weeks' time. A plan is always needed if a project is to be finished on time. In our culinary example planning is simple and informal, conducted solely within the brain of the cook. Projects such as aircraft development and assembly are more complicated and need special techniques.

This chapter begins by demonstrating simple bar charts, which can be adequate for planning and progressing small projects. They are particularly useful during the early phases of even very large projects, when there is little or no detailed information available about the tasks that lie ahead, so preventing precise planning.

BAR CHARTS

Bar charts are also widely known as Gantt charts, after their originator, the American industrial engineer Henry Gantt (1861–1919). They have long been in widespread use and are valuable planning aids. Anyone who can understand an office holiday chart can draw and understand a project bar chart.

The visual impact of a bar chart can be a powerful aid to controlling a project. Bar charts are preferred to other methods by most senior managers, on project sites and in factories. All levels of supervision and management find them convenient as day-to-day control tools. Even when projects have been planned with more advanced computer techniques, the same computer systems are often used to convert the schedules into bar charts for day-to-day use.

Bar charts can be assembled on wall-mounted boards, using proprietary kits (although these are now less common because of the alternatives available from computer systems). A wallchart using color-coded moveable strips for the bars is the simplest method for allocating resources to tasks or machines on very small projects.

Bar charts are drawn to scale, with the horizontal axis directly proportional to time. Days, months, years, or other units are used, chosen to suit the overall duration of the project. Each horizontal bar represents a project task, with its length scaled according to its expected duration. The name or description of each job is written on the same row as its bar, usually at the left-hand edge.

A Bar Chart Case Example: An Aircraft Component Project

L-F (Lock-Flouris) Controls Inc. is a company that designs and manufactures small electronic components, particularly for the aviation, defense, and space industries. It has received an order from an aircraft manufacturer to design and supply electronic control units that will be mounted in or near the engine bays of a new range of aircraft to be built in both civil and military versions. This small unit will contain a small number of electronic components, assembled on a printed circuit board, which in turn will be supported on an aluminium chassis. This assembly is to be encapsulated in epoxy resin to protect the components from the harsh environmental conditions of the engine bay. A cable connector and a pressure switch will also be mounted on the chassis, to protrude outside the encapsulated block. The small project described here is for the design and environmental testing of a small prototype batch. Our project ends with the issue of drawings for manufacture.

Figure 7.1 lists the main tasks for this project. The estimated duration, stated in days, has been entered against each task. In each case this is the best estimate of how long each task will take (the elapsed time), and it does not indicate the resources or work-hours required. The extreme right-hand column lists, for each task, the immediately preceding tasks that must be completed before the new task can start.

Figure 7.2 is the resulting bar chart. The planner has tried to observe the dependencies (logical constraints) given in the final column of the task list. For example, no environmental testing can take place before the ten prototype units have been made and functionally tested. However, the usual form of bar chart, shown here, does not allow these logical constraints or links to be shown. These can be dealt with mentally on this simple project, presenting no problem to a competent planning engineer. But, with any project of greater size there would be a considerable risk of producing a bar chart containing some logical impossibility. Also, there is a risk of introducing logical planning errors whenever the chart has to be rescheduled.

Vertical link lines can be added to bar charts to indicate dependencies (logical constraints) between two or more jobs. Figure 7.3 is a linked version of the bar chart of Figure 7.2. This shows clearly, for example, that the determination of environmental parameters and main design cannot start before the customer has specified the project requirements. But some links, even for this tiny project, cannot clearly be shown on this kind of chart. This applies, for example, to tasks which are dependent on determining the environmental parameters. Most project management computer programs are capable of plotting linked bar charts, but the results are usually cluttered and difficult to interpret except for very tiny projects.

This project will be revisited later in this chapter to see how much more effective it would be for the L-F Controls company to plan its work with critical path networks.

Task number	Task description	Duration (days)	Immediately preceding task(s)
01	Get the customer's specification	3	-
02	Determine environmental parameters	1	01
03	Design and breadboard test circuitry	4	01
04	Design printed circuit board layout	1	03
05	Specify and list electronic components	1	03
06	Design the chassis	2	04
07	Buy 10 prototype circuit boards	10	04
08	Buy components for 10 prototypes	5	05
09	Design encapsulation mold	2	06
10	Make 10 prototype chassis	5	06
11	Assemble printed circuit boards	2	07, 08
12	Write production test procedure	3	03
13	Design vibration testing clamp	1	06
14	Make 2 molds	5	09
15	Assemble and test the prototype units	4	10, 11
16	Cast (encapsulate) all units	6	14, 15
17	Make vibration test clamp	3	13
18	Retest all units after casting	1	16
19	Vibration and shock test 2 units	1	17, 18
20	Climatic test 2 units	2	18
21	Accelerated life test 6 units	10	18
22	Assess test results	1	19, 20, 21
23	Finalize and issue production documents	2	22

Figure 7.1   Task list for the aircraft component project

Bar Charts As Progress Monitoring Aids

Because bar charts are drawn to scale, they can be used to indicate progress. For this purpose a date cursor must be added, which is a vertical line placed on the chart at the review date (which is sometimes called 'time-now'). If the chart is drawn or printed on paper, the date cursor can be formed by placing a straight edge or ruler vertically on the chart at the time-now date. Adjustable charts set up as wall charts often use a scarlet elastic cord or ribbon for the cursor line.

Progress assessment is simply a matter of checking that all tasks (or portions of tasks) lying to the left of the date cursor have been completed. Late jobs are highlighted clearly by this method.

Bar Chart Limitations

The inability of bar charts to depict clearly the dependencies between different tasks has been demonstrated but bar charts have other limitations. Although it is possible to schedule more than 100 jobs using a proprietary adjustable wall chart, rescheduling is a different story. Setting up a complex plan in the first place might take a few working days but adjusting it subsequently to keep in step with changes might prove impossible. However, a project management computer system will solve this inflexibility problem. For

Day number (will convert to calendar dates when project start date is known)

Task description	2	4	6	8	10	12	14	16	18	20	22	24	26	28	30	32	34	36	38	40	44	44	44
Get the customer's specification																							
Determine environmental parameters																							
Design and breadboard test circuitry																							
Design printed circuit board layout																							
Specify and list electronic components																							
Design the chassis																							
Buy 10 prototype circuit boards																							
Buy components for 10 prototypes																							
Design encapsulation mold																							
Make 10 prototype chassis																							
Assemble printed circuit boards																							
Write production test procedure																							
Design vibration testing clamp																							
Make 2 molds																							
Assemble and test the prototype units																							
Cast (encapsulate) all units																							
Make vibration test clamp																							
Retest all units after casting																							
Vibration and shock test 2 units																							
Climatic test 2 units																							
Accelerated life test 6 units																							
Assess test results																							
Finalize and issue production documents																							

Figure 7.2   Bar chart for the aircraft component project

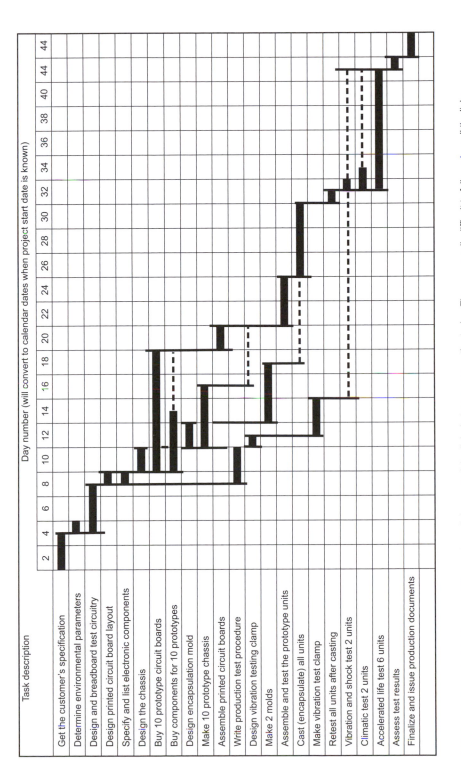

Figure 7.3   Linked bar chart for the aircraft component project

Charts such as this cannot clearly or accurately show all the constraining links between consecutive tasks. They are usually difficult to follow when all the links are included and tedious rearrangement is needed to reduce the number of crossovers. This difficulty persists even when charts are calculated by a computer. Critical path network diagrams offer a far better form of notation and they also provide many other planning advantages (see Figures 7.7 and 7.8) those who prefer to see their project plans always presented as bar charts, all competent project management software can convert plans using critical path networks into their equivalent bar charts, either with or without the links shown.

The visual effectiveness of a chart is lost when too many color codes are introduced, or when there are so many tasks shown in one view that it is difficult to trace their positions along the rows and columns.

CRITICAL PATH NETWORKS

The idea for critical path networks germinated in several places before the Second World War, but it was in the US during the 1950s that they were fully exploited. They became more popular in the 1960s when suitable computer systems became available with which to remove the drudgery of scheduling and (particularly) rescheduling.

Network diagrams show all the logical interdependencies between different jobs. The planner can ensure, for example, that a set of tires is not scheduled for fitting before the wheels manufacture has been completed and the tires have been purchased. Such logical inconsistencies are easily possible with complex bar charts, where it is impossible to depict or see every logical constraint.

Another great strength of networks is that they allow priorities to be quantified, based on an analysis of all the task duration estimates. Those tasks that cannot be delayed without endangering project completion on time are identified as critical tasks, and all other tasks can be ranked according to their degree of criticality.

Networks cannot be used by themselves for resource scheduling. In this respect bar charts are superior and easier to understand, provided that the number of activities is very small. However, one important value of networks is that they assign time-based priorities to tasks and highlight critical jobs. That is a vital contribution to the resource scheduling process, and critical path network analysis is an essential precursor to resource scheduling. Resource scheduling is described in Chapter 8. Most project management software can schedule resources.

Even if no duration estimates are made and there is no time analysis, the benefits derived from drawing a network can be worthwhile. Networking encourages logical thinking. A planning meeting can be regarded as a productive form of brainstorming. It greatly helps to develop the project process. Not only does the network notation allow expression of all inter-activity dependencies and relationships, but there is also the important possibility that activities may be brought to light which might otherwise have been forgotten, and thus excluded from schedules, estimates, cost budgets, and pricing.

TWO DIFFERENT NETWORK NOTATION SYSTEMS

Several network systems were devised during the second half of the twentieth century, but these all fit within one or other of two principal groups, determined mainly by the method of notation:

- Activity-on-arrow networks, often called arrow networks or ADM (short for arrow diagrams).
- Precedence networks, also known as PDM (short for precedence diagrams) or activity-on-node (AoN) networks.

We prefer to sketch arrow networks at brainstorming meetings and use precedence networks for subsequent computer processing. Arrow networks are faster and easier to draw than their precedence counterparts. That can save valuable time at initial planning meetings, which are invariably attended by busy senior people. Precedence networks are better suited to computer processing and take up relatively less computer memory. Now only Micro Planner X-Pert can process both arrow and precedence networks <http://www.microplanning.com>. However, if a planner chooses to sketch the first draft network in arrow notation, it is usually a simple matter to convert it to precedence notation later for the computer. There are people who prefer to sketch their networks in precedence mode at planning meetings using a Post-It™ note for every task, but that approach can soon cover a large area of paper and is suitable only for small networks.

Arrow networks are described briefly in the following section, but most of the examples in this book will be given using the precedence system.

Although precedence diagrams are not as well suited as arrow diagrams for rapid sketching on paper, it is fairly easy to draw and edit them on the computer screen. However, the limited screen area available when compared with a roll of drawing paper means that larger network diagrams require much tedious scrolling up, down, and sideways. It is not possible to see the whole picture and trace long paths through a network with an index finger or pointer unless the network is drawn or printed on a large area of paper.

CRITICAL PATH NETWORKS USING ARROW DIAGRAMS

Explanations given here are repeated in the precedence diagram section that follows, allowing readers to skip this arrow section if they wish to learn only the precedence method.

Activities And Events In Arrow Diagrams

Figure 7.4 is a simple arrow diagram. Each circle denotes a project *event*, such as the start of work or the completion of an activity. The arrow joining any two events represents the *activity* or *task* that must take place before the second event can be declared as achieved. The terms *task* and *activity* usually have the same meaning in all modern planning

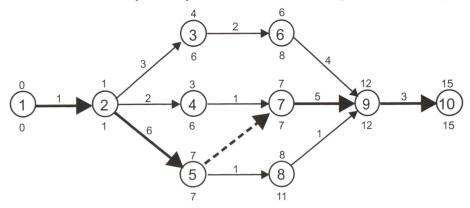

Figure 7.4   **The elements of an arrow critical path network diagram**

methods. Thus in Figure 7.4 11 activities link six events (ignore the dotted arrow for the time being).

All network diagrams are drawn so that work progresses from left to right. They are not drawn to scale and neither the lengths of the arrows nor the spacing of events have any significance.

The numbers in the event circles label the events. They allow the events and their associated activities to be referred to without ambiguity. Thus the arrow from event 1 to event 2 can be described as activity 1-2.

The logical significance of the diagram in Figure 7.4 is that each event cannot be considered achieved until the activity or activities leading into it have been finished. Only then, and not before, can activities immediately following the event be started.

The dotted arrow in Figure 7.4 is a dummy activity. Dummy activities (called dummies for short) do not represent work and practically always have zero duration. Instead, they denote a constraint or line of dependence between different events. In this case, therefore, the start of activity 7-9 is dependent not only upon completion of activity 4-7, but must also await completion of activity 2-5. Alternatively expressed, activity 7-9 cannot start until events 5 and 7 have both been achieved.

In practice, each arrow on a real project network would have its task name or description written along the length of the arrow. Lack of space in diagrams and computer report columns means that these activity descriptions are usually kept short, sometimes even abbreviated to the extent that they are barely intelligible.

Time Analysis Of Activity-On-Arrow Networks

Numbers have been written above the activity arrows in Figure 7.4 to show their estimated durations. The units are chosen as being the most suitable for the project. Once chosen, the same time units should be used consistently throughout any network.

Assume that the numbers in this Figure 7.4 are weeks. These estimates are strictly for *duration* only, which means *elapsed time*, not necessarily the work content. In fact, for some 'activities' (such as procurement lead times) there might be no work content for the project staff at all.

The first purpose of time analysis is to determine the shortest possible time in which a project can be completed, taking into account all the logical constraints and activity duration estimates. It is not usual to take resource allocation into account at this stage because that problem can be resolved at a later stage (described in Chapter 8).

Time analysis also performs the vital function of determining which activities should be given the most priority. This is achieved by calculating a quantity called *slack* or *float*, which is the amount by which any activity can be allowed to slip past its earliest possible start and finish dates without delaying the whole project.

The forward pass   In the network of Figure 7.4, the earliest project duration possible has been calculated by adding the activity duration estimates along the arrows from left to right. This is always the first step in the time analysis of any network and is known as the 'forward pass'.

The forward pass additions will depend on which path is followed. The earliest possible completion time for event 7, for instance, might seem to be $1 + 2 + 1 = 4$, if the path through events 1, 2, 4, and 7 is taken. However, event 7 cannot be achieved until event 5 has also been achieved, because of the link through the dummy. The path through events 1, 2, 5, and the dummy is the longer of the two possible paths and that must, therefore, determine the earliest possible time for the achievement of event 7. Thus the earliest possible time for event 7 is the end of week 7 (1 + 6). This means also that the earliest possible start time for activity 7-9 is the end of week 7 (which in practical terms means the beginning of week 8).

So, the earliest possible time for an event (and therefore the earliest possible start time for its immediately succeeding activities) is found by adding the estimates of all activities along the path leading into it. When there is more than one such path, the one with the highest total time estimate must be chosen. By continuing this process through the network to the end of the project at event 10 it emerges that the earliest possible estimated project completion time is 15 weeks.

The backward pass   Now consider event 9 in Figure 7.4. Its earliest possible achievement time is the end of week 12. It is clear that activity 8-9 could be delayed for up to 3 weeks beyond its earliest possible start without upsetting the overall timescale, because there are longer paths leading into event 9. In other words, although the earliest possible achievement time for event 8 is week 8, it could be delayed by up to 3 weeks, to the end of week 11, without delaying the earliest possible completion time for event 9. This result is indicated on the arrow diagram by writing the latest permissible time underneath the event circle. The result is found this time, not by addition from left to right along the arrows, but in exactly the opposite way by subtracting the estimated times from right to left (15 – 3 – 1 = 11, for event 8).

This subtraction process must be repeated throughout the network, writing the latest permissible times below all their event circles. Wherever more than one possible path exists, the longest must always be chosen so that subtraction gives the smallest remainder (the earliest time). This is illustrated for example at event 5, where the correct backwards subtraction route lies through the dummy (15 – 3 – 5 = 7). The path through events 10, 9, 8, and 5 is shorter and would give the incorrect answer 15 – 3 – 1 – 1 = 10, which would be 3 days too late. Event 5 must be achieved by the end of week 7, not 10, if the project is to finish on time.

The earliest and latest times are written above and below the event circles and also apply to the activities leading into and out of the events. Thus, for example, activity 8-9 has the following time analysis data:

- estimated duration: 1 week
- earliest possible start: end of week 8 (effectively the beginning of week 9)
- earliest possible finish (8 + 1):   end of week 9
- latest permissible finish: end of week 12
- total slack: 3 weeks

Slack (float) and the critical path   The term 'slack' indicates the amount of leeway available for starting and finishing an activity without the project end date being affected. Total slack is the difference between the earliest and latest start times for any activity (or between its earliest and latest finish times). There are other categories of slack, explained in Chapter 8, but they can be ignored for the purposes of all the examples in this chapter.

When all the earliest possible and latest permissible event times have been added to the diagram, there will always be at least one chain of events that each have the same earliest and latest times, indicating zero slack. These events are critical to the successful achievement of the whole project within its earliest possible time. The route joining these events is not surprisingly termed the 'critical path'.

Although all activities may be important, it is the critical activities (the activities that form the critical path or paths) that must claim greatest priority for scarce resources and management attention.

PRECEDENCE DIAGRAMS

This section repeats some of the text from the previous section for the benefit of readers who skipped the account of arrow networks.

A precedence diagram must be constructed with careful thought to ensure that it shows as accurately as possible the logical relationships and interdependencies of each activity or task with all the others in the project.

Activities (Or Tasks)

Figure 7.5 shows the notation commonly used for an activity in precedence notation and Figure 7.6 is the precedence equivalent of the arrow diagram in Figure 7.4. The numbers in brackets in each activity box in Figure 7.6 indicate the equivalent arrows in Figure 7.4.

The flow of work in any network diagram is from left to right. Precedence diagrams are not drawn to scale and neither the length of links nor the size of the activity boxes has any significance whatsoever. Every activity is given a unique identification number, often referred to as its ID code. These codes are essential for computer processing. ID codes can range from small serial numbers to complex alphanumeric codes containing ten or even more characters, depending on the size and complexity of the networks, the nature of the projects being planned, and the capabilities of the computer software.

The activities (tasks) comprising a project are joined by arrows which, unlike those in arrow diagrams, simply represent constraints or links. Because all arrows travel from left to right, we usually leave out the arrowheads.

Dummy activities have zero duration and do not denote work but are occasionally used to clarify logic or tidy up the drawing. For example, it is usually convenient to create artificial start and finish activities for the network. Networks that have several starts and several finishes will be found untidy for time analysis and computer processing. However, dummy start and finish activities were not needed for the network in Figure 7.6, because this network already has only one start and one finish.

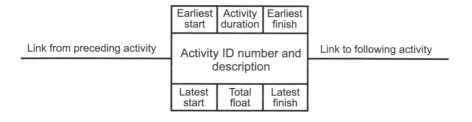

Figure 7.5   An activity in precedence notation

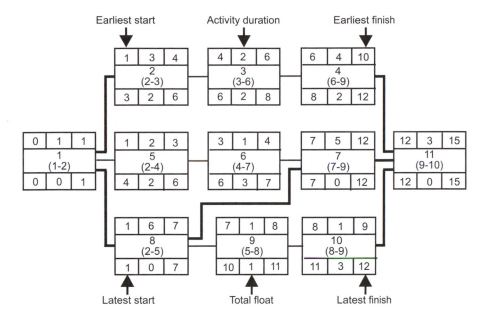

The numbers in brackets are the corresponding activity numbers in the arrow diagram in Figure 7.4

Figure 7.6   The elements of a precedence critical path network diagram

Time Analysis Of Precedence Networks

The units used for estimated activity durations are chosen by the planner as being the most suitable for the project. Once chosen, the same time units should be used consistently throughout any network. Assume that the numbers in Figure 7.6 are weeks. These estimates are for duration only, which means elapsed time, not necessarily the work content. In fact, for some 'activities' (such as procurement lead times) there might be no work content for the project staff at all.

The first purpose of time analysis is to determine the shortest possible time in which a project can be completed, taking into account all the logical constraints and activity duration estimates. It is not usual to take possible shortage of resources into account at this stage because that problem is resolved at a later stage (see Chapter 8).

Time analysis also performs the vital function of determining which activities should be given the most priority. This is achieved by calculating a quantity called *slack* or *float*, which is the amount by which any activity can be allowed to slip past its earliest possible start date without delaying the whole project.

The forward pass   In the project network of Figure 7.6, the earliest overall project duration possible has been calculated by adding activity duration estimates along the various paths, through the links, passing from left to right. There is more than one possible path through the network and the result will obviously depend on which path is followed. The earliest possible start time for activity 7, for instance, would seem to be 1 + 2 + 1 = 4 (the end of week 4) if the path through activities 1, 5, and 6 is taken. However activity 7 cannot really start until the end of week 7 (which in practical terms means the beginning of week 8) because it is constrained by the longer path through activities 1 and 8 (1 + 6 = 7).

Thus the earliest possible start time for any activity is found by adding the times of all preceding activities along the longest path in the network. By following this procedure through the network to the end of the project at activity 11 it emerges that the earliest possible estimated project duration is 15 weeks.

The backward pass   Now consider activity 10 in Figure 7.6. Its earliest possible start time is the end of week 8. This activity has an estimated duration of 1 week and its earliest possible completion time is therefore at the end of week 9. But the following activity 11 cannot start until the end of week 12, because of longer forward paths through the network. Thus activity 10 could be delayed by 3 weeks without delaying activity 11. The start and finish times for activity 10 therefore have a leeway or slack (or float) of 3 weeks.

A backward pass through the network can determine the latest permissible times at which each activity must start and finish if the project is to finish at its earliest possible time. Contrary to the forward pass, the backward pass process means subtracting the duration of each activity from its latest permissible finish time to arrive at its latest permissible start time. This backward pass must begin at the very end of the final activity in the network diagram, and at each subsequent activity it is the path with the longest combined duration (from the right) that must be chosen.

For example, the longest path to the right of activity 8 runs through activities 7 and 11. The latest permissible finish time for activity 8 is thus 15 − 3 − 5, which is 7. As this backward pass is continued throughout the network, the other quantities along the bottoms of the activity boxes can be filled in. The latest permissible start of each activity is its latest permissible finish, minus its estimated duration.

The total slack of each activity is found either by subtracting its earliest possible finish from its latest permissible finish, or by subtracting the earliest possible start from the latest permissible start.

The critical path   When all the earliest possible and latest permissible times have been added to the diagram, there will be at least one chain of activities where the earliest and latest times are the same, indicating zero slack. These activities are critical to the successful achievement of the whole project within its earliest possible time. The route joining these activities is not surprisingly termed the 'critical path'. Although all activities may be important, it is the critical activities that must claim priority for scarce resources and management attention.

PLANNING THE L-F CONTROLS AIRCRAFT COMPONENT PROJECT BY CRITICAL PATH NETWORK

Earlier in this chapter it was shown that bar charts are very limited in their ability to show the constraints between interdependent activities. The linked bar chart in Figure 7.3 could not show all the links clearly, even for the simple project carried out by the L-F Controls company.

Figure 7.7 shows how the small L-F Controls project plan looks as an arrow diagram and Figure 7.8 is the equivalent precedence diagram. Time analysis data are shown in both cases and the critical path is highlighted by the bold lines. These time analysis results are tabulated (for both the arrow and precedence diagrams) in Figure 7.9.

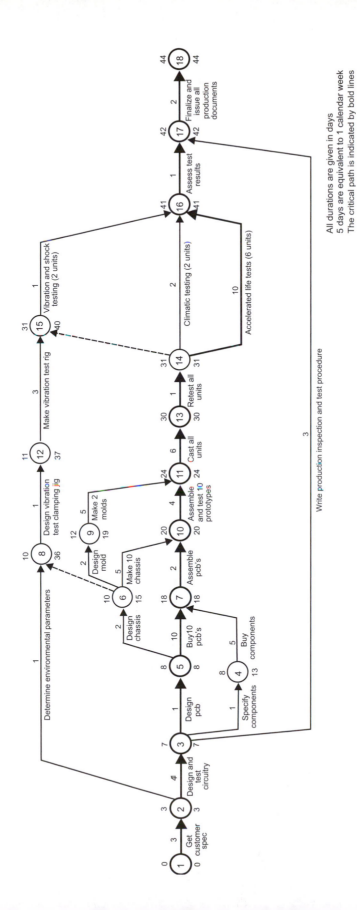

Figure 7.7   Activity-on-arrow critical path network diagram for the aircraft component project

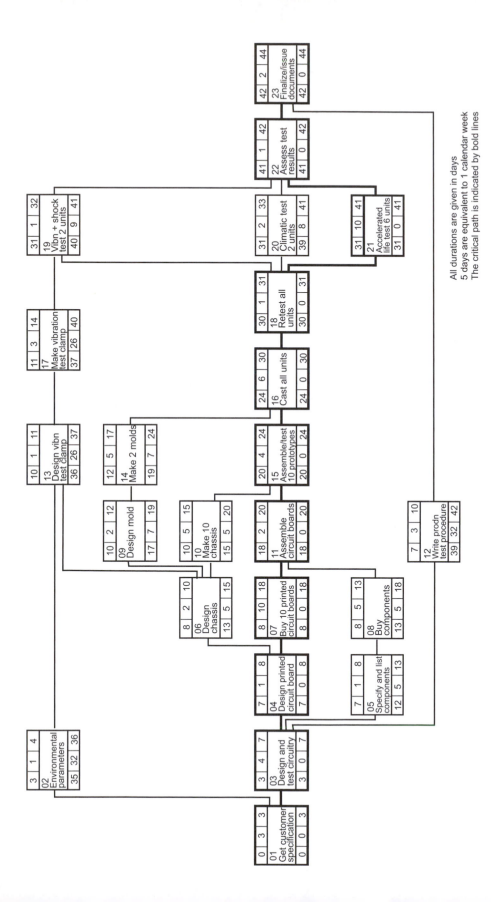

All durations are given in days
5 days are equivalent to 1 calendar week
The critical path is indicated by bold lines

Figure 7.8   Activity-on-node (precedence) critical path network diagram for the aircraft component project

ADM only		PDM							
Prec. Event	Succ. event	Task ID	Activity description	Duration (days)	Earliest start	Latest start	Earliest finish	Latest finish	Total slack
1	2	01	Get the customer's specification	3	0	0	3	3	0
2	8	02	Determine environmental parameters	1	3	35	4	36	32
3	3	03	Design and breadboard test circuitry	4	3	3	7	7	0
3	5	04	Design printed circuit board layout	1	7	7	8	8	0
3	4	05	Specify and list electronic components	1	7	12	8	13	5
5	6	06	Design the chassis	2	8	13	10	15	5
5	7	07	Buy 10 prototype circuit boards	10	8	8	18	18	0
4	7	08	Buy components for 10 prototypes	5	8	13	13	18	5
6	9	09	Design encapsulation mold	2	10	17	12	19	7
6	10	10	Make 10 prototype chassis	5	10	15	15	20	5
7	10	11	Assemble printed circuit boards	2	18	18	20	20	0
3	17	12	Write production test procedure	3	7	39	10	42	32
8	12	13	Design vibration testing clamp	1	10	36	11	37	26
9	11	14	Make 2 molds	5	12	19	17	24	7
10	11	15	Assemble and test the prototype units	4	20	20	24	24	0
11	13	16	Cast (encapsulate) all units	6	24	24	30	30	0
12	15	17	Make vibration test clamp	3	11	37	14	40	26
13	14	18	Retest all units after casting	1	30	30	31	31	0
15	16	19	Vibration and shock test 2 units	1	31	40	32	41	9
14	16	20	Climatic test 2 units	2	31	39	33	41	8
14	16	21	Accelerated life test 6 units	10	31	31	41	41	0
16	17	22	Assess test results	1	41	41	42	42	0
17	18	23	Finalize and issue production documents	2	42	42	44	44	0

Figure 7.9   Time analysis for the aircraft component project

The data in Figure 7.9 are all in terms of day numbers, which have little practical use for the project manager (who will usually need calendar dates). Conversion to calendar dates must wait until the project start date has been established. Then, computer processing of the network will automatically produce schedules with calendar dates, and will automatically allow for weekends and specified public holidays.

The table resulting from network time analysis should be of far more use to the manager of this project than any bar chart because it is not necessary to read the chart scale. Also, the relative priorities of the different tasks are clearly stated in terms of their total slack.

LEVEL OF DETAIL IN NETWORK DIAGRAMS

A question often facing inexperienced planners is, 'How much detail should we show in the network?' In other words which activities should be included in the network and which should be left out or combined with others?

To some extent this depends on the size of the project, the project duration, the size of the duration units chosen, the amount of detailed knowledge available, and the purpose of the network. A very detailed project network containing 10 000 activities might sound very impressive, but smaller networks are more manageable.

Guidelines

There are several guidelines that apply generally to the level of detail which should be shown in project network diagrams.

Activities with very short durations It is usually possible to avoid showing jobs as separate activities if their durations amount only to a very small fraction of the expected overall timescale, especially if they do not require resources. Of course these activities cannot be ignored, but they can be included in the network as parts of other activities. An example might be the preparation of a group of drawings, where a single activity 'detail and check subassembly *X*' would be shown rather than including a separate activity for detailing every drawing, and another set of activities for checking them.

As with all rules there are exceptions. Some activities with very short durations might be so important that they *must* be included (for example, an activity for obtaining authorization or approval before subsequent work can proceed).

In a short project lasting only a few weeks (for example, a major overhaul and maintenance program of an aircraft that is needed back in service as soon as possible) it would be reasonable to use network planning units of days, fractions of days, or even hours, and to include activities lasting only an hour or so.

Level of detail in relation to task responsibility A network path should be broken to include a new activity whenever the action moves from one department or organization to another — in other words where the responsibility for managing and doing work changes. Remember that the ultimate purpose of the network is to allow the project work to be scheduled and controlled. In due course, work-to lists for different managers will be generated from the network. The network must contain all the jobs needed for these lists. This means that:

- No network activity should be so large that it cannot be assigned for the principal control of one, and only one department or manager.
- Activities must correspond to actions that have a clearly definable start and finish.
- The interval between the start and finish of any activity should not be too long compared with the project timescale, so that fairly frequent progress points are provided for progress measurement and control.

A network that is sufficiently detailed will enable the following types of events to be identified, planned, and monitored or measured:

- Work authorization, either as an internal works order or as the receipt of a customer order or contract.
- Financial authorizations from the customer (especially where these might risk work hold-ups during the course of the project).
- Planning application and consent for airports or their individual buildings.
- The start and finish of design for any subassembly. If the duration of the design task is longer than 2 or 3 weeks it might be advisable to define separate, shorter activities corresponding to design phases.
- Release of completed drawings for manufacture or construction (probably grouped in subassemblies or work packages rather than attempting to plan for every individual small drawing).

- The start of purchasing activity for each subassembly or work package, signified by the engineering issue of a bill of material, purchase specification, or advance release of information for items which are known to have long delivery times.
- Issue of invitations-to-tender or purchase enquiries.
- Receipt and analysis of bids.
- Following on from the above three items, the issue of a purchase order with a supplier or subcontractor (again at the level of work packages and subassemblies rather than small individual purchases).
- Material deliveries, often meaning the event when the last item needed to complete the materials for a particular work package (or for a single item of capital equipment) is received at the manufacturing plant or airport site. For international projects, this delivery point may be to a ship or to an aircraft, with subsequent transit time shown as a separate, consecutive activity (when the change of responsibility rule applies, because responsibility transfers from the supplier to the carrier or freight forwarding agent).
- The starts and completions of manufacturing stages (in large projects usually only looking at the entries into and exits from production control responsibility, and again considering work packages or subassemblies rather than individual small parts).
- The starts and finishes of construction subcontracts, and important intermediate events in such subcontracts (see the section 'Milestones' below).
- Handover activities for completed work packages. This would include activities for handing over the finished project, or major parts of it, to the customer but would also ensure that associated items such as maintenance and operating manuals were itemized separately in the network plan.

These are, of course, only guidelines. The list is intended to be neither mandatory nor complete.

Level of critical path network detail in relation to activity costs   Some cost reporting and control measures will be impossible if sufficient attention to certain activities is not given when the network diagram is prepared.

It is possible to assign a cost to an activity, such as the purchase of materials. If an activity is included on the network for the planned issue of every significant purchase order, then the purchase order values can be assigned to their associated activities. This makes possible the preparation of reports from the computer which will set the times for these costs when the orders are placed and thus give a schedule of purchase cost commitments.

If another activity is added for the receipt of goods against each of these purchase orders, the same order value can be assigned to these later activities. Using suitable computer techniques, cost schedules can be derived that relate to the time when invoices will become due. These schedules indicate cash outflow requirements.

None of this would be possible without sufficient detail on the network.

MILESTONES

It is important to provide several intermediate points throughout the network and any resulting schedules that can be used as progress benchmarks. This is done by designating significant activities as 'milestones'. Computer programs for project scheduling allow reports to be filtered and printed so that they contain only such milestone activities, and these greatly help the assessment of progress against time and costs and are of value in reporting to higher management and to the customer.

IS THE PREDICTED TIMESCALE TOO LONG?

It is often found that the first forward pass through a network will predict a completion date that is unacceptably late. The planner is then likely to be placed under great pressure to come up with an alternative plan to meet the required timescale (which might correspond to a delivery promise already made to a customer).

One option is to consider spending more money in additional resources, use of overtime, or special machinery to speed up critical activities, a process sometimes called crashing. Crashing can add risk and cost to a project without adding value, and is to be avoided if possible.

The planner might be tempted to cut estimates arbitrarily, perhaps on the advice of other managers, until the work fits neatly into the timescale. That must, of course, never be considered as a valid option unless good reasons can be given as to how the shorter times can be achieved.

A more sensible first course of action is to re-examine the network logic. Are all the constraints shown really constraints? Can any activities be overlapped, so that the start dates of some critical activities are brought forward? 'A process called 'fast-tracking' considers the performing of activities in parallel that have traditionally been performed serially. In any case, a network diagram should always be checked to ensure that it reflects the most practicable and efficient way of working.

Most networks use only simple start-finish relationships but the planner should always bear in mind the availability of more complex notation in the precedence system and be prepared to use start-start or other complex links to overlap suitable activities and bring the planned completion date forward. Figure 7.10 shows the range of constraints that precedence diagramming allows. However, the finish-start relationship shown in Figure 7.10(a) is by far the most commonly used and is the default assumed by computer programs.

EARLY CONSIDERATION OF RESOURCE CONSTRAINTS

Nothing has been said so far about possible scarcity of resources and the additional constraints that such problems might impose on the network logic or estimated activity durations.

Consider, for example, the simplest case of a resource constraint, where one particular individual is going to have to perform several network activities single-handed. Assume that this person cannot perform two activities at the same time. The planner, knowing this, might be tempted to add links to the network to indicate this constraint and prevent any two of these activities from being planned as simultaneous tasks. But if all these activities lie on different paths in a complex network where should the constraints be placed? Before time analysis the planner cannot know in which order all these jobs should be performed.

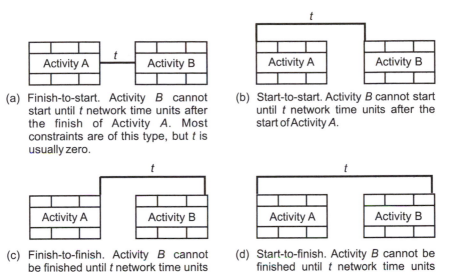

(a) Finish-to-start. Activity *B* cannot start until *t* network time units after the finish of Activity *A*. Most constraints are of this type, but *t* is usually zero.

(b) Start-to-start. Activity *B* cannot start until *t* network time units after the start of Activity *A*.

(c) Finish-to-finish. Activity *B* cannot be finished until *t* network time units after the finish of Activity *A*.

(d) Start-to-finish. Activity *B* cannot be finished until *t* network time units after the start of Activity *A*.

Figure 7.10   Constraint options in precedence networks

Similar worries about resources might attach to other activities where the resource requirements are more complex, when several activities can be allowed to run in parallel or overlap provided that the total resources needed do not exceed the total amount available.

Fortunately there is a simple solution to all these problems of resource constraints. At this stage in the planning, simply ignore them! The purpose of drawing the network is to establish the most desirable work pattern (assuming no resource constraints). Time analysis follows to establish the amount of float available, which effectively allots priority values to all activities. All of this information provides a sound basis for *subsequent* resource scheduling, which is a quite separate process (described in the next chapter).

Planning and scheduling have to be carried forward one step at a time, and consideration of resource constraints is a step that is not taken when the first network is drawn. However, the planner must use common sense in this respect. Suppose that an activity requiring skilled fitters has been estimated to require 150 man-hours, and that several people could work on the task if required (without getting in each other's way to any serious extent). The duration for this activity would therefore depend on the number of people assigned:

- 1 fitter for 20 days (20 man-days)
- 2 fitters for 10 days (20 man-days)
- 3 fitters for 8 days (24 man-days)
- 4 fitters for 7 days (28 man-days)
- and so on.

The correct approach for the planner is to ask the manager (or delegate) of the department responsible to say how many fitters would be best for this task, and write the corresponding duration on the network. The possible demands of other activities on these fitters are disregarded at this stage. However, if the company only employs two suitable fitters in total, the planner would be stupid to schedule more than two for this or any other activity. This is where common sense comes in.

CASE EXAMPLE: GENERAL AVIATION HANGAR RESTORATION

Introduction

This case example, although for a very small project, illustrates some interesting features of planning using critical path analysis. Although there are only 17 activities, the precedence logic is a little complex to draw clearly owing to the number of crossed links, and we show how this difficulty is easily overcome by inserting dummy activities at three of the crossover points.

Our case example demonstrates the application of PERT (Program Evaluation and Review Technique), in which the estimated duration for each activity can be subjected to a probabilistic study in an attempt to forecast the most likely completion time for the entire project.

Finally, this case will demonstrate how a project manager need not accept the results of time analysis without question, but can plan to apply extra effort to expedite critical activities (usually for additional cost) to bring the planned project completion date forward

Project Background

CEN-CONSTRUCT is a medium-sized business located in Sydney, Australia that is owned and operated by a family. It is principally a consulting company that specializes in aviation civil engineering, having worked on runway construction and paving projects as well as several other airport airside projects, most of which have been for smaller general airports. Having decided to extend its range of operations, the company recognized a local need for a contractor that could carry out aircraft hangar renovation. In consequence, the company has now achieved a good level of expertise in the interior design and renovation of hangars

The subject of this case example was the renovation of a hangar for a small client at a general aviation airport. The client uses the hangar to house his Cessna 310 twin-engine plane. The hangar was originally built in 1950, since when no further construction or renovation work has been carried out. CEN-CONSTRUCT had no previous integrated project management system or strategy for this type of project, so the project management planning steps described here were implemented for them. The planning exhibits are slightly simplified for clarity of reproduction.

Project Definition And Activity List

Because the total number of identified activities was small, a simple activity list (task list) sufficed for the WBS. This list, given in Figure 7.11, defines the project scope. It also defines the logical work sequence by stating the immediate predecessor(s) that must be completed before each new activity can begin. The cost estimates show that the total original estimated cost for this project was $46 900.

Readers will note that the table in Figure 7.11 contains four different duration estimates for each activity. This is because the project planner decided to use a probability assessment method known as PERT to this project. This is explained in the following section.

Application Of PERT To The Hangar Renovation Project

Almost all duration estimates are a matter for subjective judgement and the actual outcome for each activity can be quite different from the planner's intention. One branch of critical path analysis recognizes this uncertainty. The method, one of the earliest critical path analysis methods, is Program Evaluation and Review Technique (PERT). Each person who estimates the duration of an activity is asked to give three possible values which are:

t_m = the most likely estimated time
t_o = the most optimistic estimated time
t_p = the most pessimistic estimated time

The values are inserted in the following formula for each activity to give the most probable or *expected* time, which is based on the standard deviation from a normal statistical distribution curve:

$$t_e = (t_o + 4t_m + t_p)/6.$$

This method was used for the hangar renovation project, and the data are given in the four estimated duration columns of Figure 7.11.

	Activity description	Estimated duration (days)				Immediately preceding activities	Estimated cost $
		Most likely	Opti- mistic	Pess- imistic	Expected time		
1	Establish customer specification and budget	10	5	15	10.0	-	800
2	Design new hangar features	9	7	12	12.2	1	1 500
3	Agree and sign contract	2	1	3	2.0	2	3 000
4	Buy materials	5	3	10	5.5	3	3 000
5	Remove redundant fixtures	2	1	3	2.0	3	500
6	Clean and strip floor	7	5	9	7.0	5	4 000
7	Set pipes and valves	4	2	7	4.2	6,4	4 000
8	New electrical wiring	4	2	7	4.2	6,4	5 000
9	Install ventilation and air conditioning ducts	5	3	7	5.0	6,4	6 500
10	Install toilet and shower	5	3	8	5.2	4,7,8,9	4 500
11	Install storage cabinet for aircraft spares etc.	10	5	12	9.5	4,7,8,9	5 000
12	New floor screed	9	5	13	9.0	4,10,11	7 000
13	Paint	5	4	7	5.2	4,12	1 000
14	Install lamps and electrical appliances	2	1	3	2.0	4,13	500
15	Final finishing and clean up	3	2	4	3.0	4,14	600
16	Hand over hangar to the client	1	1	1	1.0	15	0
Total expected project cost:							$46 900

Figure 7.11   Activity list for the aircraft hangar renovation project

The Network Diagram And Its Initial Time Analysis

The network diagram, using expected duration values, is shown in Figure 7.12. Time analysis has revealed the critical path (shown in bold lines) and indicates a most probable project duration of 67.9 days.

Two dummy activities, identified as *A* and *B*, have been inserted to clarify the logic drawing. These dummy activities do not affect the network logic (work sequence) and as they both have zero duration they do not affect time analysis. It is quite usual to add a start dummy and a finish dummy to network diagrams that otherwise would have multiple starts and finishes, but their use within a precedence network, as here, is less common. However, a glance at Figure 7.13 shows that they can improve the clarity of a network diagram.

Measures For Reducing The Predicted Timescale

It often happens that the predicted timescale for a project is too long, and that was the case in this example, with the client specifying that he wanted to fly in and house his airplane between days 50 and 55 of this project. Clearly the originally planned completion time of day 68 would have been far too late. There are two possible approaches to shortening the planned timescale of a project. The project manager has a choice between these two methods or, to achieve maximum expedition, can use both methods together.

Fast-tracking using concurrency   Network logic often shows constraints that are not literally true, and it is known that some activities can be allowed to overlap or even run concurrently. One example is in the purchase of long-lead items, where design engineers are able to release purchasing information to the buyer before the relevant design activity has been completed. The complex constraints given in Figure 7.10 showed how the precedence system will allow such overlaps to be depicted in a network. However, that process was not considered applicable on this aircraft hangar case project and will not be described further here.

Shortening activity durations by crash action   It is often possible to shorten the duration of an activity by deploying more resources, using different processes, or working overtime. These actions usually add additional cost, and it would thus be wasteful to crash activities with large amounts of slack because, to do so, would have no effect on the total project duration.

Crash action must be considered first, therefore, only on activities which lie on the critical path. Constructing a table that compares time saved on an activity with the relevant additional cost can theoretically produce a factor for each activity that will reveal the cost per day saved for that activity.

Thus crash action can be even more selective than choosing only critical activities, because it can be concentrated on those critical activities which have the lowest cost per day saved. However, the exercise becomes complicated in practice because as one or two critical activities are crashed and the critical path is shortened, other paths through the network become critical. Crash attention must then shift to the newly created critical activities. Theoretically this process can be reiterated until *all* activities and *all* possible paths through the network become critical. It could then be claimed that the network has been optimized, but that claim needs to be taken with considerable circumspection because it is based on a false premise. Remember that every duration estimate is *only* an estimate, so the perceived mathematical precision of total network crash optimization is a myth.

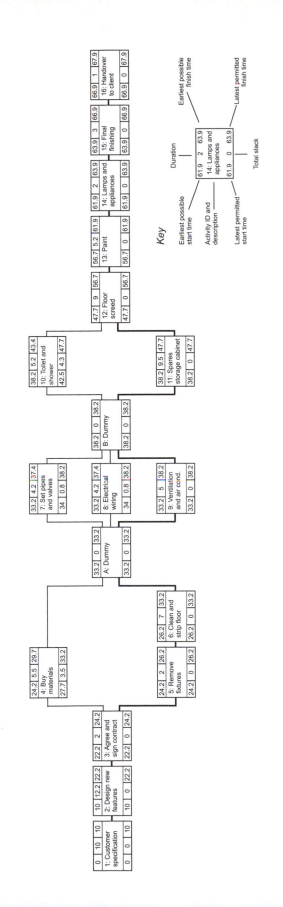

Figure 7.12   Network diagram for the hangar renovation project before crashing the times

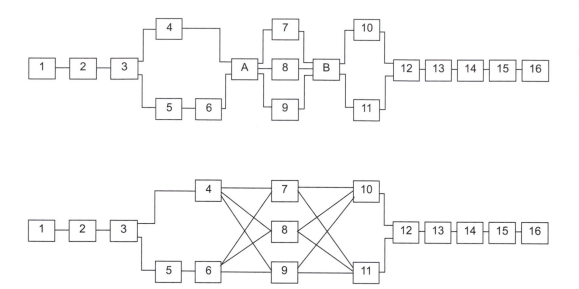

These networks have identical logic but dummies A and B in the top diagram make the logic easier to follow

Figure 7.13   Use of dummy activities in precedence networks to clarify multiple links

Activity description	Duration (days)		Estimated cost of crashing	Notes
	PERT time	Crash time		
1 Establish customer specification and budget	10.0	10.0		Task not suitable for crashing
2 Design new hangar features	12.2	6.0	1 000	6.2 days saved for $161 per day saved
3 Agree and sign contract	2.0	2.0		Task not suitable for crashing
4 Buy materials	5.5	3.0	500	2.5 days saved for $100 per day saved
5 Remove redundant fixtures	2.0	1.0	300	1.0 day saved at extra cost of $300
6 Clean and strip floor	7.0	4.0	2 500	3.0 days saved at $833 per day saved
7 Set pipes and valves	4.2	3.0	1 500	1.2 days saved at $1 250 per day saved
8 New electrical wiring	4.2	2.0	2 600	2.2 days saved at $1 182 per day saved
9 Install ventilation and air conditioning ducts	5.0	3.0	2 000	2.0 days saved at $1000 per day saved
10 Install toilet and shower	5.2	3.0	1 500	Non-critical task does not need crashing
11 Install storage cabinet for aircraft spares etc.	9.5	6.0	2 000	3.5 days saved at $571 per day saved
12 New floor screed	9.0	6.0	1 800	3.0 days saved at $600 per day saved
13 Paint	5.2	4.0	500	1.2 days saved at $417 per day saved
14 Install lamps and electrical appliances	2.0	1.0	200	1.0 day saved at extra cost of $200
15 Final finishing and clean up	3.0	2.0	100	1.0 day saved at extra cost of $100
16 Hand over hangar to the client	1.0	1.0		Task not suitable for crashing

Figure 7.14   Activity list for the aircraft hangar renovation project showing crashed times and extra costs

There is no slack in a totally crashed network, so that all or most activities are critical and that increases the risk of failing to meet the delivery date. Further, the probability results from the original PERT time analysis no longer apply, because each crashed estimate has been made on a deterministic, not probabilistic basis.

In the aircraft hangar renovation project a realistic approach to crash action produced the table shown in Figure 7.14 on the left. When the crashed times were substituted for the PERT normal duration estimates in the network diagram they produced a total estimated project time of 43 days, well within the client's requirements.

The notes in Figure 7.14 show that some activities were less costly to crash than others in terms of the dollars budgeted for each day's time saved.

Note that although activity 10 could have been shortened from 5.2 to 3 days, the additional expenditure of crashing that task was not justified because Activity 11, running concurrently, could not be crashed below 6 days. In other words, Activity 10 still had slack remaining after Activity 11 had been crashed, and there is no point in wasting money on crashing non-critical activities, because that process cannot reduce the project duration.

Summarizing, therefore, the hangar restoration project duration was originally planned as 67.9 days at a budget cost of $46 900. Crash actions brought the planned duration down to 43 days but added $15 000 to the total project budget.

8

Scheduling Project Resources

A small aircraft hangar construction project is used in this chapter to illustrate network time analysis and, more particularly, resource scheduling. Resource scheduling can be a complex subject, but the most commonly used methods are described here and we show how a logical step-by-step approach can remove much of the mystery. Cash scheduling is included in this chapter, because cash is a vital project resource and if cash flows are not correctly scheduled and managed throughout the project life cycle (especially for high-investment, long-term aircraft development projects) sudden project death will result.

INTRODUCTION TO RESOURCE SCHEDULING

Resource scheduling converts a project plan into a work schedule that takes account of the resources which can be made available. The schedule has to be practical. Workload peaks and troughs should be smoothed out as far as possible, whilst still attempting to finish the project at the earliest or required time.

In projects where most work is contracted out to others, project planning will probably be adequate if taken only to the time analysis stage. The labor resources will still have to be scheduled, but that process can be delegated to the subcontractors who employ the direct labor.

Most people think of resource scheduling in terms of people. But subjects for scheduling can include other resources such as plant and machinery, bulk materials, and cash. The treatment of these non-labor resources is generally similar to manpower scheduling, except that the names and units of quantity will change. Any commodity that can be quantified in linear units can be scheduled using the methods described here.

Physical working space is more difficult to schedule, particularly when the three-dimensional shape is important, and that problem needs solutions that are not discussed here.

Network Analysis As A Precursor To Resource Scheduling

When a critical path network is drawn, attention has to focus on the logic or the tasks themselves and no considered account can be taken of the resources which will be available when work starts. A network cannot be used by itself to demonstrate the volume of resources needed at any given point in project time. Unless subsequent resource scheduling is carried out, the start of each activity is assumed to be dependent only upon the completion of its preceding activities, and not on the availability of resources at the right time. This was explained in the previous chapter.

The results of network time analysis are however used to determine activity priorities, which in turn is a vital component of the resource scheduling process. Thus, before resource scheduling can be carried out, a network diagram must be drawn and time analyzed. Usually it is the activities with least remaining slack that should get the highest priority and first claim for scarce resources.

TIME-OUT TO TALK TERMINOLOGY

Every profession, such as accounting, medicine, the different branches of science, and so on, has its own language. Each of those languages has its special terminology or vocabulary, grammar, and conventions. As time passes, languages develop and change with use. Further, each language has its own regional variations or dialects. The language of project management is no exception to these rules.

The academic zealot who wishes to delve more deeply into the language and terminology of project management could do no better than start with one of the body of knowledge (BoK) guides produced by the professional project management associations. The most widely known of these is *A Guide to the Project Management Body of Knowledge* from the Project Management Institute (PMI).

For the practical purposes of this book we need to explain just two of the project management terms and one of the conventions (with their optional variations) that we use throughout this chapter and elsewhere in the book.

Activity Or Task

In everyday English, *activity* means the process required to *achieve* a task. But that is not so in project management. For us, the words *activity* and *task* are synonyms that we can interchange at will. Further, an activity or task in project management often involves no actual work, but might mean something as passive as waiting for materials to be delivered or watching paint dry. In those cases, the activity is still important because it takes project time. However, some of our activities do not even occupy any project time; for example, activity 01 in our hangar project simply indicates the start instant for the project.

If we are using arrow networks, a task or activity is anything represented by an arrow (including dotted dummy activities). However, when we use a precedence network, every network node is a task or activity.

We have generally used the term activity throughout this book but task would have done just as well.

Float Or Slack

So far we have described slack as being the difference between the earliest possible and latest permissible start times for an activity, or its corresponding finish times. The popular project management software Microsoft Project will report all such quantities as *slack*.

However, note that Open Plan reports not slack, but *float*, as can be seen in Figure 8.5 and all subsequent reports.

Nowadays slack and float are true synonyms, and the choice between these relies on personal or regional preferences. To some extent 'slack' is used more by American people, and float is perhaps used more by those from the United Kingdom.

Readers with an academic frame of mind might like to know that there is actually a significant historic difference between these two terms. *Slack* originally referred to the difference between earliest and latest *event* times in arrow diagrams. *Float*, on the other hand, was specific to *activities* as opposed to events. Now, no one cares any more, so it's just a matter for personal choice.

Conventions For Expressing Calendar Dates

There are different national conventions for expressing calendar dates, and since aviation and aviators routinely and frequently cross national borders the understanding of these conventions is vital. For example, tell an American project manager that their project is needed by 1/12/10 and they will assume that all work must be done by the twelfth of January in the year 2010. If an American company were to give the same project deadline to an Englishman, they would plan to deliver their project almost a year late, on the first of December 2010.

A glance at the schedule in Figure 8.5 shows that Open Plan has adopted a very sensible default convention for its dates, which is to present them in the form DDMMMYY, so that the American 1/12/10 would be written as 1Jan10. That is the convention that we recommend and always use ourselves.

In the examples presented in Chapter 7, the project start dates were not known so that all times were expressed as day numbers, counting from day one of the project. Subsequent conversion to calendar dates is painless and automatic when a project is given a start date and processed by computer. However, there are companies that operate their own internal calendars, based either on day numbers or week numbers. One or two of these companies make the mistake of expecting their suppliers and subcontractors to work to their numbers instead of calendar dates. That practice is to be actively discouraged. Imagine, for example, a supplier or contractor serving several customers, each of which operates its own different day or week numbering system. Calendar dates using the DDMMMYY convention are universal and should be incapable of misinterpretation.

INTRODUCING THE BILD-RITE HANGAR CONSTRUCTION PROJECT CASE EXAMPLE

Project Definition

Bild-Rite Inc, a specialist contractor, has been commissioned by a private owner to project manage and erect a hangar for housing a small fleet of light aircraft. The hangar is to be erected on a concrete slab using a prefabricated building, purchased as a 'flat-pack' from Sheds 'n Shacks Inc. The building is steel framed, and the walls and roof are clad with pre-coated aluminium sheets. Some of the roof panels are of transparent polycarbonate to allow daylight illumination inside the hangar. The hangar owner will subsequently be responsible for installing some simple maintenance equipment, such as a work bench, storage racks, and tool cabinets. Figure 8.1 shows the outline organization chart for this project.

The structural strength of this building will depend on the aluminium cladding being in place on at least thee of the four walls, so that work on the roof must wait until the east, west, and rear walls are finished. The hangar doors will be electrically driven, suspended from outrigged running rails. These doors require assembly from components in the flat-pack, and this assembly must be done flat on the ground before the doors are hoisted into position.

Hire plant will be required for several operations, but for simplicity and clarity only the crane is included in our schedule. Local airport regulations affect the height of plant such as cranes. Any crane that we need cannot be left in place overnight, because it would be a hazard to night flyers. Our crane will therefore be of the mobile kind, mounted on a truck and with a hydraulic jib that can easily be folded flat at night.

No materials or hire plant can be delivered to site until a security fence has been erected. Otherwise tools and materials would inevitably be lost to theft. The fence will also keep out potential vandals.

An external subcontractor will supply and pump in the ready-mix base concrete, and another external subcontractor will build a short road connecting the hangar to the airport perimeter track. That road is not part of this project and its activities are not included here.

The planned project start date is Wednesday 5 May, 2010. Completion requirement has initially been left open to 'as soon as possible', and the actual end-date target will be determined as part of the planning operation described here and by agreement with the client.

All data for this case example were processed using Open Plan, which is 'high-end' and very competent project management software that was originally developed by Welcom Software Technology but is now available from Deltek.

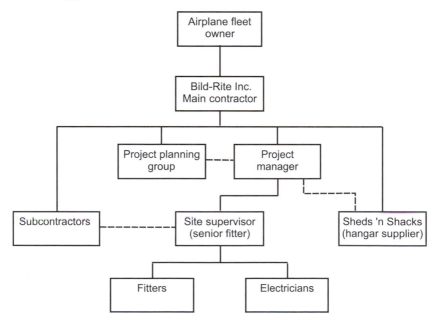

Figure 8.1   Organization of the Bild-Rite hangar project

Resources Available

The contractor's workforce includes multi-skilled fitters who can perform any project task on site except electrical installation, for which qualified electricians must be employed. The contractor can make four fitters and two electricians available, whenever required, for this project. Thus the total available resources for the Bild-Rite hangar project can be stated as:

- multi-skilled fitters: four (each coded 1M for the computer)
- electrician: two (each coded as 1E for the computer)
- mobile cranes: one (coded as 1C for the computer)

The daily cost rate for each fitter will be $400, inclusive of overheads. For each electrician it will be $450 and the crane costs $200 per day to hire. These rates are for illustration purposes only. They are not intended to be representative of actual industry rates.

The most senior fitter on site will act as the site supervisor. Bild-Rite employs one project manager to oversee all their projects, and she pays regular visits to all project sites. Her cost is an overhead, not included in the project prime cost budget.

In addition to requiring the availability limits and cost rates for each resource, Open Plan also requires the period to be stated for which those limits and cost rates are valid. This allows the planner to specify different data for different periods, which can allow for cost escalation and changes in workforce levels expected through future recruitments or downsizing.

Network Logic For The Hangar Project

The network logic and all time and cost estimates for this project have been established at an initial planning meeting, which resembled a brainstorming session. The meeting participants were:

- the project manager;
- the planning engineer assigned;
- the senior site fitter;
- an engineer from Shacks 'n Sheds.

The resulting network diagram is shown in Figure 8.2. The planner for this project has preferred to use the precedence method (activity-on-node) from the start rather than begin with an activity-on-arrow sketch. However, the activity boxes in this network do not conform to the standard set out in the previous chapter (Figure 7.5). Although that standard is an ideal format, it is generally too complex for networks sketched by hand at planning meetings. Further, because this project will be scheduled using a computer, it is not usual or necessary to show time analysis data on the initial network diagram, where there is usually insufficient space.

Practically every network printed by any computer software has to omit most time analysis data from the activity boxes in order to keep the area covered by the drawing as small as possible. However, these data are readily available in tabular reports, and most software will allow a time analysis table to be shown in the same report as the bar chart (placed to the left-hand side of the bar chart).

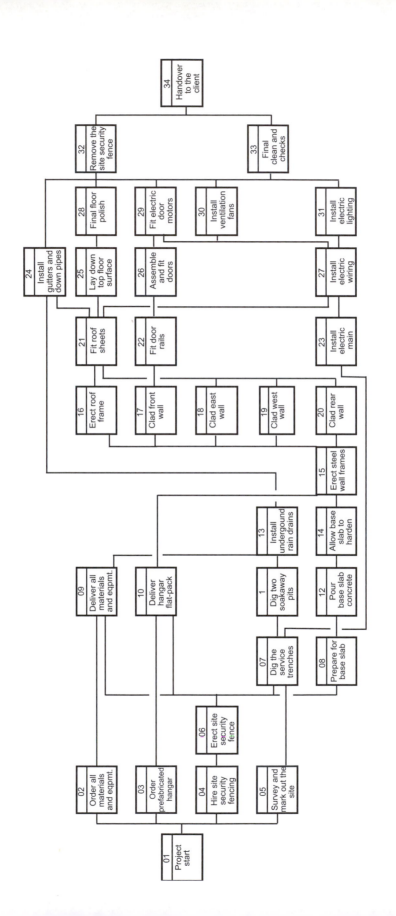

Figure 8.2   Network logic diagram for the Bild-Rite hangar construction project

In contrast to the hangar renovation case which ended Chapter 7, this planning meeting was treated as a brainstorming session to identify all the necessary tasks and their estimates. Thus the activity list (task list) described below could not be completed until after drawing the network logic.

Activity List And Cost Estimates

The activity list (or task list) for the hangar project is shown in Figure 8.3. This lists all the principal tasks identified during the network brainstorming session, together with their estimated durations and (where appropriate) the agreed resource requirements. The activity ID codes correspond with those on the network diagram of Figure 8.2 and in all subsequent reports produced from the Open Plan software.

Materials cost estimates have been bundled with their delivery-to-site activities, and they are not distributed over the relevant construction activities.

Rate-Constant Resources

Every resource requirement is considered to be rate-constant for this project. This means that if an activity with a duration of 10 days is shown as requiring two fitters, that implies two fitters working constantly on the task, every day, so that the task will have a work content (and related cost) of 20 man-days.

Competent software will allow non rate-constant resources to be specified. This principle is illustrated in Figure 8.4. The facility would be useful, for example, in an activity during which the resource requirement changed from day-to-day on a basis that could be predetermined. However, unless individual activities have very long duration or the project is very tiny, this level of resource planning detail is unnecessary, because the day-by-day fluctuations in requirements will cancel out over the total number of resources. Planners must always aim for simplicity and avoid unnecessary complication or fine levels of detail that are not justified.

Project Calendars And Time Units

All scheduling for the hangar project must be based on a 5-day working week. Saturdays and Sundays are not normally available for work. This is the default calendar assumed in most project management software. Although public holidays would have intervened in real life, they were ignored for this simple case example. All computer software will allow for public holidays to be removed from the working calendar, or for weekends to be added.

The Open Plan default calendar is appropriate for this project, which assumes a working week that includes Monday to Friday, inclusive. No work is scheduled for weekends. We have ignored public holidays for the sake of simplicity.

All good project management software allows the planner to allocate custom-defined calendars to activities, and sometimes also to specified resource categories. For example, if one group of people customarily work at weekends, a special 7-day calendar can easily be defined for them. Special calendars are also important in international projects, where companies in different nations do not share the same national festival and holiday dates. A

	Activity description	Duration (days)	Resources allocated	Cost of materials	Comment
01	Project start	0	None		Target start date is Monday 3 May 2010
02	Order all materials and equipment	15	None	$2000	Duration includes longest lead time
03	Order prefabricated hangar	20	None	$35 000	Duration includes lead time
04	Hire site security fencing	2	None	$500	
05	Survey and mark out the site	1	2M		
06	Erect the site security fencing	1	2M		
07	Dig the service trenches	1	1M		
08	Prepare for the base concrete slab	2	1M		Ground leveling with a bulldozer
09	Deliver all materials and equipment	2	None		
10	Deliver the hangar flat-pack	1	None		Transport by road trucks, cost included in 03
11	Dig two soakaway pits (east and west)	2	1M		For rainwater drainage
12	Pour base slab concrete	1	1M		Concrete delivered pre-mixed in tanker trucks
13	Install underground rain drain pipes	1	2M		Connect gutter down pipes to soakaway pits
14	Allow concrete base to harden	5	None		
15	Erect the steel wall frames	4	2M, 1C		All walls must be erected together
16	Erect the roof frame	3	2M, 1C		
17	Clad the front wall	2	2M, 1C		The fixing of pre-cut and drilled aluminium sheets
18	Clad the east wall	4	2M, 1C		to all four walls adds critical strength to the
19	Clad the west wall	4	2M, 1C		complete hangar structure
20	Clad the rear wall	4	2M, 1C		
21	Fit the roof sheets	5	2M, 1C		When finished, the internal dry trades can start
22	Fit the door rails	1	2M, 1C		
23	Install electricity mains	1			This activity is carried out by the utility company
24	Install gutters and down pipes	2	2M		
25	Lay down the top floor surface	2	2M		
26	Assemble and fit the doors	1	4M, 1C		
27	Install electric wiring	3	2E		
28	Final floor polish	2	2M		
29	Fit the electric door motors	1	2M, 2E		
30	Install ventilation fans	2	2M, 2E		
31	Install lighting	4	2E		
32	Remove the site security fence	1	2M		
33	Final clean and checks	2	2M		
34	Handover to the client	1	None		

Resource codes used: M= multi-skilled fitter; E = electrician; C = mobile crane

Figure 8.3   Activity data for the Bild-Rite hangar construction project

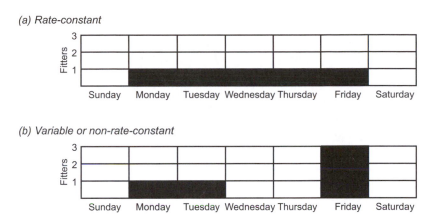

Figure 8.4   Rate-constant and variable resource usage for a project task

calendar allowing activities over all 7 days in each week might, for example, be allocated to activities such as waiting for concrete to harden.

Time units   Many programs allow time units to be mixed, the most common instance of which is to assume that each day equates to 8 hours. However, it is best not to mix hours and days as planning units because all the schedule reports become incredibly messy. Further, most project planning estimates are made to a degree of accuracy that does not justify the use of such small time elements.

TIME ANALYSIS OF THE BILD-RITE PROJECT

The data for Figure 8.5 were produced by Open Plan using the activity information from Figures 8.2 and 8.3. No resources have been entered into the system at this stage. Note that Open Plan prefers to use the term 'float' rather than 'slack', Open Plan is a powerful and versatile program and, not surprisingly, it made short work of this tiny project. The activities in Figure 8.5 are listed in ascending order of their ID numbers.

Given a start date of 5 May, 2010, Open Plan has revealed that this project should finish on 6 July, 2010, provided that nothing goes terribly wrong and that there are adequate resources to carry out all critical tasks at their earliest times. But a big question mark hangs over those resources. Will the specified resources be enough to carry out all this work in the time available? That question will be probed as this chapter progresses.

A Reporting Paradox For Activities With Zero Duration

Assigning zero duration to an activity (as we have done for the start activity of the Bild-Rite project) can lead to some apparent scheduling anomalies.

When an activity with an estimated duration of 1 day is scheduled to begin, say, on 1 June, it will be scheduled also to finish on 1 June. However, 1 June for the start is taken to mean the start of the working day on 1 June, and the finish means the end of that working day.

To the computer, the night hours between each working day and the next are not available for work, which means that those hours simply do not exist in the 'mind' of the computer. So the last second on a working day is seen by the computer as the same instant as the first second of the following working day.

Now return to that activity which is scheduled to take place on 1 June. It has a duration of 1 day, which means it begins at the start of 1 June and ends at the end of the same day. If we change the estimated duration to zero, that activity begins and ends at the start of 1 June.

Because the computer totally ignores the intervening, non-working night hours, the beginning of 1 June is the same instant as the end of 31 May. So some programs will report this zero-duration activity as beginning on start of work on 1 June and ending at close of work on 31 May. Something of the sort can be seen in activity 01 in Figure 8.5.

CONVENTIONS AND PRIORITY RULES FOR SCHEDULING PROJECT RESOURCES

Resource Agregation

Many project managers are content to avoid resource scheduling altogether. These brave folk rely only on the initial results of time analysis and attempt to schedule every activity at its earliest possible time. Thus, the tabulation shown in Figure 8.5 would be accepted as the working schedule for the Bild-Rite hangar project. For companies that outsource all their labor to subcontractors, this method can work, but then the subcontractors will have to carry out their own resource scheduling to manage their workforce deployment. For companies that employ their own direct labor to work on projects, relying on earliest start dates is not satisfactory, and some method must be found for allocating resources to jobs on a more calculated basis.

If the resource requirements for this 'earliest possible' approach were to be plotted by Bild-Rite as a resource histogram, it would be found that for every type of resource used there would be days when some people were scheduled to be idle, whilst on other days there might be severe overloads. In other words, the resource usage pattern would exhibit unacceptable peaks and troughs. Schedules such as this, where no due regard is given to the actual availability of resources, are known as resource aggregations.

Resource Scheduling Priority Rules

Activities that possess slack can be delayed beyond their earliest possible dates so that critical activities (activities with zero slack) get priority for scarce resources and are scheduled first. The planned start of each non-critical activity can be delayed up to its latest permissible time, and that often removes or reduces resource overloads. However, deliberately delaying activities to smooth resource usage is a complex process for several reasons:

- Once any activity is delayed, it will usually produce a corresponding reduction in the slack of activities that follow.
- Activities often have more than one type of resource assigned to them, and an operation to smooth the usage of one resource type can create overloads or idle periods for other resources.
- If the network diagram contains more than a few activities (some contain many hundreds) the scale of the calculation is beyond the capabilities of the average human brain.

Activity ID	Activity Desc.	Duration	Total Float	Free Float	Early Start	Late Start	Early Finish	Late finish
01	Project start	0	0	0	06May10	06May10	05May10	05May10
02	Order materials and equipment	15d	21d	0	06May10	04Jun10	26May10	24Jun10
03	Order prefab hangar	20d	0	0	06May10	06May10	02Jun10	02Jun10
04	Order security fencing	2d	10d	0	06May10	20May10	07May10	21May10
05	Survey and mark out site	1d	12d	2d	06May10	24May10	06May10	24May10
06	Erect security fence	1d	10d	0	10May10	24May10	10May10	24May10
07	Dig service trenches	1d	29d	0	11May10	21Jun10	11May10	21Jun10
08	Prepare for base slab	2d	10d	0	11May10	25May10	12May10	26May10
09	Deliver materials and equipt	2d	21d	0	27May10	25Jun10	28May10	28Jun10
10	Deliver hangar flat-pack	1d	0	0	03Jun10	03Jun10	03Jun10	03Jun10
11	Dig soakaway pits	2d	32d	11d	12May10	25Jun10	13May10	28Jun10
12	Pour base slab concrete	1d	10d	0	13May10	27May10	13May10	27May10
13	Install underground drains	1d	21d	16d	31May10	29Jun10	31May10	29Jun10
14	Let concrete harden	5d	10d	10d	14May10	28May10	20May10	03Jun10
15	Erect steel wall frames	4d	0	0	04Jun10	04Jun10	09Jun10	09Jun10
16	Erect roof frame	3d	1d	1d	10Jun10	11Jun10	14Jun10	15Jun10
17	Clad front wall	2d	11d	0	10Jun10	25Jun10	11Jun10	28Jun10
18	Clad east wall	4d	0	0	10Jun10	10Jun10	15Jun10	15Jun10
19	Clad west wall	4d	0	0	10Jun10	10Jun10	15Jun10	15Jun10
20	Clad rear wall	4d	0	0	10Jun10	10Jun10	15Jun10	15Jun10
21	Fit roof sheets	5d	0	0	16Jun10	16Jun10	22Jun10	22Jun10
22	Fit door rails	1d	11d	0	14Jun10	29Jun10	14Jun10	29Jun10
23	Install electric main	1d	29d	29d	12May10	22Jun10	12May10	22Jun10
24	Install gutters and down pipes	2d	5d	5d	23Jun10	30Jun10	24Jun10	01Jul10
25	Lay down top floor surface	2d	3d	0	23Jun10	28Jun10	24Jun10	29Jun10
26	Assemble and fit the doors	1d	11d	8d	15Jun10	30Jun10	15Jun10	30Jun10
27	Install electric wiring	3d	0	0	23Jun10	23Jun10	25Jun10	25Jun10
28	Final floor polish	2d	3d	3d	25Jun10	30Jun10	28Jun10	01Jul10
29	Fit electric door motors	1d	3d	3d	28Jun10	01Jul10	28Jun10	01Jul10
30	Install ventilation fans	2d	2d	2d	28Jun10	30Jun10	29Jun10	01Jul10
31	Install lighting	4d	0	0	28Jun10	28Jun10	01Jul10	01Jul10
32	Remove security fence	1d	1d	1d	02Jul10	05Jul10	02Jul10	05Jul10
33	Final clean and checks	2d	0	0	02Jul10	02Jul10	05Jul10	05Jul10
34	Handover to client	1d	0	0	06Jul10	06Jul10	06Jul10	06Jul10

Figure 8.5   Time analysis for the Bild-Rite hangar project before resource scheduling (data from Open Plan)

- Many companies will have several projects active at any time, all competing for common resources (that difficulty is discussed later in this chapter).

The solution to all these problems lies in tackling the calculation in a series of logical steps, many of which depend on using a computer loaded with competent project management software. Some of these steps will become apparent as this chapter progresses, and they will be summarized at the conclusion.

Resource-Limited Or Time-Limited Scheduling?

If the computer is commanded that no resource usage may exceed the numbers stated to be available, there will often be occasions when some activities have to be delayed up to or even beyond their latest permissible times if overloads are to be prevented. This drives delayed critical activities into negative slack, and the project end date will thus be delayed. A schedule made under these rules is said to be *resource-limited*.

If the client or the project manager specifies, on the other hand, that the project end date may not be delayed beyond its earliest possible time, when there are insufficient resources the computer must not delay any activity beyond its latest permissible time, even if that means causing a resource overload. The resulting schedule is then said to be *time-limited*.

Some software (including Open Plan) will allow the planner to specify two levels of availability for each resource. These two levels are the normal level and a threshold level. Threshold resources might be made available by subcontracting temporary labor or by scheduling existing labor to work overtime (which is not normally recommended as good scheduling practice because overtime should be reserved for emergencies). Threshold resources will have their own cost rates, which will usually be higher than the normal resource rates.

The resource pool for a project can be regarded as a balloon filled with an incompressible liquid. If the balloon is squashed flat to keep the vertical resource usage peaks below their maximum permitted level, the balloon has no option but to spread sideways. And, vice versa, when the balloon is constricted horizontally within time limits, it must expand vertically to exceed the upper resource-usage limits.

These resource scheduling concepts are illustrated in Figures 8.6 and 8.7. Note that the leveled histograms in Figure 8.7 are ideal solutions and, in practice, the computer will not achieve such perfect results. Generally speaking, the larger the network and the greater the number of activities, the better chance the computer will have of producing a level resource usage. However, for all practical purposes, the results of resource scheduling usually promote the efficient use of resources.

Different Kinds Of Slack

An activity can possess four different kinds of slack, but only three of these need be explained here. For precedence networks they can be defined as follows:

- **Total slack**: The amount of slack calculated by subtracting the earliest activity start time from its latest permissible start time (using the corresponding finish times gives the same result). It is also defined as the time by which an activity may

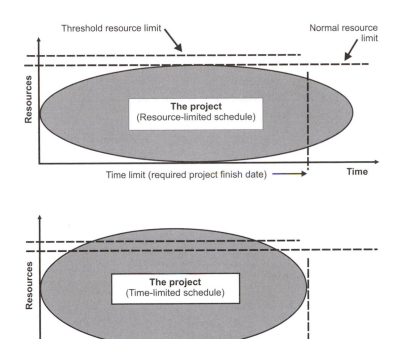

Figure 8.6 **Time-limited versus resource-limited priority rules**

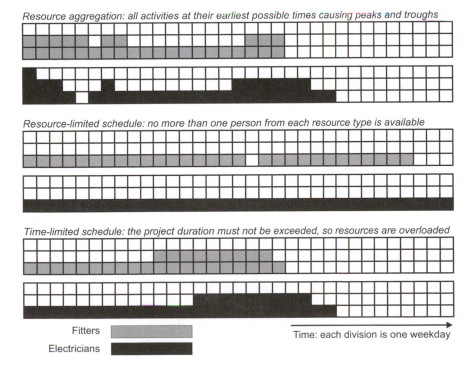

Figure 8.7 **Three different resource usage patterns for a small project**

be delayed if all preceding tasks take place at their earliest possible times and all subsequent tasks will not be delayed beyond their latest permissible times.

- **Free slack**: The amount of slack calculated by the earliest start time of the activity that immediately follows the subject activity, minus the latest permissible finish time of the subject activity. This is also defined as the amount of slack possessed by an activity if all preceding tasks take place at their earliest times and the immediately succeeding activity can still take place at its earliest possible time. This condition is less common than total slack and can only arise when more than one network logic constraint enters the immediately succeeding activity.
- **Remaining slack**: The amount of the original total slack that still remains after an activity has been delayed by late progress, or as the intentional result of resource scheduling.

These calculations become easy with practice when the network diagram displays only day numbers. They are far more difficult when calendar dates are substituted for day numbers. However the computer removes all the mental effort.

Activities with negative slack   Suppose that the critical path through a network has a total estimated duration of 100 weeks. The end activity will therefore have an earliest possible completion time of 100. Barring other considerations, the latest permissible completion time for the project will be at the end of the 100th week. Time analysis will, in the usual way, produce one or more critical paths back through to the start of the network in which all the critical activities have zero total slack.

Suppose, however, that those 'other considerations' include a promise to the customer that the project will be completed in 90 weeks. The latest permissible project end date is therefore 10 weeks before its earliest possible date. All activities that were previously on the critical path with zero total slack will now have a total slack of minus 10 weeks.

Negative slack can be caused whenever a fixed target date is imposed on the end activity (or on any other activity in a project network) that is impossible to meet. The cause may be a critical path that is longer than the time allowed by the target date. Negative slack can also occur as a result of imposing resource restrictions during scheduling, so that there are insufficient resources to carry out all the tasks in the time allowed by the critical path.

Splittable Or Non-Splittable Activities

Some software will allow the planner to specify some or all activities as *splittable*. This means that the computer is 'given permission' to interrupt a scheduled activity at some point during its planned progress so that its resources can be temporarily diverted to a more critical activity.

All software will by default assume that activities are non-splittable, so that the planner must make a conscious decision to designate any activity as splittable.

We do not generally favor splitting activities because that leads to a practical difficulty at the workplace. People do not like change, even when that means temporary interruption to a job which they are performing. Swapping people away from a job and then back to it can be disruptive and it will reduce efficiency, and could even lead to errors being made in the work.

DATA ERRORS

In a large project great volumes of input data are necessary and it is almost impossible to avoid making one or two mistakes when entering data into the computer. It *always* pays to check everything before accepting the output reports as correct.

Even for this tiny hangar construction project we made one or two careless numerical errors before producing the working resource schedules. Diagnostic routines in the software will identify some errors, but the computer cannot know (for instance) that a duration estimate entry of 10 days should have been 1 day.

In the early days it was possible to enter two or more activities with the same ID number, which could lead to absolute mayhem and error reports covering large areas of paper. Modern software puts a stop to that possibility because it will simply not allow duplicate ID numbers to be used.

Two common errors, explained below, are loops and dangles (which have absolutely nothing to do with items sold in jewelry shops).

Loops   A loop is caused when, by mistake, a logical constraint between two activities is wrongly entered into the system so that it not only connects the wrong two activities, but also creates a continuous cyclical path (loop) that might contain two or many more activities. Then, if the computer attempted a forward pass for time analysis, it could never finish because it would keep tracing round the endless path.

Early software would simply report that a loop existed and give up the time analysis attempt, sometimes accompanied by the chilling report 'fatal error'. Later, when programs became more sophisticated, the ID numbers of activities comprising a loop would be reported, allowing the planner to do some detective work and locate the incorrect constraint.

Open Plan, along with other modern software, will not even allow a loop to be created, but will produce a warning message when the attempt is made to add the incorrect constraint. The Open Plan warning reads simply and succinctly, 'This relationship will create a loop'.

Dangles   A dangle is created when a constraint between two activities is left out of the input data by mistake. The effect of omitting a constraint is to cause the preceding activity to end with nothing coming out of it (so that it looks like a finish activity) and the succeeding activity (with nothing leading into it) will be seen by the computer as a start activity. Activities that have been left high and dry through such errors of omission are called dangles.

Dangles are seen commonly among networks produced by inexperienced planners, and especially by students. However, even the most experience planner can occasionally forget to input a constraining link.

Open Plan (and most other software) will list the start and finish activities that it discovers during processing. If the network diagram has been drawn (as we recommend) with only one intended start activity and one intended finish activity, then obviously when more than one start or more than one finish is reported, something must have gone wrong.

Checking to avoid input data errors   Computer diagnostics, no matter how good, cannot be relied upon to identify every mistake. A good method for avoiding data input mistakes is to have two people entering the data into the computer. One person has prints of the network diagram and activity list, and calls out the data to the second person, who sits at the keyboard. Each activity, each piece of data, and each constraining link, is ticked off on the diagram or list as it is entered.

Then, have the computer produce a time analysis report and use that as a second check, to ensure that all dates look sensible and that all data have been correctly entered.

Data entry is a process demanding high concentration by dedicated people, without unnecessary interruption.

RESOURCE SCHEDULES PRODUCED FOR THE BILD-RITE HANGAR PROJECT

The first report for the Bild-Rite hangar project was time analysis, before any attempt at resource scheduling. That report was shown in Figure 8.5, and we used it as part of our error checking.

The crane, fitters, and electricians for the Bild-Rite hangar project were scheduled first using the time-limited rule, and then the calculation was repeated as a resource-limited schedule. Open Plan produces particularly attractive reports from a good range of standard templates. The resource histograms are made more attractive, especially for presenting to senior management, by the use of color and three-dimensional perspectives. Unfortunately for us, each report spreads over more than one A4 page, and to reproduce all of them here would have occupied too much space. All the reports have therefore been consolidated on to one page in Figure 8.8, where all the essential data are displayed.

The upper trio of histograms show the resource usage patterns that would be needed to complete the hangar construction by the earliest possible time, on 6 July, 2010. But Bild-Rite do not have those levels of resource normally available. (This is 1 day later than the latest date indicated by the resource histograms because the final 1-day activity requires no resource).

Rescheduling to avoid resource overloads has resulted in the modified schedule depicted by the lower trio of histograms. Now the project can be carried out using only the resources declared to be available, but this has caused the end date to be delayed until Monday 19 July (again 1 day later than the end of the histograms owing to the final handover activity, which requires no resource and therefore no bar on the histogram).

Work-To Lists

The most valuable and practical reports to come from resource scheduling are the tabular work-to lists. These are particularly valuable in larger organizations, where many departmental managers have responsibility for issuing work instructions and managing progressing.

Each work-to list looks very similar to the time analysis report presented in Figure 8.5. The only difference in the work-to list's presentation is that two different date columns are either added or substituted for the dates produced before resource scheduling. These dates are the *scheduled start* date and the *scheduled finish* date for each activity. These scheduled dates are the dates when each activity should start and finish if the smoothest use of resources is to be achieved, as determined by the computer's resource scheduling process.

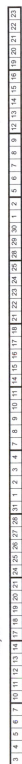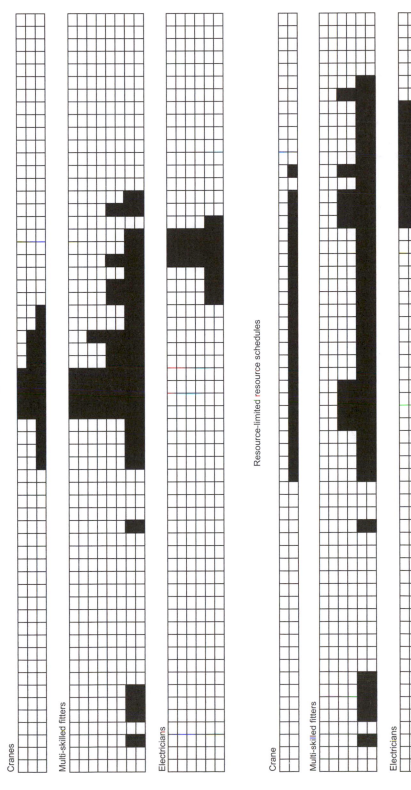

Figure 8.8   Resource usage patterns for the Bild-Rite hangar project (all calculated using Open Plan)

There are two other important attributes of any work-to list. The first of these is achieved by the computer *filtering* the data for each report, using departmental filter codes, so that each departmental manager receives reports that contain only the activities for which they have direct managerial responsibility.

The second important attribute is *sorting*, so that all the activities listed for each manager are presented in their most convenient sequence. The most common sequence chosen is to sort in order of ascending scheduled start date. However, different sequences might be more suitable in some cases. For example, a purchasing expediting clerk might find a report sorted in ascending order of expected materials delivery dates helpful. The project planner, who needs to check all the data, would need an unfiltered report (showing all activities) sorted in ascending order of the activity ID numbers.

Executive Summary Reports

Most project management software makes provision for one-page project summary reports, intended for management overview. If more than one project is contained in the system, some programs will allow summary reports to be printed out concisely for all these projects in a type of report sometimes known as a project directory. Some programs can produce imaginative graphics for this purpose, for example, including RAG reporting in which red, amber, or green signals are placed in traffic signal style against each item to show respectively whether it is running over time or budget, is at risk, or is on plan.

Particularly relevant in the context of summary reports is the identification of one or more activities as *key activities* or *milestone activities*. These are activities which the project manager or client has specified as being of particular importance in the progress of the project, or they could be linked to the release of progress or stage payments. The computer can produce reports that contain only the milestones as executive summary reports. In our tiny hangar project example, the start and finish activities would certainly be identified as milestones. Another possible milestone for the hangar project might be activity 21, because when the roof sheets have all been fixed the building is weatherproof and the internal 'dry trades' can begin their work.

SCHEDULING CASH FLOWS

Cash is a project resource, just as people, materials, and equipment, and its inflows and outflows can be scheduled using any project management software that can schedule other resources. One method is to assign each significant cash outflow (cost) item to a network activity, and the resource schedule will, among all the other resource reports, produce a schedule of cash outflows that march with the working schedules. These cash inflow amounts can be identified and isolated for reporting by giving all the relevant cash outflow activities a sort code.

Cash inflows (payments from clients or cost savings) can similarly be attached to activities, and scheduling those activities will produce a report of expected cash inflows against calendar dates. Milestone activities can often be used for this purpose.

When cash inflows and cash outflows are tabulated in a spreadsheet that has columns for the months, quarters, or other periods in a project, the project manager can calculate the expected cumulative net flows for the project (inflows minus outflows). That process is very similar to managing a checking account at one's personal bank. The results enable the company's financial vice president to budget for the project, or alternatively scream that the project cannot be afforded.

Like so many other project management processes, setting up a cash flow statement and reporting mechanism begins with a series of logical steps. These are illustrated in Figure 8.9.

Given detailed cost estimates and a practicable project plan, the scheduling of project cash outflows becomes fairly straightforward arithmetic. However, it is very important to set each item of expected expenditure in the period when the payment will actually become due. For example, the cash outflow for purchasing an item of equipment or a bulk supply of materials takes place not when the purchase order is placed (the time of cost commitment) but at the time when the invoice will be paid. Of course the act of committing the project to any significant new cost is important, but that comes within the context of *cost* control and not *cash* control.

Every item in any cash flow schedule, whether for outflows or inflows, is the best estimate of two different things, which are:

1. the amount of cash involved;
2. the date when that amount of money will actually change hands.

First consider the cash outflows. Everything starts from the WBS or detailed task list that specifies what has to be done. Then, a combination of the project work schedules and detailed cost estimates enables each cash outflow item to be placed in its appropriate period.

Returning to Figure 8.9, it can be seen that knowing both the prices to be charged to the client (as progress payments for this construction project) and the project schedule will enable a schedule of cash inflows to be made. When that has been done, the forecast cash inflows and outflows can be compared to assess how much cash will flow in or out of the contractor's bank each month (the *net* flows). That, in turn, will enable the project manager to report the effect that these cash movements will have on balances at the bank. Figure 8.10 is an outline format for a summary cash flow spreadsheet.

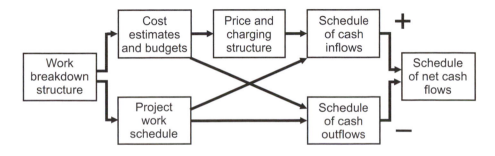

Figure 8.9   Essential elements of a project net cash flow schedule

LOX-COPTERS	The tree hopper chopper project												Project # Issue date			
Cost item	Quarterly periods - all figures $1000s															Total budget
	2010				2011				2012				2013			
	1	2	3	4	1	2	3	4	1	2	3	4	1	2	3	4	
INFLOWS Agreed loans Share issue Pre-orders																	
Total inflows																	
OUTFLOWS Engineering Purchasing Manufacture Trials Certification																	
Total outflows																	
NET FLOWS Periodic Cumulative																	

Net flows are cash inflows minus cash outflows

Figure 8.10   Pro-forma for a net cash flow spreadsheet

SCHEDULING THE RESOURCES FOR ALL PROJECTS IN AN ORGANIZATION

In organizations which employ their own permanent direct labor force for a number of simultaneous projects (often called a program of projects) multi-project resource scheduling is essential. A multi-project schedule has benefits for an organization beyond the planning and control of existing work. The schedule, if properly prepared, is a model of a company's total workload. As such, it becomes a powerful aid to manpower and corporate planning. It is possible to run 'What if?' trial schedules, testing possible new projects in the multi-project model to see what effect these might have on the company's future workload and capacity requirements.

All of this can still present an apparently difficult problem. The system has to digest a vast amount of data, priority conflicts must be resolved, and all logical task interdependencies need to be observed. In addition, the result has to be dynamic and responsive to changes, such as design modifications, technical problems, work cancellations, the introduction of new projects, or fluctuations in total resource capacities. Most of the software products that can schedule resources for single projects are capable of dealing with these problems.

Projects And Subprojects

In multi-project scheduling there is an important difference of scale from single project scheduling. The organization's total workload can be regarded as 'the project', although other terms are 'project portfolio' or simply 'program'. Each of the former individual projects becomes, effectively, a 'subproject' within the new total project.

Network Activity Identifiers

There is a probability that the same activity identifying code numbers will crop up on different subproject networks. This will be true particularly if the tasks for each subproject are numbered in a simple numeric series. With some software this can be disastrous. When presented with two or more subprojects containing duplicated numbers, the computer sees the whole conglomeration of data as one huge error-laden network. The confusion and number of errors generated can be imagined, with all sorts of complex constraints and paths being created across all the subprojects by mistake. There are several possible solutions to this problem, which depend largely on the capabilities of the software chosen.

One solution is to ensure that duplicate numbers can never arise between different subnetworks. A good way to prevent duplication is to prefix all the activity ID codes within each subproject with a unique string of characters. The length of this string will depend on the number of subprojects to be managed, but it is unlikely to be more than two or three characters. Some software can add such prefixes automatically across all the tasks in a subproject network. Project numbers, or parts of them, can often provide useful and logical prefixes. It is, however, easy to build up very long activity ID codes. These are best avoided if possible because long numbers increase work and the risk of human errors. Some of the cheaper software systems can only accept ID codes containing perhaps four or six characters in total, which does not allow much space for a prefix.

Fortunately, most software packages do not demand that every number in the overall multi-project model is unique. It is only necessary to make certain that every identifier is unique within its own subproject network diagram. The vital point then becomes that each subproject *must* be given its own identifying subproject code.

Managing The Multi-project Model

The multi-project model can be expected to have a continuous but constantly changing existence. It will comprise a variable number of subprojects, each with its own different finite life. At regular or irregular intervals, new projects must be added, completed projects removed, and progress information or other changes injected for current projects. Managing such a model can be a formidable (but worthwhile) task. Even though individual project networks might be of manageable size, perhaps containing only one or two hundred tasks, the total multi-project model for a medium-sized company can easily contain many thousands of tasks.

Strict attention to data preparation, system security, and updating disciplines must be observed if the whole model is to be maintained in a useful state. This usually means that access levels to the system must be carefully controlled through entry passwords. Certainly the data should be accessible for all authorized people to view, but only those with the necessary training and skills should be allowed to enter data or commands that could materially affect the project files and the resulting schedules. Access that can change the system parameters must be even more jealously guarded. Figure 8.11 shows the arrangement that we favor for maintaining the integrity of the multi-project model, while still allowing adequate access for the system users.

The coordination function need not be expensive. It can often be performed by one skilled, appropriately trained person. Training and hands-on experience must, however, be given to at least one deputy. In larger organizations the ideal home for administering the multi-project model is the project support office.

Data Preparation For The Multi-project Model

Preparation for multi-project scheduling is very similar to that required for single-project scheduling. Anyone who has mastered the problems associated with single-project resource scheduling will find the step up into multi-project modelling very easy.

A separate network must be drawn for every significant, definable subproject in the organization. Estimates for durations, costs, and resources are made in the normal way and prepared for input to the computer. All of this follows the methods explained in previous chapters.

Calendars and holiday files will normally be the same as those used for carrying out single project scheduling in the organization.

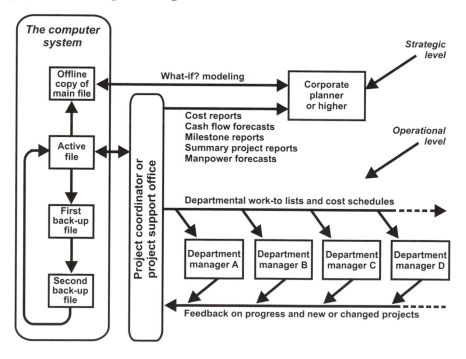

The integrity of the model must be preserved. This can be achieved by allowing access for system changes only through an expert person or group such as a project support office.

Figure 8.11   Managing a multi-project model

Allocation Of Priorities Between Subprojects

Planners are always able to choose from a number of priority rules for allocating resources to activities within each subproject, just as in single-project scheduling. In the multi-project case, however, there is a further level of priorities to be decided, namely the allocation of resources between different subprojects.

The ideal solution is very simple and it works well. First, it is necessary to specify target start and completion dates for every subproject. These dates should be the contractual dates committed and agreed with the various customers. The computer will carry out time analysis for all subprojects independently and calculate float from these imposed target dates. After that, priority claims for scarce resources during multi-project processing can be decided automatically according to the amount of float possessed by each activity.

Senior managers undoubtedly have their own views on priority differences between all the subprojects in the model. There are occasions, for example, when one customer might be regarded as being more important than another. There is then a risk of interference with the scheduling process, with a desire to force the progress of one or two projects at the expense of others. If the project planner cannot overcome these undesirable external influences, the most favored subproject will have to be given some form of higher priority by artificial means. This can be achieved by placing an artificially early target completion date on the relevant subproject.

When a successful multi-project scheduling operation has been established, it should earn the benefit of management trust and be left to deal with priorities in its own logical and equitable fashion. Allocation of resources according only to remaining float is an elegant solution that is easy to apply.

PRACTICAL HINTS ON RESOURCE SCHEDULING

There is a tendency among novices to try to schedule every possible resource employed in an organization. However, consider just one example, namely paint sprayers. If all the manufacturing tasks have been scheduled, work should reach the paint bays in a steady, uniform flow. It is, therefore, not necessary to schedule the paint sprayers.

It is also unnecessary to schedule indirect staff, such as administrators, project planners, managers, and others who do not work full time directly on specific project activities. The best approach is to examine the organization, pick out no more than three or four resource categories that employ most labor, and schedule just those resource categories. Care must be taken to include any resource category that is known to be in short supply or prone to causing progress bottlenecks.

Another problem facing beginners is how to specify the number of resource units available within each category. This problem is actually easier to solve when the total company is being scheduled as a multiple project model, because one simply declares all active resources as being available within each chosen category. However, the emphasis here is on the word 'active'.

Take any group of people in an office or factory, and you will find that at any given time some of them are not available for work on projects, for a number of different reasons. Some might be sick. Others could be away on training courses. Then, there is always a sludge factor to take into account, to deal with all the after-issue or rework issues, and ad hoc non-project jobs that always seem to crop up, but which cannot be planned. Again,

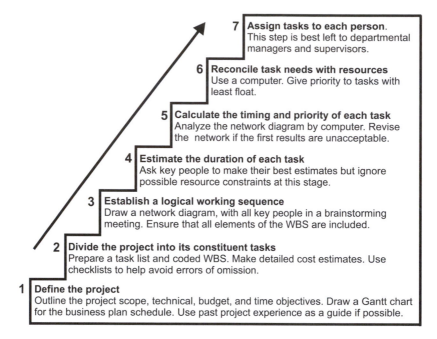

Figure 8.12   Seven logical steps to a practical project resource schedule

one must always look for the simple solution. In this case, the answer is to declare the total number of resource units available as being somewhat less than the total number of people employed. Try starting with 85 per cent, leaving 15 per cent of each resource type free to fill the sludge factor.

Many project management processes depend on logical thought. Making sense of the myriad of problems and pressures that face any project organization can seem to be an insurmountable problem because there are simply too many variables. But in mathematics the way of dealing with a large number of unknown variables is to solve them one at a time. So it is in project planning.

Figure 8.12 above identifies seven logical steps that can solve most of the variables and lead to a practicable plan of work. When a project organization can implement resource scheduling effectively, very significant savings in costs result and fewer projects will be delivered late.

REFERENCES

PMI (2004), *A Guide to the Project Management Body of Knowledge* (PMBOK® Guide), 3rd edn, Newtown Square, PA, Project Management Institute.

9

Implementing the Plan

Once authorization has been received, the project ceases to be merely an object for planning and speculation and becomes instead a live entity, to which all who work in the project organization are fully committed. To achieve the project objectives, whether technical, budgetary, or timescale, the appropriate project organization has to be set up. All participants must be made aware of the particular role they will be expected to play.

A common risk to projects is failure to start work on time. Very long delays can be caused by prevarication, legal or planning difficulties, shortage of information, lack of funds or other resources, and a host of other reasons. All of these factors can place a project manager in a difficult or impossible position because if a project is not allowed to start on time it can hardly be expected to finish on time.

PROJECT AUTHORIZATION

Project authorization by the customer or project owner means giving formal written instruction that authorizes the contractor or project organization to proceed with the project on previously agreed terms. (For in-house management projects, remember that the 'customer' is the company itself and the 'contractor' is the internal division or department responsible.)

Initial Registration And Numbering

A new project has to be formally 'entered into the system' so that all the necessary accounting, planning, progressing, and other administrative procedures can be put in place.

One of the first steps is to add the new project to the project register and allocate a project number. This number should preferably be built in as an identifying component of drawing and equipment specification numbers, cost codes, timesheets, and all other important project documents.

Whenever it is necessary to retrieve information about a project, current or long past, the project register or its archived information is usually the best, even the only, starting place. In most management information systems and archives the project number is the essential element leading to the various document files and project data. However a well-kept register should also allow any project and its former manager's name to be traced from the customer's name, project description, approximate date, or other information, long after the project number has been forgotten.

Internal Project Authorization Document

An authorization document, entitled 'project authorization', 'works order', or even 'project charter' should define the departmental and purchasing cost budgets, give planned start and finish dates, details of the customer's order, pricing information, invoicing and delivery instructions, and so on. An essential item on a project authorization is the signature of a member of the company's senior management to signal that the project is authorized and that work can begin. Project authorizations come in many designs but an example is given in Figure 9.1.

PROJECT AUTHORIZATION

Client ____________________

Scope of work ____________________

Source documents ____________________

Project number (to be entered by accounts department) ☐☐☐☐☐☐

Project title (for computer reports) ☐☐☐☐☐☐☐☐☐☐☐☐☐☐☐☐☐☐

Project manager (name) __________ Staff number ☐☐☐☐

Project engineer (name) __________ Staff number ☐☐☐☐

Project start date (enter as 01-JAN-10) ☐☐-☐☐☐-☐☐

Target finish date (enter as 01-JAN-10) ☐☐-☐☐☐-☐☐

Contract type:

Reimbursable ☐ Lump sum ☐ Other (Specify) __________

Estimate of labor hours

Standard cost grade	1	2	3	4	5	6	7	8
Labor hour totals								

Notes:

....

Authorization (1) *Authorization (2)*

Project manager		Marketing		Contracts dept.		Purchasing			
Project engineer		Central registry		Cost/planning		Accounts dept.			

Figure 9.1 An authorization form for an airport construction project

Project authorizations are distributed to all company departments, but the supporting technical and commercial documents go to the project manager. It becomes the project manager's responsibility thereafter to ensure that all other managers in the organization are made aware of project requirements in detail and sufficiently in advance to enable them to make any necessary preparations.

PRELIMINARY ORGANIZATION OF THE PROJECT

Even when a clear technical specification has been prepared there are often many loose ends to be tied up before actual work can start. The extent and nature of these preliminary activities naturally depend on the type and size of project.

When the project manager has been named, an organization chart should be drawn and published to show all key people or agencies concerned with the project. It must include senior members of all external groups who are going to have any responsibility in the project. If the organization is very large, the usual arrangement is to produce an overall summary chart and then draw a series of smaller charts which allow some of the groups to be shown in more detail.

Responsibility Matrix

People must know what is expected of them. One tool which can assist the project manager to allocate responsibilities is the linear responsibility matrix, an example of which is shown in Figure 9.2. The job titles of key members of the organization are listed above the matrix columns and important task categories are listed along the rows. Symbols placed at the appropriate matrix intersections show primary and secondary responsibility-listed task category.

Distribution Of Correspondence And Other Paper Documents

The principal project company (which we call the contractor in the remainder of this chapter) will be well advised to take control procedures for project correspondence seriously. The contractor could easily find itself in a difficult position if it were to lose vital letters or other documents. Positive steps must be taken to deal with the routeing and control of documented information across all external parts of the project organization.

In large projects it is good practice for each different company involved to nominate a person to act as a control point for receiving and sending all formal written communications and technical documents. Each nominated addressee is made responsible for seeing that the documents or the information contained in them is made known to all the relevant people within their own organization. Of course this procedure can apply only to documents that have legal or technical significance, and not to communications such as informal emails.

It is necessary to consider and list the types of documents that will be generated throughout the life of the project, and then decide who needs to receive copies as a matter of routine. This should usually be on a 'needs to know' rather than 'wants to know' basis (except that all requests for documents from the customer must be looked upon favorably unless these would give away information that the contractor wishes to remain confidential).

Document distribution matrix

Recipient:

Document type:	The customer	General manager	Project manager	Project engineer	Works manager	Production control	Buyer	Quality manager	Accountant	and so on
Bought-out parts lists						1	2	1		
Material specifications				1		1	1	1		
Purchase requisitions				1			1*			
Purchase orders							1		1	
Shortage lists			1			1	1			
Committed cost reports		1	1	1			1		1	
Drawing list		1	1	1	1					
Drawings for approval	1			1*						
and so on										

1	Number of copies per recipient
1*	Retains the original signed document

Linear responsibility matrix

Responsibility:

Task type:	The client	Project manager	Project engineer	Purchasing manager	Drawing office	Construction manager	Planning engineer	Cost engineer	Project accountant	and so on
Make designs		+		●						
Approve designs	●	■	+							
Purchase enquiries		■	+	●						
Purchase orders	■	■	+	●						
Planning	■	■	+	+	+	+	●			
Cost control		●		+		+		+		
Progress reports		●	+	+	+	+	+	+		
Cost reports		●		+		+		+	+	
and so on										

- ● Principal responsibility (only one per task)
- + Secondary responsibility
- ■ Must be consulted

Figure 9.2   Two very useful matrix charts

If the documents are to be made available in electronic form, accessible over a network, it might be necessary to impose different levels of access for security purposes, thus preventing unauthorized people from seeing sensitive or confidential data.

Once the regular distribution or availability of documents has been agreed, the decision can be depicted on a matrix chart, arranged in similar fashion to the responsibility matrix already described. An example is shown in the right-hand section of Figure 9.2. The document types are listed down the left-hand side, and their authorized recipients are put at the heads of the columns. A tick in the square at each grid intersection shows that access is permissible. Alternatively, a number written at each intersection shows how many hard copies of the relevant document each person should receive.

Design Standards And Procedures

The contractor will have to investigate whether or not the project calls for any special design standards, safety requirements, or compliance with statutory regulations. These issues usually have cost implications, so that most of the requirements should have been established at the project definition stage.

Drawings made for a project sometimes become the property of the customer, who will expect to take possession of all the original drawings at the end of the project and file them in their own system (the contractor would, of course, retain a complete copy). The contractor might be asked to use the customer's own drawing numbering system. Usual practice in such cases is to number each drawing twice, using the customer's system and the contractor's normal standard. These dual numbers must be cross-referenced, but that is simple with the drawings register filed in a computer.

Choice Of Project Planning And Control Procedures

Companies that regularly carry out projects may have at their disposal a considerable range of planning and control procedures. At the start of each new project these can be reviewed to determine which should be used. Factors affecting this choice are the size and complexity of the project, the degree of difficulty and risk expected in meeting the end objectives, the number and locations of outside organizations, and the wishes or directions of the customer.

Project Handbook

For large projects contractors will compile a project handbook (also known as a project procedures manual). This lists the procedures that will apply to the project. It will include such things as the names of key personnel, organization charts, responsibility matrix, document distribution matrix, and the names and addresses of all key organizations with their relevant incoming and outgoing correspondence contact points. A short version, containing only matters pertaining to correspondence, can be issued as a secretaries' manual.

PHYSICAL PREPARATIONS AND ORGANIZATION

It is obvious that physical preparations must be made for any project that requires accommodation, plant, equipment, services such as gas, electric power, compressed air, water, and so on. It is equally obvious that there is no typical case, because the requirements of every project depend very much on the nature of the project and the practices of its contractor. At one end of the scale is the project that will simply follow another in a factory or assembly hangar, using the same staff, management, and facilities. At the opposite extreme is the international airport project involving several large companies and a construction site in the middle of a newly developing area, where good road and rail communications have not yet been established. At that extreme, making physical preparation for the main project is, in itself, a collection of subprojects. Any discussion of physical preparations in this chapter must, therefore, be in general terms.

Checklists

All project managers will know the frustration caused during the initial days and weeks when, keen to start and with deadlines to meet, work cannot start because there is no information, no staff, and a general lack of other facilities.

Lack of information is often the worst of these problems: not necessarily about the main objectives and features of the intended project but more likely about a hundred and one annoying details which have to be resolved before work can start.

The value of checklists is mentioned in several places in this book, and no apology is needed or made for giving additional space to this subject here. Standard checklists, applicable to all projects, present and future, can be used as questionnaires to pre-empt information requirements. The best checklists are developed and refined through experience, so that lessons learned on each project are remembered and put to use on projects that follow.

Here, again, we should mention the analogy with cockpit checklists. Every flight can be regarded as a new project. Pre-flight checklists that have been developed through considerable experience help to ensure that each new flight 'project' will proceed safely from take-off to landing exactly as intended,

Construction site checklist example   An example where a checklist is particularly useful is when an airport construction site organization has to be established, especially when this is to be overseas. Even for an experienced organization, that can be an enormous operation. All sorts of questions have to be asked, and answered. Some questions should already have been answered when the proposal was researched (see Figure 2.2, for example). When the project becomes real, the questions and answers have a more definite and detailed aspect, as shown in the checklist fragment in Figure 9.3. It is important to get answers as completely and as early as possible. The better the checklist, the earlier and more completely these answers are likely to be obtained.

Workplace checklist for a Lox Aviation project to inspect and recondition landing gear
The list shown in Figure 9.4 is the initial issue of a checklist designed to ensure that safe and efficient working conditions can be provided in work areas that are being prepared in readiness for a project to inspect and recondition an aircraft landing gear. In practice this list would need further consideration and development, but we have shown the principles.

How many people will be working at the airport site?
How many of these people will be:
- our own permanent staff?
- our own fixed-term contract staff, hired for this project only?
- local recruits? (will they need training?)
- client's staff?
- subcontractors' staff?
What accommodation must be provided?
- how much?
- what standard?
- who will provide it?
- rent free?
What are the local immigration rules?
- passports and visas?
- work permits?
- any racial prejudices?
Local employment laws and practices?
What about expatriates' wives and families?
Standard terms of employment?
Pay and personal taxation?
Insurances:
- staff related?
- work related?
Staff medical, welfare, and leisure facilities?
Climate?
Site access:
- road?
- rail?
- air?
- other?
Vehicle fleet:
- personnel carriers?
- goods and heavy materials?
- how provided?
- how managed and maintained?
Construction plant:
- what is needed?
- when?
- how provided?
- how maintained?

Figure 9.3   **Fragment of a site checklist for an overseas airport construction project that employs interacting contractors**

If the workplace conditions are safe and ideal, the turnround time for each aircraft will be reduced and there will be less risk of poor quality work or an on-the-job accident.

GETTING WORK STARTED

The Kick-Off Meeting

When the newly appointed project manager has collected their wits and absorbed the contents of the project specification (which will probably entail some late nights), the most urgent job is to mobilize all the project resources and tell the key participants what is expected of them.

Lox Aviation Inc.

Temporary landing gear maintenance bay – facilities checklist

1   *Areas alongside aircraft*
    Space for equipment trolley
    Safe working clearances for lifting gear
    Adequate equipment storage space

2   *Dismantling area*
    Individual work stations within easy conversational distances of each other
    Adequate access for trolleys and forklift trucks
    Tool racks
    Work benches of adequate strength
    Wheeled racks and cradles for dismantled parts
    Local lifting hoists
    Good local lighting

3   *Cleaning area*
    Safe disposal arrangement for cleaning agents
    Good ventilation to clear fumes
    Adequate working space

4   *Paint stripping area*
    Efficient fume extraction
    Clear working space
    Good access for trolleys

5   *Used parts inspection area*
    Ensure inspectors are included in resource schedules
    Racks for storing inspection equipment and instruments
    Good local lighting

6   *Painting area*
    Ensure painters are included in resource schedules
    Ensure paint area not too far from wheel shop
    Efficient fume extraction

7   *Reassembly area*
    Individual work stations within easy conversational distances
    Adequate access for trolleys and forklift trucks
    Tool rack
    Safe storage for replacement components and consumable spares
    Work benches of adequate strength
    Wheeled racks and cradles for dismantled parts
    Local lifting hoists
    Good local lighting
    Facilities for inspectors

8   *Leak test area*
    Provide safe protection cages

9   *Dispatch bay*
    Remember clean desk and filing facilities for dispatch paperwork

10 *General*
    Health and safety throughout, including first aid and fire precautions

    Document reference LG45   Rev 0   June 2011

Figure 9.4   Workplace creation checklist for a landing gear inspection and reconditioning project

This process takes place in different stages and by a variety of methods. The first executive action of the project manager is usually to call an initial meeting, often called the 'kick-off' meeting, which gives the project manager the opportunity to outline the main features of the project to managers whose departments will work on the project, and to the most senior design staff and other key people.

If the project is organized as a team, the project manager will have the advantage of talking to people who are going to be directly responsible to him or her. If the organization is a functional matrix, the task is more difficult—even getting people to attend the meeting becomes a question more of invitation or persuasion rather than a direct summons.

Whatever the circumstances, the skilled project manager will make the best possible use of the kick-off meeting to get the project off to a good start. Everyone should leave the meeting with a clear picture of the project's objectives, the part that they are expected to play in achieving them, and a sense of keenness and motivation to get on with the job.

Initial Planning Information

It is unlikely that early plans will exist in sufficient detail for issuing and controlling work on mainstream activities, but two aspects of initial plans have to be mentioned:

1. Even though the first bar chart or outline critical path network plan might have been made in very coarse detail, with gaps in knowledge of how the project is going to be conducted, those early plans will probably have been used in the project proposal. Thus, when authorization is received, the project timeframe will already have been agreed with the customer.
2. The absence of very detailed plans at the start often does not matter, when the very first project tasks are either administrative or are intended to finalize design concepts.

Two sets of initial plans should, therefore, be available for issue at the start. These are:

1. A summary plan giving committed dates for the whole project. This should accompany the works order or other project authorization document. It might be a bar chart but for this early use it can be a simple list key dates or milestones.
2. A checklist and plan for preliminary activities. Every contractor learns the preliminary activities needed to set up a new project and establish its procedures and design standards. One company in our experience designed a checklist in the form of a standard network diagram for use at the start of every project. Time estimates were not used on this network. Its value was as a checklist of preliminary activities, arranged in their logical sequence.

One job during the early period covered by this preliminary checklist must, of course, be to make detailed plans and work schedules for the project. These often have to be worked and reworked until they satisfy the delivery promises already made to a customer.

DETAILED PLANS AND WORK INSTRUCTIONS

Importance Of Personal Agreement And Commitment

Enough has been written in earlier chapters about the methods available for producing plans and working schedules. It must be taken for granted that detailed planning will be performed, and that this will involve at least one senior representative from every key project function. Each key participant should have some share in formulating and agreeing the detailed plan because no plan can be imposed successfully in isolation. It must carry the acceptance and support of those who are to be bound by it.

Issuing Work Schedules: Targeting Instructions For Action

Dissemination of programme information must be made far more effective than simply issuing complete work schedules to all and sundry. As soon as the first detailed plans and resource schedules are available, the computer can produce a work-to list that is specific to every project department, showing only those tasks for which each departmental manager is responsible.

Instructions are often ignored when they are issued to too many people, instead of being targeted to the person who is expected to arrange for action. If an instruction is put in a document that goes to several departments, each may do nothing and rely on the others to carry the instruction out, or the same task could be performed in two or more places (such as duplicating orders for equipment and materials).

Carefully filtered work-to lists have the advantage of being specific to their addressees, so that management responsibility for every item on each list is the clear responsibility of the recipient.

Work-to lists need only be provided in detail to cover a few weeks ahead, but longer-term summaries should be provided to help departmental managers to recruit or reserve the necessary people. All of this is readily achievable with the filtering and sorting capabilities of project management software.

Work-To Lists And The Authority Of Departmental Managers

The instructions or reminders contained in work-to lists should in no way detract from the personal authority vested in each departmental manager.

Although the source of these working schedules is the project manager's office (or project support office), the data in them should derive from the detailed project plan that was previously reviewed and agreed by the departmental managers. The authority of these managers, far from being undermined, is reinforced.

Each manager receives a timed list of the work required of their department but, within that timeframe, is free to allocate the work to groups or individuals within the department and to direct and control it (the last of the seven steps described at the end of the previous chapter). With work-to lists resulting from sensible resource scheduling, there should be no chronic overloads, although temporary overloads are always a risk.

Work-To Lists In Relation To Departmental Work Procedures

Work-to-lists can be regarded as departmental orders or as planning reminders, depending on the department to which they are sent.

Work-to lists for aerospace manufacturing   Work-to lists for aerospace manufacturing would usually be sent to the production manager or production controller, who would continue to issue works orders, job tickets, route cards, and other documents used throughout the manufacturing organization. The levels of detail shown in project networks (and, therefore, in their resulting work-to lists) are bound to be far coarser than those needed for the day-to-day planning and control of factory operations. For example, work-to lists can provide the scheduled start and required finish dates for each assembly and subassembly but they will not usually specify a greater degree of work breakdown.

Thus the manufacturing organization will use its own production engineering, planning, and control facilities to interpret drawings, identify the parts and materials required, and carry out detailed production scheduling. This must be done to satisfy the dates scheduled on the work-to lists but, when project resource scheduling has been used, the overall rate of working requested by the project manager should lie within the capacity of the manufacturing plant.

Work-to lists for design engineering   In engineering design departments, the work-to lists will contain some tasks that can be allocated to individuals with no need to plan in any greater detail. However, networks are not always drawn with sufficient breakdown detail for the day-to-day allocation of all work, and it may often be necessary for managers and supervisors to arrange for very detailed activities to be listed by clerical or other means.

For instance, a design task shown in a network diagram (and in the resulting work-to lists) usually summarizes a group of drawings needed for a small work package or subassembly. It is not usually desirable or possible to have a separate network activity for every individual project drawing or for every small item to be purchased. Drawing lists or drawing schedules, and purchase control schedules, bills of materials or material take-offs, and parts lists will always be needed to show a greater level of detail than is possible in the network diagram and its associated work-to lists. Thus design managers and their staff will often have to carry out some planning in fine detail themselves to produce these more detailed control documents and records.

The inclusion of estimated costs and target dates on work-to lists can help to make highly trained technologists aware that they have time and cost responsibilities—in addition to the creative aspects of their work that they enjoy most.

MANAGING PROGRESS

This section starts from the premise that an effective schedule has been produced, and that all key project participants know, and have willingly agreed to, what is expected of them.

Project Progressing As A Closed-loop Control System

Project progressing can be regarded as a closed-loop control system. For every instruction issued, the system response has to be monitored and feedback information must be generated.

Otherwise there would be no way of knowing when corrective actions are needed. The project manager will ensure that these corrective actions take place, so that a control system is created. Electronic engineers will recognize the similarity here with a negative feedback circuit that is designed to reduce distortion in amplifiers and other devices when the feedback loop is closed. Feedback systems ensure that mechanical movements are measured so that positional errors in some aircraft controls are kept within acceptable tolerances. Thus the process of regular progress monitoring and the application of corrective measures in project management is sometimes called cybernetic control. Figure 9.5 illustrates this concept.

With any system of control feedback, it is the errors that are given most attention. In the management context these errors are called 'exceptions' or 'variances'. In all branches of management (including financial management) this sensible approach of concentrating reports and management attention on exceptions is known as 'management by exception'.

There is an alternative management approach to management by exception that relies only on outgoing instructions, with no feedback or error signals. This open loop method is called 'management by surprise', because the manager feeds in work instructions at the front end of the system and is surprised when the expected results do not come out at the end!

PROGRESS MONITORING AND SCHEDULE UPDATING

In order for a closed-loop progress management system to work effectively it is apparent that two-way communication between the project manager and every departmental manager must exist. Departmental managers, in their turn, will ensure that they have effective day-to-day or even hour-by-hour communication with their subordinates. For every work instruction issued, information must be available regularly on the resulting progress and especially on any exceptions or variances that need correction.

Use Of Work-To Lists As Progress Returns

If the instructions are to be conveyed from the project manager to participants by way of work-to lists, there is no reason why the same procedure should not be used in reverse to

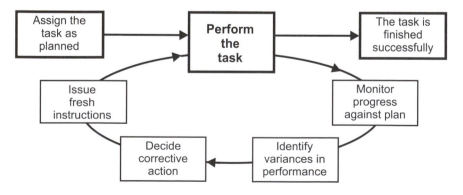

Figure 9.5   A control cycle: an example of management by exception sometimes known as a cybernetic control loop

feed back progress information. The only missing item is a document complementary to the work-to list. This gap can be filled by one of the following:

1. the use of specially designed progress return forms;
2. line managers annotating and returning copies of their work-to-lists;
3. direct input to the project computer or server by managers and others using their own computers.

Option 1 introduces more forms and clerical work, which should be avoided if possible. For option 2, work-to lists can be specially configured with space to allow feedback reports. Open Plan is an example of a software package that can print a combined work-to list and questionnaire progress return in its standard range of reports. It is usually possible to arrange work-to list layouts from other software packages with a blank column that leaves space for comments and progress feedback.

For option 3, it is often practicable for departmental managers to access the project computer files through their own terminals. The project manager will want to be assured that progress information fed directly to the computer in this way emanates from truthful and reasonably senior staff. False input statements could lead to subsequent errors in network analysis, resource scheduling, and future work-to lists. If the computer is holding a large, complex multi-project model, the group or person responsible for scheduling will always be wary of any input that could corrupt the model and cause many hours of restoration work.

Although project progress information can be updated continuously, work-to lists and other schedules will probably only be revised and reissued when the planner decides that this is necessary to keep issued instructions up to date.

Quality And Reliability Of Progress Information

Whatever the method used for progress feedback, care must be taken to avoid either ambiguity or undue complication. The simpler the method, the more likely will be the chances of persuading all the managers involved to return data regularly on time. Even so, training key participants to adopt the regular routine of progress reporting often provides project managers with a real test of their mettle. Many attempts at project control break down because this particular process cannot be reliably established.

Nature Of Progress Information Required To Update Schedules

Whether the system's progress input starts from a paper questionnaire or direct keyboard intervention by line managers, the following facts or estimates are usually required for each task that has been started, finished, or worked on since the previous report or keyboard visit:

- If started since the previous report, what was the actual starting date?
- If started but not finished, either:
  - the estimated percentage completion at time now or;
  - the estimated remaining duration after time now.
- Is the activity finished?
- If finished, what was the actual finish date?

Time-now means the start date given to the computer from which the next schedule update will be calculated. No tasks or remaining portions of them will be scheduled to take place before time-now.

Questions Of Logic

There is another question that the perceptive project manager needs to know for each task reported as complete. The vital question is: Can this activity's immediate successor(s) be started? This is the acid test of whether or not an activity has truly been completed. If the network logic is correct, then an activity cannot strictly be reported as complete if its immediately following tasks cannot be started.

An alert project manager will recognize the danger behind a progress return which says that the percentage progress achieved is 99 or 100 per cent, but that the next activity cannot start. This could mean that the progress claimed has not been made. This anomaly also occurs when a design engineer has completed a batch of drawings, but refuses to release them for issue through lack of confidence in the design, or because they feel that (given more time) the drawings could be improved.

Sometimes a following activity can be started even though one or more of its predecessors is still in progress. For example, an activity, although not complete, could be sufficiently advanced to allow the release of procurement lists for long-lead items. A network diagram may not always indicate such possibilities, and very often these opportunities for expediting progress would be missed by individuals who had not regularly asked the right questions.

Activities are quite often reported as started before one or more predecessors have been reported as finished. This is in contradiction to the logic enshrined in the network so that, when it happens, it indicates that the network constraints were not absolute. Nonetheless, if that is the situation, then it has to be accepted and reported to the computer accordingly: most software should be capable of accepting 'out of sequence' progress data.

Management By Walking About

The methods described so far for collecting progress information can work properly only in an ideal world. They paint a picture of the project manager sitting behind a desk, issuing instructions and receiving reports while the project proceeds smoothly to its successful finish. But while efficient routine systems are commendable and necessary, more is needed. The project manager must be prepared to depart from the routine and their desk from time to time, making visits and spot checks, giving praise or encouragement where due, and viewing physical progress at first hand. This process is sometimes called 'management by walking about'.

Visits to design offices, production areas, construction sites, or assembly hangars (depending on the project category) are particularly useful when two or more visits are made some little time apart, so that progress (or lack of it) can be noted. Where relevant, photographs should be taken on such visits, both for checking progress and as a permanent record of the project as it develops.

Global Checks

One useful occasional check is to ask how many people in a department (or of a particular grade) are currently working on the project. The answer can then be compared with the human resource usage planned for that date.

Comparison of scheduled and actual cost curves can also be made, but the head count is quicker, more positive, and likely to produce the earlier warning. Suppose that 35 design engineers are scheduled to be working on the project on the check date. If only 18 people can be counted, something is obviously very wrong somewhere. Although routine progress returns might indicate that everything is on schedule, the 'head count' shows that work on the project in the design department is not taking place at the required rate.

When action is taken, it may be found that project design is held up for lack of information, that other work has been given priority, or that the department is seriously under-staffed. The project manager must investigate the reason and take steps to set the right number of people to work.

WHEN THE NEWS IS BAD

How Bad?

When jobs start to run late, the first thing that the project manager must do is to consider the effect that this is likely to have on the following:

1. the current project;
2. projects or other work queuing in the pipeline;
3. the customer.

On rare occasions, late running might be acceptable and require no action. Usually, however, corrective action is needed. The project manager must then assess the situation, decide the appropriate action and implement it.

Jobs with free slack   If a late-running task has enough free slack to absorb the delay, all that needs to be done is to ensure that the work is expedited and finished without further interruption, within the available free slack.

Jobs with some total slack   Total slack has to be treated with more circumspection than free slack, because total slack used up by late working will rob later tasks of their slack. So, even jobs that possess total slack should be expedited to bring them back on schedule if possible.

Purchasing and manufacturing departments have always suffered at the hands of project managers by being expected unfairly to perform miracles when all the total slack has been used up long before work enters the purchasing and manufacturing phases.

Jobs with zero or negative slack   If critical tasks (tasks with zero or negative slack) are late, then special measures must be taken. It might be necessary to accept more expensive working methods to expedite these late jobs and bring them back on schedule. If a task expected to cost $2000 is in danger of running several weeks late and jeopardizing the handover date of a project worth $1m, then it might be worth spending $20 000 or even more on the problem task if that could rescue the overall programme. The project manager must always view the costs of expediting individual activities against the benefits gained for the whole project.

Corrective Measures

Corrective measures will only be effective when they are taken in time, which means that adequate warning of problems must be given. This will depend on having a well-prepared schedule, keeping it up to date, and monitoring progress regularly.

Working overtime, perhaps over one or two weekends, can sometimes recover time. The project manager will be relieved, on such occasions, that overtime working was not built into the normal schedules. Used occasionally, overtime can be an effective help in overcoming delays. Used regularly or too often however, the law of diminishing returns will apply, with staff permanently tired and working under fatigue, with no adequate reserves of energy.

If problems are caused by shortage of resources, perhaps these could be made available from external sources by subcontracting. Or, there might be additional capacity somewhere else in the company's own organization that could be mobilized.

The network logic should always be re-examined critically. Can some tasks can be overlapped, bypassed, or even eliminated?

Special motivational measures, incentives, or even unorthodox actions can sometimes give progress a much needed boost, provided that these measures are not repeated too often and are used sensibly.

In dire circumstances, when many tasks are running late, setting up a task force to drive the remaining work can be an effective solution.

PROGRESS MEETINGS

Any project manager worthy of the title will want to make certain that whenever possible their tactics are preventative rather than curative. If a special meeting can be successful in resolving problems, why not pre-empt trouble by having regular progress meetings, with senior representatives of all departments present?

Regular progress meetings provide a forum where essential two-way communication can take place between planners and key project participants. The main purposes of progress meetings emerge as a means of keeping a periodic check on the project progress, and the making of consequential decisions to implement corrective action if programme slippages occur or appear likely.

Frequency Of Progress Meetings

The frequency with which meetings are held depends to a large extent on the nature of the project, the size and geographical spread of its organization, and its overall timescale.

On projects of short duration, and with much detail to be considered, there may be a good case for holding progress meetings frequently, say once a week, on an informal basis at supervisor level. For other projects monthly meetings may be adequate. Meetings at relatively junior level can be backed up by less frequent meetings held at more senior level.

Project review meetings, which can cover the financial prospects as well as simple progress, can also be arranged. Senior managers may wish to attend such meetings and for some capital projects the customer might also want to be represented.

Meetings held too frequently create apathy or anger. Departmental supervisors and managers are usually busy people whose time should not be wasted.

Keeping To The Subject

There are dangers associated with the mismanagement of progress meetings. For instance, it often happens that lengthy discussions between specialists concern technical issues that should be resolved outside the meeting. Such discussions can bore the other members of the meeting, waste their scarce and expensive time, and cause rapid loss of interest in the proceedings. It is never possible to divorce technical considerations from progress topics, but design meetings and progress meetings are basically different functions and should be kept apart. Discussions should be kept to progress topics, with irrelevancies swept aside.

Was The Meeting Successful?

When a meeting breaks up, it will have been successful only if all the members feel that they have achieved some real purpose and that actions have been agreed which will benefit the project. Demands made of members during the meeting must be achievable, so that promises extracted can be honoured.

Issuing The Minutes

Minutes must be published without delay, so that they do not become outdated by further events before distribution. Minutes should be clearly and concisely written, combining brevity with clarity, accuracy and careful layout, allowing each action demanded to stand out from the page. If the document is too bulky it may not even be read. Short, pointed statements of fact are all that is required.

No ambiguity must be allowed as to who is directly responsible for taking each agreed action. Every person listed for taking action must receive a copy of the minutes (although this seems obvious, the point is sometimes overlooked). Times must be stated definitively. Expressions such as 'at the end of next week' or 'towards the end of the month' should be discarded in favor of actual dates.

Progress Meetings Abandoned

The above account of progress meetings adheres to the conventional view that progress meetings are an accepted way of project life. Here is some food for less conventional thought.

An engineering company held progress meetings at regular intervals or whenever things looked like going badly wrong. Several large projects were in progress at any time, and the permanent engineering design department of about 60 people was often augmented by as many as 80 subcontracted staff working either in-house or in external offices.

Meetings typically resulted in excuses from participants as to why actions requested of them at previous meetings had been carried out late or not at all. Each meeting would end with a new set of promises, ready to fuel a fresh collection of excuses at the next meeting. This is not to say that the company's overall record was particularly bad, but there was room for improvement and too much time was being wasted through too many meetings.

Senior company management supported a study which led to the introduction of critical path network planning for all projects, using a computer to schedule resources and issue detailed work-to lists. Two progress engineers were engaged, one to follow up in-house work and the other to visit subcontractors. Both these engineers had the benefit of work-to lists, which told them exactly which jobs should be in progress at any time, the scheduled start and finish dates for those jobs, how many people should be working on each of them, how many people should be working in total on each project at any time and the amount of slack left for every activity.

By following up activities on a day-by-day basis from their work-to lists, these two progress engineers succeeded in achieving a considerable improvement in progress and a smooth flow of work. If a critical or near-critical activity looked like running late, stops were pulled out to bring it back into line (by working overtime during evenings and weekends if necessary). Fortunately, all the staff were cooperative, grateful (in fact) for the new sense of order created in their working lives.

After a few months under this new system it dawned on managers that they were no longer being asked to attend progress meetings. Except for kick-off meetings at the introduction of new projects, progress meetings had become unnecessary.

PROJECT PROGRESS REPORTS

Internal Reports To Company Management

Progress reports to company management must give the technical, fulfilment, and financial status of the project and compare performance in each of these respects with the scheduled requirements. For projects lasting more than a few months, such reports are usually issued at regular intervals. For many reasons it is important that data on the condition and management of the project are presented factually, supported where necessary by carefully reasoned predictions or explanations.

Information in these internal reports may contain detailed information of a proprietary nature. They might, therefore, have to be treated as confidential, with their distribution restricted to a limited number of people, all within the company.

Exception Reports

There is another type of internal management report in addition to the detailed management reports just described. These are the reports of exceptions, and are confined to those project factors which give rise to acute concern, and which demand immediate attention.

If the report is to do with costs, the exceptions will probably be listed as 'variances', but variances can be either adverse or advantageous divergences from plan.

Exception reports can be contained in documents such as cost reports, materials shortage lists, or computer printouts of jobs running late. At the other extreme, an exception report might be the frenzied beating on a senior manager's door by a distraught project manager who feels that their project and their world have fallen apart.

Before allowing any exception report to be passed to more senior management, the project manager must be certain that some remedy within their own control cannot be found. However, once it has been established that events are likely to move out of control, the project manager has a duty to appraise senior management of the facts without delay.

All of this is, of course, follows the sensible practice of 'management by exception'. This seeks to prevent senior managers from being bombarded with large volumes of routine information that should be of concern only to supervisors and junior managers. The intention is to leave executives free to concentrate their efforts to the best advantage of the company and its projects.

Reports To The Client Or Customer

The submission of formal progress reports to the client or customer is often a condition of contract. If the customer expects regular reports then, quite obviously, these can be derived from the same source which compiled all the data and explanations for the internal management reports. Some of the more detailed technical information in the internal reports may not be of interest to the customer or relevant to its needs. Customer progress reports, therefore, are to some extent edited versions of internal management reports.

Whether or not financial reports of any type are to be bound in or attached to customers' progress reports will depend on the main contractor's role in each case. Under some circumstances cost and profitability predictions must be regarded as proprietary information, not to be disclosed outside the company. In other cases, the project manager may have to submit cost summaries or more detailed breakdowns and forecasts.

Although customer reports may be edited to improve clarity and remove proprietary information, they must never be allowed intentionally to mislead. It is always important to keep the customer informed of the true progress position, especially when slippages have occurred which cannot be contained within the available slack. Any attempt to put off the evil day by placating a customer with optimistic forecasts or unfounded promises must lead to unwelcome repercussions eventually. Nobody likes to discover that they have been taken for a ride, and customers are no exception to this rule.

CASE EXAMPLE: THE FREEZELAND COMMUNITY AIR SERVICE IMPLEMENTATION PROJECT

Freezeland is an island republic in the Northern Hemisphere, with much of its territory above the arctic circle. Most of the population and commerce inhabit one large island, some living in scattered communities. There are also several small islands, many of which are home to small communities. The mainland has principal airports in Northville and Southville, plus smaller airstrips or airports where there are clusters of local communities.

The Project Background

Freezeland Airlines is a company that is wholly owned by a number of corporate and private shareholders, all of whom are located either in the north of Freezeland in the city of Northville or in the southernmost city of Southville. It is the largest carrier that is based in Freezeland.

This carrier serves a small number of destinations in Canada, Scandinavia, and Northern Europe using a mix of Boeing 737-200 combi and Fokker F-100 aircraft. All international services terminate at Southville airport, which is Freezeland's only international airport.

Northville has its own airport, upon which the residents place particular reliance because road transport facilities in the north are very poor owing to the climate and terrain. All of Freezeland Airlines' inland operations are between Southville and Northville, and this service is appreciated by Northville residents, who like to take their vacations in Southville. Business travelers, who include some Freezeland Airlines shareholders, rely on this service as a vital link. The service also carries freight and mail, and delivers fresh food to the north.

All the offshore island dwellers rely on air transport, especially during the frozen winter months. However, these islands have only small airstrips. A number of independent carriers operating small fixed-wing aircraft or helicopters, ply between the various islands shore airstrips, and there are links with Southville. These local services carry passengers, light cargo, and mail.

A significant proportion of Freezeland Airlines' international passengers rely on these smaller independent carriers connecting flights from Southville to their destinations in small inland or offshore communities. Thus all these small inland and island carriers feed some of Freezeland Airlines' international business.

Generally, Freezeland Airlines' existing arrangements with these local secondary carriers have not been very effective. There is little or no coordination of schedules, and no attempts to interline passengers or cargo. Passengers arriving at Southville from other countries often have been unable to book seats on these local carriers in advance, and thus have to suffer the inconvenience of buying their local tickets on arrival.

The nature of travel within Freezeland has changed in recent years. Some areas in the north have become targets for overseas venture holiday tour operators. Some northern communities have built accommodation facilities to cater for these tourists, and this business has increased their retail outlets and consequent requirements for food and freight consignments. Some smaller airports have been upgraded to cater for the increased numbers of travelers, although in general the airside facilities are suitable only for light aircraft.

Other international airlines operate out of Southville airport but, unlike Freezeland Airlines, none of these service any other Freezeland airports. Freezeland Airlines thus currently enjoys a monopoly of services between Southville and Northville. However, the managers of Freezeland Airlines have been aware for some time that the international company which is first able to offer schedules with planned connectivity for local flights will have a market advantage.

The Community Air Service Strategy

Freezeland Airlines' management team considered various ways in which they might overcome the gap between their scheduled services and the schedules operated by the secondary local airlines. One option considered was to begin buying out the local operators, but this was rejected owing to the wide variations in aircraft types and differences in the operating methods employed. These differences would have been difficult to overcome and would have complicated Freezeland's well established and successful operating systems. Further, the buy-out schemes would have been expensive.

Thus an alternative solution was formulated, which would mean that Freezeland would introduce new services of its own into two or three of the more well-used community airports. This would mean the eventual acquisition of at least three smaller aircraft.

Freezeland's management considered that once their airline began to compete with the smaller local operators, their investment would be rewarded in two significant ways:

1. There would be a competitive advantage over other airlines for international flights. Passengers would be able to transfer at Southville to (or from) connecting local flights, on one ticket, with the same airline. Further, the aircraft used for local flights would offer more comfort than the light aircraft currently used by the small independent carriers.
2. On any local route where Freezeland Airlines did not immediately choose to operate alongside the existing small carrier, that small carrier might be more willing to cooperate with Freezeland Airlines on providing schedule information and on taking international connectivity more seriously. In other words, they would feel an implied threat of being supplanted by a superior Freezeland Airlines service if they failed to cooperate.

These strategies found favor with the senior management of Freezeland Airlines, and a business plan was drawn up as a precursor to obtaining finance for establishing the new local community services. The company considered that three routes would be chosen as pilot schemes, which would mean buying or leasing three aircraft, providing the crews, updating airport facilities at the targeted destinations and, most important, collaborating throughout with FRAOA, the Freezeland Air Operations Authority for various stage approvals. The scheme was given the title Community Air Services Enhancement, which soon became abbreviated to CASE. The following three destinations were chosen for the pilot scheme:

1. Westport, a fishing community about 300 miles to the west of Southville on Freezeland's south coast. This location was chosen because its small airport was capable of conversion for increased traffic and slightly heavier aircraft for relatively little expense. Further, Westport was used by independent operators as an air gateway to five small island communities as well as for providing a link to Southville.
2. The reasons for selecting Easthaven as the second community target destination were similar to those applying to Westport. Easthaven lies 150 miles east of Southville and its local air operator provides services to three thriving offshore communities as well as providing an Easthaven-Southville link.
3. The third chosen target destination was Mid-town. This community has grown considerably in recent years, due in no small part to the activities of venture holiday tour operators. The airport will need upgrading, but land and labor are cheap in this area. Mid-town is in the north of Freezeland, and it connects with Northville. As is typical in this region, there are no viable alternative road routes.

Lack Of Progress On Implementation For CASE

The CASE scheme was approved more than a year ago, and Freezeland Airlines had no problems in identifying potential investors or loan sources. FRAOA were notified of the airline's intentions, and approval requests were set in motion for outline permission to operate these three new routes. However, there has otherwise been no tangible progress on this scheme. Freezeland Airlines' managers have obviously been disappointed, and they investigated the reasons for such slow progress. They reached the following conclusions:

- The CASE scheme should have been authorized with project status, Then a project manager could be appointed to plan, organize and drive this project through to its successful conclusion.
- Not all managers within Freezeland Airlines had been consulted about the proposed new project, and there was no determined or combined consensus to make the project a success. Another way of stating this is that the management, as a body, did not wholly own the project or feel totally committed to it.
- There was a lack of supporting data. For example, information on existing traffic volumes and the revenues generated on the relevant routes was very unreliable. The company conducted traffic counts at the target destinations over a 3- week period, but the data obtained were disappointing, suggesting to some managers that the whole project would be financially unviable. Against that, no corrections could be made for seasonal variations, and the observations were made during a slack period.
- Other issues distracted Freezeland Airlines' managers and diverted their attention from the project. The company had endured a number of changes in the past year, including the introduction of a new aircraft type. This caused significant operational challenges which, together with the normal demands of day-to-day airline operations, meant that management time was limited, with their attention being pulled in many directions.
- Perhaps the most serious problem of all was failure to appoint a proficient project manager to take charge of this project. To date, no clear mandate has been given to anyone to drive this project through to its intended conclusion.

A Project Management Solution For Implementing The Community Air Service Enhancement

The requirement for Freezeland Airlines to enhance its community air service will not go away. The company must deal with this issue, even if it ultimately recommends the company's board not to proceed with the implementation of its own service. Abandonment seems an unlikely outcome as none of the alternatives are viable in the long run. Consequently, Freezeland Airlines needs to institute good project management techniques to ensure that:

- the project moves forward;
- the best information possible is used to help make the most appropriate recommendation to the board and to allow the board to support the proposed initiative with confidence.

Careful management of this project will be necessary to ensure the timely commencement of service, assuming that a decision to proceed will be made. An ideal time for introducing the new service would be the spring of 2011 and the company will need every bit of time between now and then to ensure that all the necessary work is completed in time.

The project manager The immediate appointment of a project manager is imperative. They must be given the full support of the senior management group and must also be given full authority and responsibility for timely completion of all the necessary tasks to see the airline launch its own local aircraft services by May 3, 2011. This is the most desirable start date, because improving weather conditions and a seasonal increase in traffic can be expected at that time.

If no person can be found within the company with the essential skills and experience for managing this project, one must be recruited (probably on a fixed-term contract basis).

Principal functions in the project organization and subsequent community air service operation Because the decision will be made to give the project manager overriding authority, a strong matrix organization is indicated (the relative advantages and disadvantages or different organization structures were described in Chapter 5). A strong matrix is a virtual team because, although some of its functional managers remain in their normal posts and do not report directly to the project manager, it is nonetheless the project manager who has the most power.

The following are functions or external organizations that will have to be taken into account as part of this project and the subsequent community air service operations:

- Maintenance: Freezeland Air does not have its own approved maintenance organization (AMO). Thus an appropriate outside maintenance provider will have to be contracted to provide all line and heavy maintenance services. Freezeland Airlines do, however, employ a maintenance manager, and they purchase and own specialist maintenance equipment. The maintenance manager must ensure that ground support equipment is in place and operational at all times.
- Flight operations: This function must provide expert input into operational requirements and suitability of aircraft type; dispatch procedures; operations control centre procedures; manual amendments connected with the amendment to the Air Operator Certificate for small aircraft operations and to ensure smooth pilot hiring and training.
- Inflight attendants and catering: The new community service operation will require flight attendants. This department will also be responsible for all inflight catering arrangements.
- Scheduling and fare pricing: The schedule development is very important to the success of the operation, particularly for passengers who will change flights at Southville and Northville. The company's pricing structure must be competitive.
- Marketing and sales: This group is critical for ensuring a sound marketing program in advance of the service launch, as well as providing planning and implementation of launch activities. Subsequently it will help to ensure strong continuing sales after launch.
- Finance: This project will include providing financial incentives to local airports to upgrade their facilities and the acquisition of three aircraft, in addition to all the project costs to be incurred at the company's headquarters.
- Cargo: This is expected to form a substantial part of the new local community services and is expected to earn a large percentage of Freezeland Airlines' on board revenue.

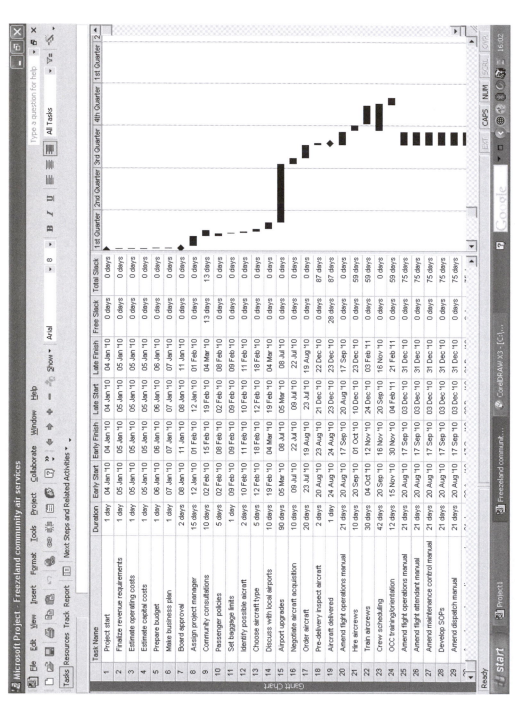

Figure 9.6   Freezeland air community project outline plan

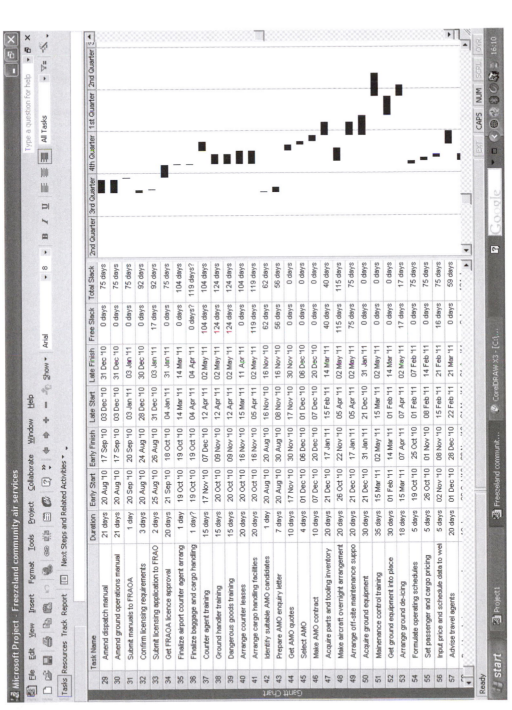

Figure 9.6   *Continued*

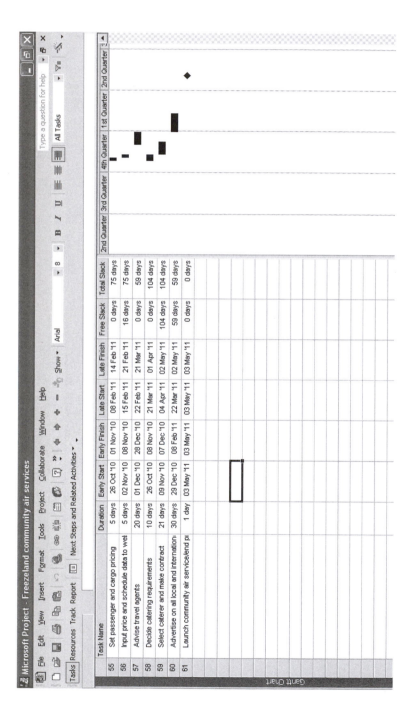

Figure 9.6   Concluded

Abbreviations:

AMO	Approved maintenance organization
FRAOA	Freezeland Air Operations Authority
OCC	Operation control center
SOP	Standard operating procedure

- Airports: Handling at the stations for cargo and passengers will be provided by contractors in all cases. Freezeland Airlines' airport manager will have to ensure that the contractors are carefully selected and that their actions are well-coordinated with other airline operations. A considerable amount of careful negotiation will be needed between Freezeland Airlines and those airports which must be upgraded to accept the new services. The airports will expect either some financial incentive or contribution from Freezeland Airlines.
- Community air service manager: This person will assume overall responsibility for managing the community air service after launch. Although not part of the initial project team, it is recommended that they should join the team before launch to gain advance familiarity with all aspects of the new service. This appointment could be a new recruitment but Freezeland Airlines will investigate whether a person on the existing staff might be suitable for promotion to this post.

Project Planning   Project planning is clearly an area requiring focus and dedicated effort. The project manager will have to lay out a clearly defined set of objectives and, from these, produce a WBS. An initial plan for this project is shown in Figure 9.6, (processed by Microsoft Project). This might have to be expanded into more detail later, possibly as one or more critical path networks, when the project manager would do well to call a brainstorming session involving the key participants.

Controlling the project for a successful conclusion   The other essential ingredient to the successful completion of this project will be the continual monitoring and control of the project work. This is when the critical path network time analysis and the resulting work-to lists come into prominence. The project outline plan shown in Figure 9.6 will serve as a road map for the project team. The project manager will attempt to have all tasks performed at their scheduled times, but will pay particular attention to those tasks that are critical, or which have only a small amount of slack. If the project manager can do this well, there is a very good prospect for the community air service being launched as planned on May 3, 2011.

10

Managing Purchasing, the Supply Chain, and Aviation Project Materials

Purchasing is part of a wider materials management function that can include vendor appraisal, contract negotiation, goods inwards inspection, and the safe handling and storage of goods received. It extends beyond the boundaries of the purchaser's premises to embrace supervisory expediting and inspection visits to suppliers, packing and transport arrangements, port and customs clearance for international movements, and involvement whenever special provisions have to be made for insurance, credit guarantees, and other commercial arrangements.

AN INTRODUCTION TO AVIATION PROJECT PURCHASING

Airlines provide interesting examples of multidimensional purchasing. They are in the business of offering all weather services to a wide range of passengers as well as cargo. They have to operate to timetables, giving uninterrupted services upon which their customers can rely. Thus they need to buy a very wide range of goods and equipment that must be durable and reliable. Airlines purchase anything from fine china, blankets, and bottled water to maintenance equipment and replacement parts, high-end avionics, and complete aircraft. In addition to all that hardware, the services that airlines purchase from outside service providers (such as catering) must also be of consistent good quality if the customers are to perceive that they get value for money.

Purchasing is a greedy function, because it consumes time and money in prodigious amounts. Purchased goods and services account for over half the total costs of most aviation development projects (even up to 80 per cent in some cases). Efficient purchasing and supply chain management are essential to avoid serious over-expenditure or delays through shortages and the acquisition of goods that are unfit for their intended purpose. Yet, with very few exceptions, project management writers either give purchasing little prominence, or they ignore it altogether (Figure 10.1). Try an experiment. Visit your nearest technical library and look in the index of every available project management book for the word 'purchasing' or 'procurement'. In too many cases you will search in vain.

Cost, of course, is not the only consideration for the purchasing organization. In no industry other than aviation are reliability and safety more important. Every company engaged in the aviation industry, whether in manufacturing, maintenance, or in flight operations has to put safety and reliability at the top of its list of priorities. A major aircraft manufacturer will,

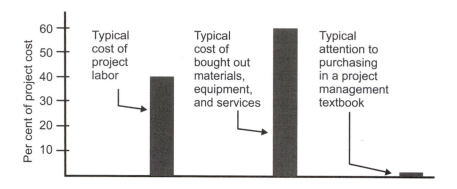

Figure 10.1   Value of purchasing in project management

of course, understand the importance of creating a quality culture throughout all its design and manufacturing operations. But in aviation projects that is not enough. That quality culture has to extend through all branches of the project organization, from the most senior designer in the controlling company right down to the lowliest machine operator in the smallest subcontractor or supplier. The purchasing department of the main project contractor controls many of the channels through which that quality culture must be encouraged.

Purchasing is at the leading edge of that part of the project organization which is generally known as the supply chain. As such it plays a critical role in ensuring that materials and components are obtained of the right quality, in the correct quantities, at the right time, at an appropriate price, and delivered in good condition to the place where they are needed for the project. This aspect of the supply chain applies not only to new development projects, but also to airlines (the customers of the airplane developers).

AN OUTLINE OF AVIATION PROJECT PURCHASING ORGANIZATION AND PROCEDURES

Purchasing methods and procedures depend to some extent on the total cost of the item or items being purchased. At one end of the scale is the urgent item of stationery obtained by sending someone to the nearest mall or high street store with petty cash. At the other extreme is the purchase of a fleet of wide-bodied passenger aircraft.

Figure 10.2 charts the more common functions of purchasing against order value and complexity. This chapter describes activities that generally lie towards the middle and right-hand columns of this chart, concerned with purchasing materials, components, equipment, and services of moderate to high value. Clearly not every procedure shown in this illustration or described in this chapter would apply to the routine purchases of low-cost goods from supplier's standard lists or catalogues.

The Purchasing Cycle

Contrary to popular belief, the role of the purchasing organization is not simply to issue purchase orders. Activities for all significant project purchases start well before an order is placed and do not end until the materials have been delivered and put to use in the project.

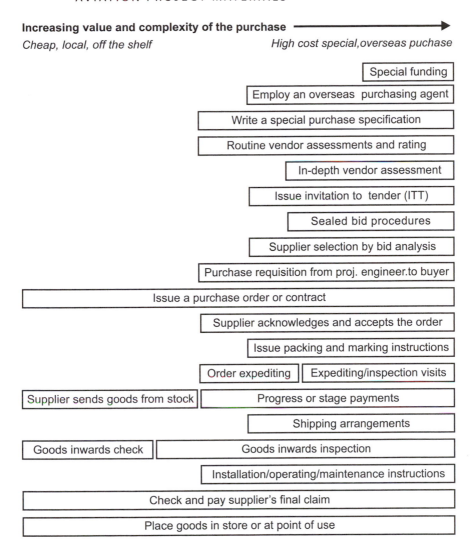

Figure 10.2   Typical range of purchasing procedures

Where international freight movements are needed to deliver materials and components to a project or an aircraft maintenance station, the purchasing department typically makes the arrangements, either directly or (more usually) by engaging a shipping or freight forwarding agent. Routine purchasing functions often include the establishment of preferred vendors lists, and the rating of vendors' performance.

The procedures for any purchasing event will depend to a very large extent on the value and importance of the goods. If the project desperately needs a sheet of plywood for temporary use, the procedure can be as simple as sending someone to the nearest lumber store to buy it with petty cash, without even involving the purchasing department. But most project purchases need far more care and attention, to ensure that goods are fit for purpose and available when they are needed. In many aviation projects the sources of all purchases have to be meticulously recorded, to allow retrospective traceability in the event of subsequent failures in service (a subject dealt with more fully in Chapter 11).

The usual sequence of events for a project purchase is cyclical. The cycle begins and ends with the person or department that needs the purchase for use in the project. The outline of a typical purchasing cycle is shown in Figure 10.3 and, to a great extent, the sequence of this chapter is modeled on the phases of this cycle. The purchase life cycle is similar in some respects to a project cycle and indeed the purchase of a special or expensive piece of equipment or parcel of goods can be regarded as a mini-project in itself, with the buyer or purchasing manager acting as a kind of project manager.

Where goods are being obtained from distant locations, especially from overseas, the transportation phase must be added to our illustration of the purchasing life cycle. Those parts of the purchase cycle that involve the purchaser, the supplier, and the transport organizations are often collectively and appropriately called the supply chain. The management processes of studying and solving problems in supply chains are known as logistics.

Roles In The Purchasing Organization For A Large International Project

Before embarking on a journey round the purchasing cycle it is necessary to outline how the purchasing and supply chain management functions might be organized. In this chapter we are considering a fairly complex case, such as the purchasing organization for an international project that might exist in connection with the development and manufacture of a new aircraft. 'International' in this sense means that the main aviation company (which we are henceforth calling the main contractor), some major subcontractors, and many of the

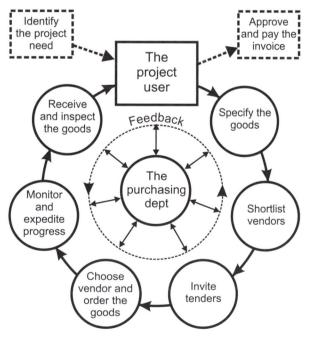

A purchasing sequence can be regarded as a small project, with the purchasing department acting as the principal project manager

Figure 10.3   Purchasing cycle

suppliers are situated in several countries or even in different continents. Figure 10.4 shows the key players who might be involved in the purchasing and supply chain logistics for such a project. This organization cannot be claimed as typical because there are so many possible variations, but it does include the important roles that can be expected.

The organizational role with ultimate responsibility for this aircraft development project is the main contractor. That company will house the design team responsible for the overall concepts, and it will also be responsible for the final assembly and flight testing and proving of one or more pre-production aircraft before commercial sales are possible. The project manager with overall responsibility for the project will almost certainly be a member of the main contractor's team.

The main contractor will undoubtedly have its own experienced purchasing department, responsible for all purchasing activities from supplier selection to receipt of finished goods. However, when there are to be a significant number of overseas purchases, a company such as this will often appoint additional purchasing agents in or close by the relevant countries, because those agents can act as local representatives. Overseas purchasing agents have the tremendous advantages of local knowledge and relative ease of access to the suppliers' premises. For example, they are often aware of local laws, regulations, standards, and other factors of which the project manager would otherwise be unaware.

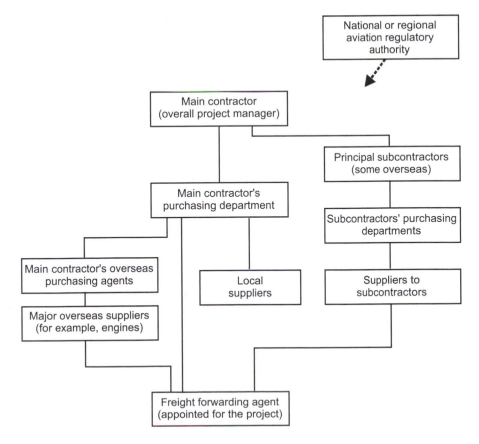

**Figure 10.4   A purchasing organization for an international aircraft
development project**

Purchasing agents typically either employ or have access to professional engineers who can carry out inspection and expediting visits to local suppliers on behalf of the main contractor. That enables such visits to be made more frequently and at less expense than if engineers were sent out every time from the main contractor's home office.

Some of the subcontractors in this aviation project will probably have very substantial roles, so that one subcontractor might, for example, be engaged to carry out the detailed design and assembly of large components (which could even mean the wings). One or more of the most significant 'subcontractors' could even be partners to the main contractor in a consortium (and thus not really subcontractors in the strict sense of the word). Each subcontractor or partner will have its own purchasing organization that will carry out purchasing for the relevant parts of the aircraft.

The main contractor will be concerned that all companies working on the project operate to the same technical standards. For purchasing standards the main contractor's purchasing department will probably have a supervisory (or at least advisory) role over all the supply chain operations.

Last, but never least in the supply chain organization, is the shipping agent or freight forwarder. That role may not be as glamorous or powerful as some of the others, but it is so vital to international projects that it deserves (and gets) its own section later in this chapter.

PURCHASE SPECIFICATIONS: DEFINING WHAT HAS TO BE BOUGHT

Once the need has been recognized for any significant purchase, action must be started by a request from the project staff to the organization's purchasing department or agent.

Buying Standard Goods From A Catalogue Without A Project Purchase Specification

Bought-out parts, equipment, and materials can often be specified by reference to a manufacturer's catalogue or part number. This would appear to be a sufficiently rigid description of the goods. However, most manufacturers reserve the right to modify their product designs without informing purchasers and, indeed, many add notes in their catalogues to that effect. If goods are ordered through stockists or factors, then even the company of manufacture might be liable to change without the purchaser's knowledge.

Here is an example of the pitfalls of relying totally on a supplier's catalogue description. A manufacture might decide to change one or more of the raw materials used in a product. Suppliers and manufacturers do not always change their part numbers when that happens. To all intents and purposes the catalogue description and illustrations could appear to be identical to the previous design. Such a change could be slight and insignificant to most users of the item concerned, but to other purchasers it could render the product utterly useless or even dangerous. This is particularly true in aviation projects. To an aircraft manufacturer, a supplier's replacement of aluminium with composite materials could mean that the catalogue description and illustration of a component part might be identical for both versions but the strength, weight, and other physical properties would be dangerously different.

Some companies take no chances with their project purchases and produce their own drawings and specifications and allocate part numbers themselves. This practice costs a considerable amount of time from professional or technical staff, but has much to commend it. Apart from removing any ambiguity about what is being ordered, the purchases can be allocated part numbers (which are the same as the relevant drawing numbers), thus allowing every bought-out component to bear a part number that fits in with the parts lists, WBS, cost accounts, and stock listing systems. A common part-numbering system simplifies procedures, eases the burden of the cost office, and greatly assists subsequent information search and retrieval.

Preparation Of Purchase Specifications

A purchase specification is a document that defines in words and quantified parameters a material substance, manufactured part, component, piece of avionics equipment, treatment process, or service that the contractor wishes to buy in for a project. Purchase specifications may be used to supplement manufacturing drawings.

In many cases, purchase specifications start life in provisional form, and are developed as other design work proceeds. When potential suppliers are approached, they might make suggestions that could affect the final content of some specifications. Thus it is convenient to identify two stages in the preparation of a purchase specification. These are:

1. **The enquiry stage**: Most purchase specifications start life as enquiry specifications. Each of these is issued by a senior member of the project staff to the purchasing agent under cover of a 'request for enquiry' or similar document. The purchasing agent sends the enquiry specification to potential suppliers along with a standard 'invitation to tender' (ITT), 'request for quotation' (RFQ), or 'enquiry letter'.
2. **The purchase order stage**: When a supplier has been chosen, the enquiry specification is reviewed and updated to include any changes that might have resulted from discussions with the supplier. The original enquiry specification has now been transformed into the purchase specification, which is reissued to the purchasing agent by the project staff with a purchase requisition. The purchasing agent then issues a purchase order to the chosen supplier, with the purchase specification and all relevant drawings attached.

There need be no difference in the method for preparing enquiry and purchase specifications, and the same format can be used for both. An example of a set of specification sheets is shown in Figures 10.5, 10.6, and 10.7 but in practice there are probably almost as many different formats as there are different companies.

Often the enquiry and purchase specifications are identical but if, during the course of pre-contract discussion with a supplier, amendments are made to the enquiry specification, the resulting purchase specification must contain all the agreed amendments.

Specification Serial Numbering

A common method for numbering purchase specifications in large projects is to allocate their serial numbers from purchasing schedules. A purchase schedule begins life as a document listing all the major purchases that can be foreseen for the project. Purchase schedules are usually developed along with drawing schedules or drawing registers by the design office. All the schedules can be grouped in sets according to each specialist

Lox Aviation Inc.		SPECIFICATION									
This specification comprises the sheets listed in the following table. At each revision only revised or additional sheets will be issued, together with a revision of this front sheet.											
Sheet	Rev	Sheet	Rev	Sheet	Rev	Sheet	Rev	Sheet	Rev	Sheet	Rev

ATTACHMENTS
The following attached documents form part of this specification:

SUMMARY OF REVISIONS

Rev No	Date	Brief description of each revision

APPROVALS

Originated by:	Checked by:	Senior engineer:	Project engineer:

Customer:
Project:
Used on:
Discipline:

Specification title:		Spec No:	Rev No:	Sheet
				1

Example of a form used to head enquiry and purchase specifications.

Figure 10.5   A purchase specification: front sheet

group in the project organization, which allows each of those groups to allocate its own serial numbers within the overall project numbering system.

Purchase schedules entries are listed in sequence of the relevant purchase specification serial numbers, whilst drawing numbers drive the sequence of entries in drawing schedules. Note that purchase schedules and drawing schedules are made for the whole project, or at least for very large parts from the WBS. The finer details of materials and drawings needed for smaller parts of the project will be taken care of using parts lists or bills of materials.

Lox Aviation Inc.	SPECIFICATION

DRAWINGS AND OTHER DOCUMENTS

1   SCOPE OF SUPPLY: Complete engineering drawings, installation instructions, operating/maintenance manuals, parts lists, and recommended spares lists for all equipment and services covered by this specification.

2   QUANTITIES:
    Drawings for approval — 3 prints
    Final drawings   — 1 transparency or master in approved electronic format
    Test certificates   — Original plus 5 copies, all signed
    Other final documents — 6 copies

3   LANGUAGE: English

4   IDENTIFICATION: All documents shall bear the purchase order number under which this specification is issued, appropriate equipment and tag numbers as specified, and the purchaser's drawing numbers (when supplied).

5   REVISIONS: Any drawing revised after initial submission shall be resubmitted immediately, showing details of changes and the new revision number.

6   CERTIFICATION: Final drawings shall be certified as accurate.

7   AS-BUILT DRAWINGS: Where the specification includes installation and erection, as-built drawings reflecting any on-site changes shall be submitted as soon as possible after the work.

8   DATE OF SUBMISSION: All documents shall be submitted on or before the dates specified in the purchase order delivery schedule.

9   APPROVAL: All drawings for equipment specially designed to meet this specification shall be submitted for approval before manufacture unless otherwise agreed.

10 TEST CERTIFICATES: These shall show the British or other agreed national standard or code under which the tests were performed.

11 LUBRICATION REQUIREMENTS. Recommended lubricants and quantities sufficient for 1 year's operation shall be specified.

12 SPARES LISTS. Lists of recommended spares shall be given, suitable for 1 year's operation under the specified conditions. Each items shall include:
    Identification, part, or serial number
    – Maker's name and reference
    – Quantity recommended
    – Current price and delivery

EQUIPMENT MARKING AND IDENTIFICATION

Each item shall be identified by its mark, equipment, or tag number by the method indicated thus: ✓

☐ Painting   ☐ Wired-on stamped metal tags   ☐ Stamped nameplates

☐ Other, as specified later in this specification. See sheet number: _____

INSPECTION AND TESTING

Documented inspection and testing is required, as indicated in the following tables thus: ✓

Inspections by the purchaser	Required?	Testing required	Unwitnessed	Witnessed
During manufacture		Standard works		
Final inspection		No load running		
Of packing		Full load performance		
As specified later on sheet number		As specified later on sheet number		

Title	Spec No:	Rev No:	Sheet
			2

This pro forma lists various standard requirements and also acts as an engineer's checklist. The main technical description for the item follows on one or more continuation sheets (see Figure 10.7).

Figure 10.6   A purchase specification: second sheet

Since each final purchase specification is derived from (or may even be identical to) an initial enquiry specification, the serial number allocated to the enquiry specification should be used again for the corresponding purchase specification, if possible, so that the two documents can always be correlated. This seems logical and straightforward, but for various reasons (such as when several specifications are grouped for one purchase order) this may not always be possible.

Figure 10.7   A purchase specification: continuation sheet

Specification Library

For equipment which is purchased often, such as pumps, valves, motors, and so on, an experienced project engineering organization will avoid the chores and risks associated with preparing a new specification for every occasion by developing a library of standard material and equipment specifications. The texts of these can be held on a computer file, to be extracted, adapted as necessary, and used to prepare the specification for each new requirement.

SUPPLIER SELECTION

The buyer's first responsibility is to identify a suitable source of supply for every purchase. Occasionally only one supplier can be found, or one may be specified by the design engineers on the purchase requisition. Limitation of choice usually arises when goods are highly specialized but, even where there is only one possible manufacturer, there may be a choice between different stockists. There are, of course, occasions when urgency is the most important factor, so that there is simply no time in which to conduct a proper supplier selection procedure. In all other cases (except for low-cost purchases) the supplier should be chosen after the collection and perusal of several competitive quotations.

To start the enquiry process, the project staff will send copies of the enquiry specification to the purchasing agent or buyer, asking the agent to issue a formal ITT or RFQ. The project staff may have a good idea of which suppliers should be asked to bid and, indeed, they may already have discussed the project's requirements with some possible suppliers in advance. Provisional quotations might have been obtained from potential suppliers for some of the more expensive items when the project cost estimates were first prepared.

The project staff can use a form similar to that shown in Figure 10.8 to convey their instructions and suggestions to the purchasing agent. Some of the information may be commercially confidential, not to be disclosed to bidders, and the purchasing agent will substitute their own official covering letter or standard form when sending out the enquiry specification to potential suppliers. The purchasing agent would usually be given some freedom to add possible suppliers to any list put forward by the project engineers.

Enquiries should always be conducted in such a way that they encourage suppliers to submit their quotations according to a common format. Then all the bids can be compared on a like-for-like basis.

A Formal Bidding Procedure

Figure 10.9 illustrates the principal stages in one form of bidding procedure. At frame 1, the purchasing agent sends all the possible suppliers a formal ITT, which sets out all the commercial and technical requirements and fixes a date by which all quotations must be presented.

Dealing with suppliers' queries during the bidding period Some main contractors' technical staff become involved in discussions with suppliers during the bidding period, answering questions and perhaps listening to alternative proposals. It is necessary to preserve fairness, and allow all suppliers to compete on equal terms, with the same supply of information. To that end, if one supplier asks a question, a copy of the question and the resulting answer is sent to all the competitors, as indicated in frames 2 and 3 of Figure 10.9. However, the purchasing agent should not reveal the source of any question.

To give an example, one of us (DL) was once on the receiving end of an ITT from a government department for a project management consultancy assignment. One condition of the contract was that the supplier (DL) would take out professional indemnity insurance cover of $20 million. That seemed rather too high for this modest proposal for a one-person project, so DL asked if cover could be reduced to $2 million. This request was allowed, and as a direct consequence, all the other bidders were informed of both the original query and of the decision to reduce cover to $2 million.

REQUEST FOR PURCHASE ENQUIRY

To: (Purchasing agent)   Date:
                                                    Our reference:
                                                    Your reference:

Please obtain bids for the goods or services described in the attached specification.
Note the following requirements:

       Vendors   *Bids*

☐ Only those listed below   ☐ Forward bids as soon as received
☐ Those listed plus those of your choice ☐ Forward all bids after closing date
☐ Suitable vendors of your choice   ☐ Supply a commercial bid summary

The closure date for receipt of bids should be:
Our required on-site delivery date is:
The recommended standard packing category is:
Your technical contact for this purchase is: Telephone:
Recommended vendors:

Notes and special requirements:

Project engineer

Client   –
Project –
Plant   –
Discipline –

Title		Spec No:	Rev No:	Sheet

Example of a form used by design engineers to instruct their purchasing agent to
issue an enquiry letter request for quotation (RFQ) or invitation to tender (ITT)

Figure 10.8   A purchase enquiry request

Late tenders   Any supplier who misses the deadline set for submission of the tender is
automatically disqualified (frames 5 and 6 in Figure 10.9). This is a very reasonable and
prudent step for a purchaser to take for three reasons:

1. proposals received late delay the process and disrupt the bid comparison procedure;
2. it would be unfair to allow one supplier more time for preparation of the proposal
    than that granted to all the others;
3. a supplier that is unable to submit a proposal on time will be more likely to run late
    in fulfilling the contract.

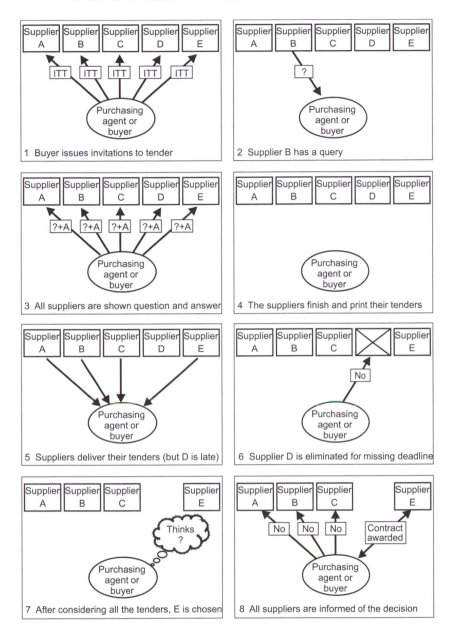

Figure 10.9   A common arrangement for inviting and considering bids

Bid evaluation   When all the bids are in, they have to be compared so the best option is selected. In a *sealed bid procedure*, each proposal is presented in two separate packages, one technical and the other commercial. The buyer opens all the technical bids first and rejects out of hand those that fail to meet the specification. Then the surviving commercial bids are compared.

The buyer would normally be expected to favor the lowest bidder, but this choice must be tempered by knowledge of the bidder's reputation for quality, delivery performance, and commercial standing. The lowest bid is by no means always the best bid.

It is usually undesirable and risky to allow the buyer to choose a supplier without the knowledge and agreement of the relevant technical staff. In some organizations vested interests or jealously guarded power means that this essential partnership between the purchasing agent and the project staff is lacking. That is always unfortunate and should be corrected, if necessary by intervention of more senior management.

An essential part of bid comparisons requires that information received from bidders is tabulated on a summary form which allows direct comparison of quoted prices, promised delivery times, and other critical factors. An example of a bid summary form is shown in Figure 10.10. This is a matrix that is intended to convert all bids into one common currency, and to include all required items that some bidders might quote as optional extras, so that the bottom lines of the bid summary allow the buyer to compare the cost delivered at the point of use. Thus estimated packing, carriage, insurance, port, and customs costs arising from foreign bidders have to be included. These steps ensure that the total delivered costs are compared in every case on a like-for-like basis.

Similarly, delivery times are adjusted where necessary to include shipping and port delays, so that all quotations are compared according to the estimated delivery time at the point of use.

Technical evaluation of quotations must, of course, be a matter for the relevant technical staff. The bid summary form illustrated in Figure 10.10 is not suitable by itself for making a detailed technical analysis. It is, as its name implies, only a place where information can be summarized to aid the purchasing decision.

PURCHASE REQUISITIONS AND ORDERS

Moving further round the purchasing cycle, when a supplier has been chosen, the enquiry specification is reviewed and updated to include all changes resulting from discussions with the supplier. The enquiry specification has now become the purchase specification, which is reissued to the purchasing agent by the project staff, attached to a purchase requisition. The purchase requisition (Figure 10.11) gives the purchasing agent formal permission to issue a purchase order.

Issuing the purchase order is the most routine and obvious job, usually consisting of typing all the special commercial details into the order, checking it, signing it, and the mailing it to the supplier (electronically or as hard copy) along with a fresh copy of the purchase specification.

What has this short explanation of routine purchase order preparation got to do with project aviation management? One answer is that it takes time. Several days or even weeks of valuable project time can be consumed by this mundane, relatively simple activity. Procurement lead-time estimates on the critical path network must always allow for such delays. In fact, unless emergency measures are contemplated, 2 weeks should often be regarded as a minimum estimate for purchase lead-times, even for items that can be obtained off-the-shelf from a local supplier's stock.

An example of a purchase order form is given in Figure 10.12. This example is based on forms used by a British company, whose identity we have disguised.

BID SUMMARY						
SELLERS ⟶	A	B	C	D	E	F
Country of origin						
Bid reference						
Bid date						
Period of validity						
Bid currency						
Project exchange rate						
Item	Qty	Description	Price	Price	Price	Price	Price	Price
Total quoted ex-works						
Discounts (if any)						
Packing and export prep cost						
Shipping cost						
Customs duty and tax						
Local transport cost						
Estimated total cost on site						
Delivery time ex-works						
Estimated total transport time						
Total delivery time to sit						
RECOMMENDED BY THE PURCHASING AGENT:						
For purchasing agent						
RECOMMENDED BY THE ENGINEER:						
Project/ senior engineer						
DECISION:						
Project manager						
Specification title:				Specification number:		

Bid summaries are used to compare bids on a like-for-like basis. Prices should be
compared on the basis of total delivered cost to the project location. All currencies
should be converted to the project control currency.

Figure 10.10   A bid summary example

Conditions Of Purchase

Many high-value purchases will be made using specially written contract documents, drawn
up specially and scrutinized by lawyers before they are signed by all parties to the contract.

In aviation construction projects, many subcontracts (such as the civil engineering and
electrical contracts) will be made using model forms of contract that have been developed as
industry standards by the relevant professional associations over many years of experience.

PURCHASE REQUISITION

To: (Purchasing agent)	Date:
	Our reference:
	Your reference:

☐ Please issue a purchase order
☐ Please also make all arrangements for transportation
☐ Please issue an amendment to the purchase order
for the equipment, materials, or services detailed in the attached specification.

VENDOR (name and address)

Quotation reference and date

CONSIGNEE (name and address)

SPECIAL INSTRUCTIONS

Inspect in accordance with specification ☐
Recommended degree of expediting is: intense ☐   normal ☐   none ☐
Recommended standard packing category is ☐
Other (see continuation sheet attached)

PRICE		DELIVERY	
Basis		Original delivery promise:	
Original budget			
Original quote		Current delivery promise:	
Previous amendments			
This amendment		Required delivery to consignee:	
TOTAL PRICE NOW			

APPROVALS			
Originated by	Senior engineer	Project engineer	Project manager

Client —		Project number:	
Project —			
Plant —		Specification number:	Revision
Discipline —			
Title:		Requisition number:	Amendment

When properly approved (and usually supported by a purchase specification) the requisition instructs and authorizes the purchase agent to issue a purchase order.

Figure 10.11   A purchase requisition

However, millions of everyday purchases for all kinds of goods and services are made every day on the basis of purchase order forms that carry pre-printed standard conditions of purchase. We have taken the following example from the reverse of the British order form shown in Figure 10.12, and again we have disguised the actual company name.

1. **Definitions**
    Company   –   means Dennis Engineering Company Limited.
    Seller   –   means the person, firm or company to whom the company's order is
                  addressed.

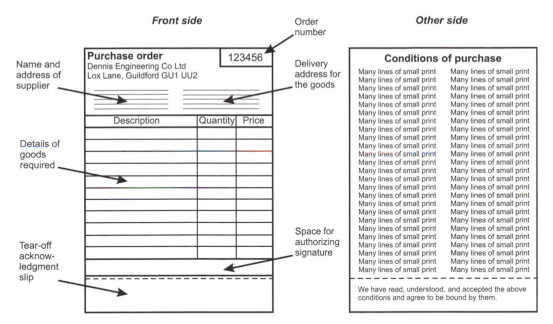

Figure 10.12   Elements of a typical purchase order

Goods   – means the supply and delivery of the goods, materials or equipment in accordance with the company's order together with any subsequent modifications specified by the company.

Contract   – means the agreement between the company and the seller for the supply of goods.

2   **Payment**: Net cash against shipping documents or other proof of delivery unless otherwise agreed (subject to any deductions and retentions authorized in the terms of the order, and subject to the seller carrying out all his obligations).

3   **Prices**: All prices are fixed for the duration of the contract and, unless otherwise agreed, are not subject to escalation charges of any description.

4   **Quality and description**: The goods shall conform to description, be of sound materials and quality, and be equal in all respects to any specification given by the company to the seller.

5   **Indemnity**: The seller shall at his own expense make good by repair or replacement all defects attributable to faulty design and/or workmanship which appear in the goods within the period of 12 months from date of delivery. The seller shall also indemnify the company in respect of all damage or injury occurring before the above-mentioned period expires to any person or property and against all actions, suits, claims, demands, costs, charges or expenses arising in connection therewith to the extent that the same have been occasioned by the negligence of the seller, his servants, or agents during such time as he or they were on, entering on to or departing from the company's premises for any purpose connected with this contract.

6   **Intellectual property**: The seller will indemnify the company against any claim for infringement of letters patent, trademark, registered design or copyright arising out of the use of sale of the goods and against all costs, charges and expenses occasioned thereby except in so far as such infringement is due to the seller having followed the design supplied by the company.

7   **Loss or damage**: All responsibility for any loss or damage, whether total or partial, direct or indirect from whatsoever cause, shall lie with the seller until full and complete delivery in terms of the order shall have been made by the seller. But it is agreed that the company will take all necessary steps to ensure that it does not in any way invalidate any claim which the seller may have against the carrier.

8   **Changes in the work**: No variations of, or extras to the order shall be carried out by the seller unless specifically authorized by the company on its official amendment form.

9   **Sub-suppliers**: The seller shall provide a list of all subcontractors or sub-suppliers when requested by the company.

10   **Expediting**: The company's expediting staff or staff of its purchasing agents shall be given access at all reasonable times to the seller's works or offices or those of any subcontractor in order to view or discuss work in progress.

11   **Rejection**: The company may at any time, whether before or after delivery, reject (giving reasons therefor) any goods found to be inferior, damaged or if the seller commits any breach of the order. This condition shall apply notwithstanding that the goods may have been inspected or tested by the company.

12   **Arbitration**: Any dispute or difference arising from the contract shall, on the application of either the seller or the company, be submitted to arbitration of a single arbitrator who shall be agreed between the parties or who failing such agreement shall be appointed at the request of either party by the President for the time being of the Law Society.

13   **Time for completion**: The seller's promised delivery date must be firm, but if delivery is delayed through any cause beyond the control of the seller and immediately such cause arises the seller notifies the company in writing giving full particulars then a reasonable extension of time shall be granted. If delivery is not made within the time stipulated or within any extension of time the company shall be at liberty to cancel the contract without prejudice to any right or remedy which shall have accrued or which shall thereafter accrue to the company.

14   **Title to goods**: Title to the goods passes to the company on delivery to the specified place of delivery as requested by the company.

15   **Law of the contract**: Unless otherwise agreed the contract shall be subject to the laws of England.

PURCHASE ORDER DELIVERY TIMES

Those responsible for initiating project purchases have a duty to identify items that are likely to have long lead-times and ensure that ordering instructions are passed to the purchasing department as soon as possible. This might mean issuing advance information on such things as special bearings, motors, castings, and other bought-out components, at times when the relevant assembly drawings and final bills of material remain unfinished or even unstarted.

It is sometimes desirable to issue advance information even when the goods cannot be specified in exact detail, because this gives the purchasing department the chance to get started on obtaining provisional quotations and (in a really urgent case) on reserving capacity in a manufacturer's works by issuing a *letter of intent*.

Any company with sufficient project experience will attempt to follow such practices as a matter of course. If a project has been planned using a critical path network any need to issue advance purchasing instructions will almost certainly be highlighted.

In some cases these urgent steps might preclude the possibility of operating a formal bid procedure, in which case the order will be given, wherever possible, to a supplier that has performed well in the past.

Just-In-Time

The phrase 'just-in-time' took on a specific meaning with the adoption by some companies of the Japanese approach to purchasing and manufacture which attempts to reduce stockholding to zero and, among other things, relies on suppliers to deliver direct to the workplace 'just-in-time' (JIT). Many manufacturers have reaped huge benefits in reduction of capital tied up in work in progress and stores inventories.

This system relies heavily on establishing a great deal of trust, and the suppliers are expected to be fully responsible for delivering the supplies in the right quantities, at the right time, and of the right quality without day-to-day supervision from the purchaser. But these ideals cannot be achieved overnight and cannot be expected to operate for project purchasing where regular use of suppliers and repeat orders are not the norm.

However, JIT is best suited to manufacture from proven drawings, such as (for example) a production run when building a fleet of aircraft. As a general rule, it is late or incorrect deliveries (and the shortages which they cause) that will always produce the biggest headaches for project managers, where purchasing is seldom routine because every part of the project and its manufacture is a new venture, laden with risk. Any decision to delay the issue of a project purchase order must be tempered with extreme caution. Time must be allowed wherever possible for unforeseen contingencies. What would happen, for example, if an important consignment of specially manufactured components arrived just in time for assembly into a prototype aircraft, only to be rejected as damaged in transit or otherwise unfit for project use?

Retarding Deliveries

There are often reasons why deliveries of project materials should not be called for too early. Materials which are ordered so as to arrive long before they are needed will have to be paid for earlier than is necessary, inflating the amount of money tied up unprofitably in inventory and work in progress. Another problem is that storage difficulties can arise for items delivered prematurely. Some goods have a short shelf life and will deteriorate if kept too long in store.

Call-Off Orders

If an order is for a large quantity of parts, deliveries can be arranged to take place in batches, at an agreed rate over a specified period. Of course the suppliers must be willing to accept such arrangements, but the practice is common. The supplier can either store the balance of the order or manufacture to suit the schedule. This is known as a 'call-off' procedure, because the items are called off as they are needed for the project. It is older than, but not too far removed from, the JIT approach.

Although the deliveries of items in large, repeating quantities brings batch or mass production to mind, some single projects do consume large quantities of materials. For instance, one would hardly consider the building of airport terminal building as mass production, but enormous quantities of building supplies may be involved. There would be very obvious difficulties if all the supplies were to be delivered before work had begun on the airport site. Chaos would reign, with cement, sand, ballast, bricks, and other supplies strewn all over the area. Access for site work would then be impossible, and those supplies which survived without being pilfered or ruined by exposure to the elements would have to be moved before work could start. By indicating the total quantities required for the project, the contractor can gain the benefits of quantity discounts, but the deliveries must be called off only when they are needed.

Now consider a manufacturing project requiring 10 000 small, identical electro-mechanical components, costing $60 each, to be incorporated in subassemblies over a period of some 2 years. These components are small and present no storage problem. But they are not all needed at once, so why commit expenditure of $600 000 too early? Again, a call-off order is indicated, allowing the contractor to delay expenditure, keep inventory down, and improve cash flow, whilst still reaping the benefits of the discount that can undoubtedly be negotiated because of the large quantity involved.

Common-Sense Timing

Once it is agreed that materials should be ordered to a project plan, there remain one or two questions regarding the common-sense application of that plan. Returning to the case of the 10 000 components costing $60 each, there is no question that the order for these items should be arranged on a call-off basis if possible. But what about the inexpensive items such as bolts, nuts, washers, solder tags, pipe clips, and so on? It would be nonsensical to attempt ordering these items to any plan. Rather, one would see to it that the whole quantity was ordered in advance, and with a generous supply to spare. Rigid control would not be necessary. The application of planning and control would probably cost more than the total value of the materials themselves, and might attract ridicule from the suppliers into the bargain.

EXPEDITING

The period following the issue of a purchase order will be one of waiting, and a great deal of reliance will have to be placed on the supplier to meet its obligations. That is not to say that the buyer can do nothing. This is the time when the company's expediting clerks earn their money by keeping the supplier reminded of its obligations. Expediting also provides an early warning system, revealing any difficulties which the supplier might be experiencing.

If a satisfactory reply to a routine expediting enquiry is not received, considerable activity is needed from the purchasing department. Their special efforts should not stop until the supplier has either shown the necessary improvement or has delivered the goods.

Alternative Sourcing

When expediting appears to be failing, the design engineers might be able to suggest an alternative item that can be obtained more quickly. The solution might instead mean finding another source of supply. If the original order does have to be cancelled because the supplier has failed to make the agreed delivery, there should be no kickback, because the supplier has broken the contract by failing to perform.

Combining Inspection On Suppliers' Premises With Expediting Visits

For some large-value purchases or purchases that have critical safety requirements or are otherwise of complex build, the purchaser will often wish to arrange on-site inspections at the supplier's premises at agreed intervals or when the supplier's progress reaches certain pre-agreed milestones.

Companies that regularly make purchases for projects sometimes employ expediters who are technically qualified, and are thus able to combine expediting visits to suppliers with inspection visits. The purpose of such visits is both to verify that the progress status claimed by the supplier is valid, and to witness tests or physically examine the products during their manufacture or construction.

It is wise and common to record the results of each inspection and expediting visit in a standard report format, an example of which is given in Figure 10.13.

PURCHASE ORDER AMENDMENTS

Should it become necessary to change any aspect of a purchase order after issue, the supplier's earliest agreement should be sought to determine the effect on price and delivery, and to ensure that the proposed change is within the supplier's capability. Once these facts have been successfully established, an amendment to the original purchase order must be issued.

Each purchase order amendment should bear the same reference number as the original purchase order, suffixed by a serial amendment number (amendment 1, 2, 3, and so on). Purchase order amendments should be prepared on a standard format and authorized in the same way as purchase orders. Amendments must be distributed so that they are received by all recipients of the original purchase order or its copies.

Amendment Or New Purchase Order?

The amendment procedure is often used to add one or more items to an existing order. If, however, the introduction of a new item is likely to jeopardize the previously agreed delivery date of any other item on the purchase order, the best policy is to issue a fresh order for the new item, so leaving the supplier to carry on unhindered and with no excuse for failing to meet the existing commitments.

The practice of adding a succession of new items to an existing order can result in a number of partial deliveries, none of which completes the order, so that administration becomes messy. The need to wade through a purchase order plus a pile of amendments

INSPECTION/EXPEDITING REPORT

Report number	Sheet 1 of	Date this visit	Date of last visit	Inspector/expediter

MAIN SUPPLIER DETAILS	Contract delivery date

Name _____

Address _____

_____

Supplier's reference _____

Persons contacted _____

_____

Equipment _____

_____

_____

_____

Current delivery estimate

Plans for next visit

Date _____

To expedite ☐

To continue inspection ☐

Final inspection ☐

To inspect packing ☐

SUB-SUPPLIER DETAILS	Agreed delivery to supplier

Main supplier's order number _____

Name _____

Address _____

_____

Sub-supplier's reference _____

Persons contacted _____

_____

Equipment _____

_____

_____

Current delivery estimate

Plans for next visit

Date _____

To expedite ☐

To continue inspection ☐

Final inspection ☐

To inspect packing ☐

ORDER STATUS SUMMARY (see attached sheets for details)

Assessed progress by (weeks)	Tests witnessed?	Complies with specification?	Released for packing?	Released for shipping?
Early ☐	Yes ☐	Yes ☐	Yes ☐	Yes ☐
Late ☐	No ☐	No ☐	No ☐	No ☐

ACTION REQUIRED	ACTION BY	
	Specification No	Revision
Title	Purchase order No	Amendment

Figure 10.13   An inspection and expediting report

in order to discover its total extent and the balance of deliveries and payments outstanding is time-consuming and irritating. Invoice control is likely to be made difficult and payment disputes can result. Issuing separate orders will prevent these difficulties.

LOGISTICS: A MORE DETAILED DESCRIPTION OF THE EXTERNAL SUPPLY CHAIN

This section is concerned with the safe carriage of aviation project materials and equipment.

Terms Of Trade Used In International Business (Incoterms 2000)

A purchaser needs to know, and agree with the seller, exactly when responsibility transfers from one party to the other when goods are shipped. For local purchases this might have very little financial effect but international shipping is a different matter and it is important that the boundaries of responsibility for transportation are clearly defined in proposals, contracts, and on purchase orders.

Incoterms, defined and published by the International Chamber of Commerce, are accepted worldwide as the succinct and definitive method for setting out these boundaries (International Chamber of Commerce, 2000). These Incoterms are outlined below, in ascending order of the seller's scope of responsibility:

Group E Incoterms (departure)
EXW   Ex works
Group F Incoterms (main carriage unpaid)
FCA   Free carrier
FAS   Free alongside ship
FOB   Free on board
Group C Incoterms (main carriage paid)
CFR   Cost and freight
CIF   Cost, insurance, and freight
CIP   Carriage and insurance paid to
Group D Incoterms (arrival)
DAF   Delivered at frontier
DES   Delivered ex ship
DEQ   Delivered ex quay
DDU   Delivered duty unpaid
DDP   Delivered duty paid

Marking And Labeling Goods Before Transit

The purchasing agent must ensure that every consignment is clearly marked before it leaves the supplier's premises. It is customary to include instructions for marking in the purchase specification or as a subset of conditions to the purchase order. Marking will usually involve suppliers stencilling easily recognizable markings on packing crates so that each item can be clearly identified through all stages of its journey and, not least, by the project personnel when it finally arrives. The purchase order number usually has to be included in all markings.

Shipping And Freight Forwarding Agents

It is best to entrust arrangements for long-distance transport, shipping, airfreight, seaport and airport, and international frontier formalities to a specialist organization. The purchasing agent (or agents) will undoubtedly have considerable experience and expertise, but the employment of a reputable freight forwarding agent will be invaluable to any project manager faced with all the commercial and strategic complexities of moving project materials and equipment around the world.

Freight forwarding agents operate through their own worldwide organizations. They have staff or representatives stationed at most of the world's ports and airports and, through modern communication networks, are able to monitor the progress of every consignment through all stages from export packaging at the supplier's works to delivery at the project site.

Collaboration between the purchasing department and a freight forwarding agent can achieve benefits from the economy of scale obtained when different consignments are consolidated to make up complete container loads. In an international project, such as a joint aircraft design and development venture, there is a good case for appointing one freight forwarder to serve all project materials movements, irrespective of which partner or subcontractor initiates the dispatch or where the goods are going.

The combined expertise of the purchasing agents and the freight forwarding agent can be a great comfort to project staff confronted for the first time with the need to deal with the formidable array of documents associated with the international movement of goods. Failure to get the documentation right first time can lead to delays, the impounding of goods, and to financial penalties.

Local knowledge provided by the freight forwarding agent's contacts in the countries along the delivery route can yield important information about the type and capacity of port handling facilities, warning of any unusual congestion or industrial disputes (with suggestions for alternative routes), and details of inland road and rail systems (including size and weight restrictions). For example, one agent prevented a mistake in the shipment of some long prefabricated sections by pointing out that the local railway company operated a particularly tight restriction on the maximum length of loads, because their route included tunnels with unusually sharp curves. In another case, the freight forwarder was able to warn about a peculiar security problem at a seaport, where the local shantytown inhabitants were always on the lookout for fresh supplies of building timber. If such timber happened to exist in the shape of well-constructed packing crates protecting expensive project equipment standing on the dockside—well who could blame them?

Freight forwarding agents, and their subsidiaries, acquire good knowledge of local customs office practices and can often expedite customs clearance. This service can be invaluable to airlines that are attempting to establish stocks of replacement parts required for aircraft maintenance at various airports. If those spares and consumables are held in customs sheds instead of being delivered to the maintenance bays there is a serious risk that some aircraft maintenance operations could be delayed beyond their recommended times.

Some customs officers can be very awkward. We remember a case, in one of the major developed nations (that we shall not name), where a complete set of project prints was dispatched from a London, UK engineering company by airfreight to the project site. The consignment was held at the destination airport by customs officers pending the payment of duty pro-rated not on the intrinsic value of the prints but on the entire multimillion dollar capital value of the project. The freight forwarder on that occasion was able to advise the London company of an alternative route and a duplicate consignment was airfreighted to a different airport, where it was cleared by customs staff with no problems. The original consignment was abandoned, left to gather dust in a distant customs warehouse.

GOODS RECEIPT

Receipt of the goods is not the end of the purchasing story. The consignment must be examined at the receiving bay to check for possible lost items or damage caused in transit. There might also have been some mistake by the supplier, either in the quantity supplied or in the nature of the goods.

Goods inwards inspectors may wish to examine the goods more thoroughly to ensure that they comply with the purchase specification although, in recent years, the tendency has been to place more reliance on suppliers' own quality procedures.

If the goods are accepted, the goods inwards personnel will record the consignment, usually by preparing and distributing a goods inwards certificate or by copying and distributing the supplier's own dispatch note (to act as a certificate). At least one copy of the certificate will go to the accounts department, who will need it before they can pay the supplier's invoice. Another copy will go to the buying department, to cut short any further expediting action and close off the file on that particular order. Routeing of other copies might include other departments such as the stores, but this depends on the nature of the company and the goods.

If the consignment is not received in satisfactory condition for any reason, it will be sent smartly back whence it came accompanied by a rejection note. Distribution of rejection notes generally follows the same pattern as acceptance certificates, but will produce opposite reactions from the various recipients. For example, the accounts department will not pay any associated invoice, and the purchasing department will redouble its expediting efforts.

When the correct goods have been received they will be passed into stores or placed with project stocks to await use.

NOTES ON STORAGE

Physical Pre-Allocation Of Project Materials

Pre-allocation is a stores procedure that usually entails placing a marker on the bin or the stock record to show that the particular item has been earmarked for use on a particular project. However, the only safe method for pre-allocating materials for use on forthcoming project work is to withdraw them from general stock and place them in a separate, securely locked, project store. If this is not done it is certain that, pre-allocation or not, some of the stock will be used on other work, and so will be unavailable for the project when needed. Cheery assurances from the storekeeper that the deficient items are 'on order' or 'expected any day now' will not be well received. A project cannot be completed with empty promises.

Preservation

Any materials which are particularly susceptible to deterioration through mechanical shock, heat, cold, or damp must be suitably protected. Some articles, such as batteries, will deteriorate under any conditions, and must be used before their 'use-by' date. Thus the storekeeper must issue goods for use on a first-in first-out basis.

Certain raw materials are not suitable for storing in close proximity to each other because of the risk of damage through cross-contamination. An every day example, a prudent person would not store strongly scented soap alongside food. In an industrial store there can occasionally be unfortunate chemical reactions that degrade objects when two different plastic materials come into contact with each other.

Security

Safe custody and security of stock demand that the storage area can be locked up outside normal working hours. At all other times stores entry will usually be restricted to authorized stores personnel. Regulations such as these are designed not only to prevent theft, but also to minimize the possibility of irregular or unrecorded withdrawals. External airport construction site stores are particularly vulnerable and need special protection, which can include a full-time watchman, dogs, patrols, high fencing, alarms, closed circuit television, security lighting, and so on.

Irregular removals from stores are not all due to theft. They might arise from surreptitious attempts at making good losses, scrap, or breakages on the site or workfloor. Over-zealous activity to clear shortages on one project could lead to unauthorized taking of stock pre-allocated for other projects.

Stores Records And Information Systems

Information systems must be designed and implemented to provide accurate feedback of all material movements (arrivals and withdrawals) for stock control and cost accounting purposes.

Stores receipts are documented by goods inwards notes or, in the case of items manufactured within the premises, some form of completed job ticket, inspection ticket, or stores receipt note. Serviceable items returned to stores for stock because they are no longer required for any reason must be similarly documented.

Issues from stores are usually authorized and documented by stores requisitions, bills of materials, stores issue schedules, or parts lists. These withdrawals have to be reported against job numbers to the cost office or accounts department. Those responsible for stock control will rely on this information to maintain stock records as accurately as possible, and reorder items for general stock as appropriate.

Stores records can be particularly important in aviation projects. The storekeeper and all those involved in materials handling have to ensure that the goods do not become separated from their individual inspection release notes and batch identities. Otherwise the traceability chain would be broken. Then, should these goods be issued and used on a project that is later connected with an operational failure or accident, the accident investigators would be unable to trace the source of a defective component back to its manufacturer, and would also be unable to state which other aircraft were built using components from that suspect batch. Thus even the mundane and routine job of storekeeping has its important part to play in the ever present need for safety and reliability.

VENDORS' DOCUMENTS

When components or equipment are purchased, they will be accompanied by vendors' documentation. At the simplest this could be a packing note plus a final inspection release note. But complex equipment such as avionics units or larger assembled components might require accompanying certified test results, operating and maintenance instruction, and a recommended spares holding list. All these comprise what are collectively known as the vendors' documentation, although the providers of the goods might also be referred to as manufacturers, sellers, suppliers, partners, or subcontractors. In many cases, those supplying the goods will be required to supply documents translated into different languages, for the benefit of the many foreign airlines, aviation maintenance companies, or airports who will be the end-users of these products.

The first step in ensuring the timely receipt of vendors' documents that satisfy an aviation project is to make certain that the obligations for providing them are always spelled out clearly on the purchase orders or their attached purchase specifications.

Serial Numbering Of Vendors' Documents

A great number of vendors' drawings and other documents can accumulate in a large project, and the main project contractor has to make certain that it will be able to find any of these quickly if any customer requires replacements or reports operating difficulties. Once again, the subject of traceability arises and vendors' documents can be an important link in the traceability chain.

Thus, copies of vendors' documents are usually serially numbered and recorded in registers before filing. To ensure that any of these documents can easily be found again in the future (location and retrieval are the buzzwords) the files must be arranged in some recognizable and logical sequence. This might be based on specification numbers, requisition numbers, purchase order numbers, or the company's standard project work breakdown coding system.

Of course the original vendors will have given all or most of their documents serial numbers of their own, but one can be certain that there will be as many different methods for allocating such serial numbers as there are vendors. For filing and retrieval a common system is needed, which means that the project staff must renumber every vendor document in the project contractor's own system. At one time this used to be an immense clerical chore, requiring thousands of index cards so that all systems could be cross referenced. Now that job is simple using any computer system.

CASE EXAMPLE: A SUPPLY CHAIN LOGISTICS PROBLEM SOLVED BY A FREIGHT FORWARDER

The Problem

The head office, design, manufacturing, and assembly facilities of Lox Aviation Inc., are situated on the outskirts of Newark, NJ, where the company has its own airfield. The flagship aircraft in this company's production is currently its BIZJET123, which is a long range twin-jet passenger aircraft with a maximum payload of ten passengers in its all-business class configuration. Lox Aviation is about to begin deliveries of 12 of these planes to one of its oldest and most valued customers, Laurence Airlines.

Laurence Airlines operate flights out of many international airports, and they intend using this new fleet to open up new scheduled routes between Canada and South America. The flight operations strategy of Laurence Airlines involves setting up a maintenance facility at the airport in Newville, in the (imaginary) republic of Obezia, down in the southern regions of South America. Thus, Laurence Airlines have ordered a range of recommended maintenance spares from Lox Aviation, and one set of these will have to be transported to Newville Airport, followed by regular shipments of replacement spares. The initial shipment will contain items of heavy equipment such as inspection and test rigs and complete replacement engines. Subsequent regular shipments will be lighter, but a requirement has been foreseen to establish a method for shipping emergency spares in the event of an aircraft breakdown at Newville.

The Initial Investigation

Lox Aviation decided that it was necessary to set up a small project to investigate the possible cargo routes from Newark to Newville to cover all the three principal requirements, namely:

1.   the initial heavy consignment;
2.   regular, non-urgent, planned shipments of replacements spares stock;
3.   rare emergency spares shipments to deal with aircraft grounded at Newville with malfunctions.

Wisely, Lox Aviation decided to consult a freight forwarding company, Shiftit Inc., a worldwide organization with long experience in moving cargoes by all modes of transport worldwide. Shiftit had local offices or agents in most important world centers, including Newville, Obezia.

Shiftit identified and investigated several different possible routes and reported that the most feasible, before consideration of cost and border formalities, included the following:

*   airfreight direct from Lox Aviation's airfield to Newville airport;
*   overland by heavy trucks. Good roads were available for the entire route;
*   rail, with delivery and collection from the railheads at both ends by heavy truck;
*   by sea, since both Canada and Obezia had seaports with good handling facilities for container ships. This method would require seaport to destination connections at both ends by heavy truck.

Familiarity with all these possible routes meant that Shiftit had good knowledge of journey times, freight rates, and customs formalities at international borders.

The Freight Forwarder's Recommendations

Where journey time was of no importance, the overland routes by road or rail offered the cheapest solutions, but Shiftit strongly recommended that neither of these options should seriously be considered because the consignments would have to cross five international borders, at some of which considerable delays could be expected by the various customs authorities. This would also complicate the export-import documentation considerably and could incur excessive payments of duty.

For immediate shipment of spares to repair aircraft grounded by malfunction at Newville, airfreight was the only option that could deal promptly with the emergency and get the plane airborne again. For light spares Lox Aviation usually had an aircraft of its own that could be used, but a large aircraft would need to be chartered to transport heavy equipment.

However, Shiftit recommended to Lox Aviation that the most economical route by far would be by a combination of trucks and sea. The initial heavy consignment could go by a combination of heavy truck and container ship, whilst the lighter regular replacement consignment could use lighter road vehicles.

The road/sea route journey times would be longer, but for routine replacements this would not matter provided that Lox Aviation carried out advance planning, enabling them to ship the supplies well in advance of the dates when they would be needed at Newville.

Thus Shiftit recommended airfreight to cope with emergencies and the road/sea route for all routine purposes.

Advantages Of Employing The Freight Forwarder

Lox Aviation gained several advantages from following the recommendations of Shiftit, and of entering into a contract with Shiftit for the management of all transport operations.

Cross-border formalities, which can be a complete nightmare for the non-professional, would be smoothed over and delays at customs points would be minimized.

Lox Aviation would benefit from the economy of scale because Shiftit would be able to combine these aircraft spares shipments with freight from Shiftit's other clients to make up complete container loads.

There would never be any problem of Lox Aviation having to pay for a vessel's round trip (returning under ballast to Canada) because Shiftit would load the same vessel with export cargo from its other clients who were based in Obezia.

Just imagine that you were the materials handling manager at Lox Aviation Inc., and that you had been faced with the solution of these problems all by yourself, without the aid of an expert freight forwarder.

11

Managing Changes

No project of any significant size can be expected to run from start to finish without at least one change. The exception to this rule might exist as a project manager's dream of Utopia, but is unlikely to assume any more tangible form. Our definition of a project change is:

> A departure from the approved project scope or design as indicated by a change to any contract, drawing, or specification after its approval and issue for action.

Thus, for example, suppose that a design engineer has been working for 6 weeks on a complex set of drawings before realizing that there was a fundamental mistake in the first outline sketch, so that much of the design must be reworked. That might be serious. It could set the project back a few weeks and add cost. But it is not a change to the project as specified, or to its scope. No drawing has been issued and no actual work is taking place. Only the design engineer is involved. Therefore this new start to design is not a modification or change that needs approval from anyone. The new work simply has to take place to restore the project to the original intentions.

If, in the same case, the design mistake is not found until the drawings have been issued for manufacture and it is too late to withdraw them, then the change affects others outside the design department and will change work in progress. Now a formal change procedure must be invoked to ensure that the original mistake is rectified and that all processes are corrected and both the error and its rectification are recorded.

Along with purchasing, change management is one of the subjects most neglected in project management literature and teaching. Yet, in aviation projects, it is vital for all post-project operations. The regulatory bodies and all aircraft manufacturers know from long experience that failure to manage changes (and the associated procedures of version control and traceability) during the design and development of aircraft and aviation equipment would have severe consequences later when the aircraft or associated aviation components are put into service.

THE IMPACT OF CHANGES IN RELATION TO THE PROJECT LIFE CYCLE

Changes are usually unwelcome to a project manager at any stage, but changes that occur toward the end of a project have the potential to cause greater cost and disruption than those which are mooted before the project begins.

When a project is in its proposal or business plan stage, any proposed change in the scope or nature of the project may cause some annoyance and result in more investigations, revised financial appraisals, and fresh planning. However, the same change when a project is nearing completion could be disastrous, meaning that much of the work in progress or completed would have to be scrapped and restarted.

Thus it is a general rule that the later the change happens, the greater the cost and disruption it will cause. This is illustrated in Figure 11.1.

ORIGIN AND CLASSIFICATION OF CHANGES

Changes can arise from a customer's request that changes the project scope or specification, a self-inflicted engineering design modification, or through some reason during work on the project that causes the finished result to differ in some respect from the issued drawings, specifications, or other formal instructions. Changes (and therefore change management) can sometimes be needed even after the project has been finished and handed over to the customer. Figure 11.2 shows many routes through which changes can develop in, for example, an aviation or defense manufacturing project.

Classification Of Changes

Changes can usually be placed in one of two principal commercial categories namely:

1. changes originating from within the contractor's own organization without any involvement from the customer or client;
2. changes requested by the customer or client.

There are, however, some borderline cases which cannot be put into either of these two classifications but which contain elements of both.

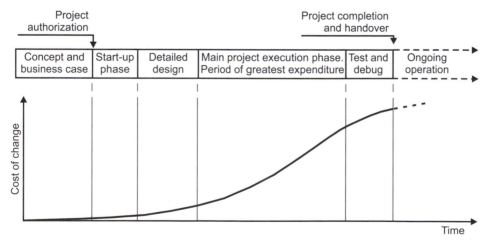

Figure 11.1   The cost of a given change in relation to project life cycle phases

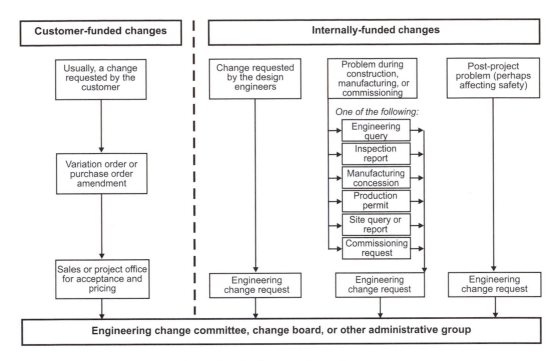

Figure 11.2   Some origins of aviation project changes

A more useful way of classifying changes from the commercial point of view is to label them as either 'funded' or 'unfunded'. For a funded change the customer must take responsibility for the change and pay for it. For unfunded changes the contractor will have to absorb all the costs, with consequent risk to budget limits and expected project profits. Whether or not a change is to be funded or unfunded will greatly influence how it is considered for authorization.

Funded changes   Changes to the specified project requested by the customer automatically imply a corresponding change to the contract, since the project specification should form part of the contract documentation. If, as usually happens, the modification results in an increase in project costs, a suitable change to the contract price must be negotiated. The delivery schedule may also be affected and any resulting delays must be predicted, discussed, and agreed.

Customer-funded modifications may possess nuisance value and can disrupt the smooth flow of logically planned work, but they do nevertheless offer the prospect of compensation through an increase in price and possibly an increase in profit. When a customer asks for a change, the contractor is in a strong price-bargaining position because there is no competitor and the contractor has a monopoly.

Customer-funded changes are usually documented as purchase order amendments or contract variation orders (otherwise known as project variations).

Unfunded changes   If a contractor finds it necessary to introduce changes for reasons unconnected with the customer, it is hardly likely that the customer could be expected to pay (unless the changes are covered by some contingency for which provision was made in the contract). The contractor must be prepared to carry the additional costs, write off any scrapped work, and answer to the customer for any resulting time delay. For these reasons, contractors have to be particularly cautious about allowing unfunded (which really means contractor-funded) changes to proceed.

The procedure for introducing an unfunded modification into an active project usually starts by raising a document called an engineering change request, engineering change order, modification request, or some permutation of these terms. Some reasons for unfunded changes are shown in Figure 11.2 and the relevant documentation is described later in this chapter.

Permanent and temporary changes   Changes can be further classified as permanent or temporary.

Permanent changes are carried out with the intention of leaving them permanently embodied in the design and execution of a project, and which will remain recorded in drawings and specifications to show the true as-built condition of the completed project.

Temporary changes may be needed for expediency in getting a project finished, but they are carried out with the intention either of removing them or converting them to some alternative permanent change at a later, more convenient time.

AUTHORIZATION ARRANGEMENTS

The effects of any change, whether customer-requested or not, may be felt far beyond the confines of the project area that is most obviously and directly affected. This could be true of the technical, timescale, or cost aspects. Most projects have to be regarded as a combination of technical and commercial systems, in which a change to one part can react adversely or beneficially with other parts of the system. That, of course, is particularly true with an aircraft, where several different systems are interdependent and operate together to determine the performance and handling of the plane. Thus these reactions can bring about consequences that the change's originator may not have been able to foresee.

For these reasons alone it is prudent to ensure that every proposed change is considered and approved by selected key members of the project organization before it can be implemented. This precaution means that the overall effects can be predicted as reliably as possible. These selected referees form the 'change committee' or 'change board'. In some organizations, perhaps in larger companies, the change committee might be a constituted body that meets regularly in formal meetings. In small project organizations the arrangement is usually far less formal, but there must nevertheless be some means for change consideration and approval at senior expert level.

The Change Committee Or Change Board

In many companies engaged on project work a regular panel of experts is appointed to consider changes and decide how they are to be handled.

Managers in (or represented on) the committee must include those who are able to answer for the safety, reliability, performance, cost, and timescale consequences of changes. Other considerations include the effects on work in progress, on purchases, on finished stocks, and on the feasibility or otherwise of introducing the change into active manufacture or construction.

In projects involving the nuclear industry, aviation, defense, or other cases where reliability, safety, or performance assume great significance, two key members of the committee represent:

- the design authority—typically the chief engineer;
- the inspecting authority—a person such as a quality manager who should be independent and able to make assessments on the basis of quality alone, without commercial pressure. In aviation and defense projects this inspecting authority will usually be a national organization, probably affiliated to a government department. A typical arrangement is for the project organization's own quality manager to be accredited to represent the relevant national body. The national body will probably wish to have one or more of its inspectors visit the manufacturing plant or assembly hangar at intervals to ensure the integrity of the quality function.

Change Committee Meetings

Change committees for large projects often meet on a frequent, regular basis, dealing with change requests in batches. Others avoid meetings by circulating requests around the committee members, so that each member considers the effect of the proposed change on their own area of responsibility. Each method has its advantages and disadvantages. If formal committee meetings take place at monthly intervals, the wait for change decisions can hold up progress or result in the greater disruption to work that late changes cause. On the other hand, frequent committee meetings take up too much of members' time. Informal committees, not meeting collectively but relying instead on the circulation of documents, suffer from a communication problem and can take longer to discuss and resolve misunderstandings or make decisions. Neither approach can be classified as right or wrong, but it will be assumed here that a formal procedure exists, with a change committee meeting at regular intervals (perhaps weekly).

Decision Criteria

When each change request is considered for approval, the committee must weigh up all the possible consequences before making its decision. Points which need to be examined are listed below (not necessarily in order of importance):

- Is the change actually possible to make?
- Is it a customer-requested or a self-inflicted change?
- What is the estimated cost of the change?
- Will the customer pay? If so, what should be the price?
- If the change is not customer-requested, is it really necessary? Why?
- What will be the effect on the project timescale?
- How will safety, reliability, and performance be affected?
- If several identical sets of equipment are being produced, at what point in the production sequence should the change be introduced?
- Will scrap or redundant materials be created?

- Are any items to be changed retrospectively? Are these:
  — in progress?
  — in stock?
  — already delivered to the customer or otherwise built into the project?
- What drawings, specifications, and other documents will have to be modified?

Figure 11.3 illustrates some of the steps in the change handling process.

The Change Committee's Response

When the committee has considered all these questions, it has the following options:

- authorize the change as requested;
- give limited approval only, authorizing the change with specified limitations;
- refer the request back to the originator (or elsewhere), asking for clarification or for an alternative solution;
- reject the change, giving reasons.

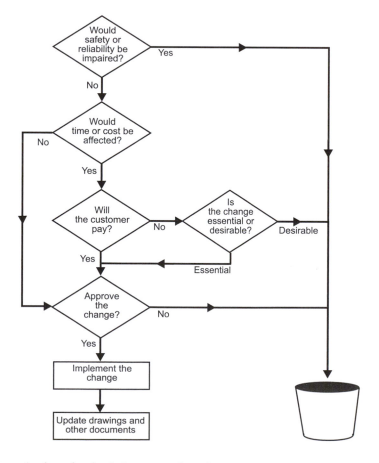

Figure 11.3   A simple decision tree for change requests

GENERAL ADMINISTRATION OF CHANGES

Use Of Standard Change Request Forms

Individuals who wish to request a change should always be asked to put their request in writing. This chapter is written on the assumption that all such requests will indeed be addressed to a formally constituted change committee (which should be the norm for aviation projects). If the organization does not operate a formal change committee, a suitably senior member of the organization, such as the chief engineer, should be designated as the person responsible for considering and authorizing changes.

To save the committee's time and to ensure that all requests are effectively controlled and progressed, some kind of standard change request form must be used. This form should be designed in such a way that the originator is induced to answer in advance all the questions that the change committee will want to ask. In some projects, even the customer can be persuaded to submit change requests using the contractor's standard forms.

Because there are several routes along which changes can arise within any organization (please refer back to Figure 11.2) there are usually several different forms that can result in change requests. Some of these forms are illustrated later in this chapter, in the section 'Forms and procedures'. However, the administration procedures described here are generally applicable to all of these different forms.

Change Coordinator

In any project organization where changes are expected (which really means all project organizations) it is advisable to nominate a change coordinator. Unless the project is very large this will not usually be a full-time role, and the person chosen will probably carry out other clerical or administrative duties for the project. A technical clerk often does this job. The change coordinator may reside in a contracts office, the project manager's administration group, project support office, the engineering department, or in some other department. The change coordinator's duties are likely to include:

- registering each change request and allocating serial numbers;
- distributing and filing copies of the change documents;
- following up to ensure that every request is considered by the change committee without avoidable delay;
- distributing and filing copies of the change documents after the committee's instructions have been given;
- following up to ensure that authorized changes are carried out and that all drawings and specifications affected by the change are updated and reissued.

Numbering And Registration

Upon receipt of any change request, the coordinator should enter brief details in a register. Apart from their initial use in allocating serial numbers, change registers are important for several other reasons, which include the following:

- to provide a base from which each change request can be progressed through all its stages, either to rejection, or to approval and subsequent full documentation and implementation;
- to record changes in budgets and, if appropriate, prices so that the current valid budgets and prices will always be known. This is part of project cost control, which is discussed further in Chapter 12.;
- to provide a search base that allows tracking back (traceability) so that the origins of all design and commercial changes can be found or verified, both during the life of the project and afterwards when the relevant aircraft are in service.

Change registers can be pages in a loose-leaf folder or, subject to safeguards against accidental erasure and loss, they can be held in a computer. Separate registers should be kept for project variations, engineering change requests, engineering queries, production permits, and inspection reports. Usually a slightly different register format is used for each of these registers, but Figure 11.4 shows a fairly typical layout.

The change coordinator must allocate serial numbers from the appropriate register. The numbering systems should be kept simple, but must be designed so that no number is repeated on another project or in another register. The simple solution is to prefix each change with either the project number or a shorter code that is specific to the project, and to add one or two letters which denote the type of change. For example, if the project number is P123, engineering change request forms might be numbered in the series P123/ECR001, P123/ECR002, P123/ECR003, and so on. Concessions or production permits for the same project could be numbered in the series P123/PP001, P123/PP002, P123/PP003, and so on.

Register					Project number:		Sheet number:	
Serial number	Originator		Date requested	Brief details or title		Approved? (Yes or no)	Date of final distribution	Budget change (if any)
	Name	Dept.						

This can be used to serial number, register, and progress change requests. Requests might be received as project variation orders, engineering change requests, engineering queries, concessions, and production permits. A separate register should be used for each of these document types.

Figure 11.4   A general purpose change register

Distribution Of Change Request Forms

The change coordinator's first duty after registering each change request is to arrange for its distribution. This process will be speeded up if the forms are stocked in multipart sets or distributed via a network.

A typical distribution for any change request might be:

- engineering manager or chief engineer (who may wish to arrange further distribution within their department);
- change committee chairperson (the original 'top copy');
- other change committee members.

The change request originator should retain a copy, and the coordinator will keep another on a 'changes pending file', with a different file for each type of form in use.

Progressing

To prevent undue delays, or even the risk of forgotten requests, change registers should be designed to highlight all those requests that are 'active'. That means all requests which have yet to be approved or rejected. For example, a column can be provided on the register sheet headed 'final sign-off date' or something similar. The absence of a date in that column tells the coordinator that the change is still active and in need of monitoring and progressing.

The coordinator will be able to use the same registers to follow up the action after approval, to ensure that the relevant drawings and specifications are updated and reissued. That, of course, is a vital part of recording the true as-built state of the aircraft or other product.

ESTIMATING THE TRUE COST OF A CHANGE

Most changes will add to the cost of a project. As we said at the beginning of this chapter, changes made late in a project often attract higher costs than those introduced earlier, because sunk costs are then higher and late changes can cause greater disruption to work in progress, causing scrap and rework. It is not always appreciated that the total costs of an engineering modification can far exceed the straightforward estimate of costs directly attributable to the modification itself.

Assessing All The Possible Cost Factors

Just as changes tend to cost more later in the project cycle, so they become more difficult to evaluate as project time passes. In an ideal world all individuals would include all possible costs of modifications in their estimates. Unfortunately the project manager must expect that some cost factors will be overlooked, whilst others might be impossible to evaluate. Checklists and searching questions can help to reset an estimator's train of thought:

- Is there to be no inspection and retesting on this job?
- Will existing stocks be affected?

- Will there be any purchase order cancellation costs?
- Will this change affect the prototype too?
- What about work in progress—how much of that will have to be scrapped and done again?
- How much will all the resulting delays cost?

Such questions must always be asked about the possible costs of changes, but the true answer will often be very difficult to establish.

Recording The Actual Cost Of A Change

Some of the difficulties to be expected in assessing the true costs of a change have now been outlined, and it is apparent that there are many factors which can easily be overlooked. Nevertheless, an estimate can be made in most cases, and this can be used to work out and justify any possible increase in price that the contractor feels able to demand.

Recording the actual costs of a modification can prove to be a far more difficult undertaking: it may even be impossible. Difficulties underlying the measurement and recording of actual modification costs may not always be appreciated by some managers and others who, quite reasonably, would like to know just how much their budgets are being affected by changes.

Case example Suppose that a modification is to be performed on a 'fuzzelbox', which is a complex piece of avionics equipment containing over 1 km of wire, thousands of electrical connections, piping and valves, and many other components.

First, take the case where the fuzzelbox has already been assembled, inspected, and fully tested. Here there need be no problem in identifying the cost of the change, because a fresh works order or job ticket can be issued for the modification work and materials, complete with a new cost code. All the subsequent work of stripping, changing, inspecting, and retesting can be attributed directly to the change.

Now consider the different (but frequent) case in which drawings and specifications are modified during the course of manufacture. The fuzzelbox is in a semi-completed state, so that the modification will add new wires, delete others, re-route wires and pipes not yet installed, and result in changed connections and components. How can anyone be expected to record accurately that part of the work which is directly attributable to the modification?

It is quite possible that many changes will occur on a job of this size before it is finished, so that the only apparent and measurable effect on costs will be an increase of expenditure compared with the initially estimated production costs. This situation has to be accepted and, if the modification costs are needed for any purpose, they will have to be estimated.

FORMS AND PROCEDURES

This section describes some of the routes through which changes can reach a project, together with their origins and associated forms (these routes were illustrated in Figure 11.2). The authorization and general administration procedures already described in this chapter will apply generally to all of these forms.

When Is A Formal Change Procedure Necessary?

Some rule or criterion is needed to determine at which point in the design or other project process the formal change procedure should be introduced. We gave clues to this answer when we indicated in the opening paragraphs of this chapter what is meant by a change in the context of engineering design or project management. The key question to be asked is, 'Would the proposed change affect any instruction, drawing specification, plan, or budget that has already been issued to and agreed with other departments, the customer, or other external organization?' If the answer to this question is 'Yes', formal change committee approval will almost certainly be needed.

Another reason for invoking formal procedures is found whenever there is an intention to depart from the design specification, especially when the development work is being carried out for an external customer. This is an exceptional case for using the formal change procedure before any drawing has been issued for manufacture or construction.

Some companies circulate early, pre-issue drawings for discussion, advance information, or approval. These issues are often distinguished from the fully released versions by labelling them as revision A, revision B, and so on, changing the revision numbers to the series 0, 1, 2,and so on to denote official full releases. A rule might, therefore, be suggested that formal engineering change procedures need only be applied to drawing revisions made after the first issue for manufacturing or construction. But such a rule can fall apart if preliminary issues are made for the manufacture of a prototype, in which changes must be properly controlled.

Design Freeze

Sometimes project organizations recognize that there is a point in the design and fulfilment of a project after which any change would be particularly irksome, inconvenient, or potentially damaging. This leads to the announcement of a 'design freeze', after which the change committee will refuse to consider any change proposal unless there are compelling reasons, such as safety or a customer request. Ideally the customer should also agree to be bound by the design freeze. In some companies the design freeze stage is called 'stable design'.

Project Variation Orders Or Contract Amendments

Changes requested by the customer which affect price, delivery, or any other aspect of the original purchase order or contract require formal documentation. The request document should fulfil the following functions:

- it amends the purchase order or contract and describes the change;
- it authorizes the contractor to make the change;
- it promises payment;
- it records agreement to any associated timescale revision.

Where the original contract was in the form of a purchase order, the customer will usually request a change by issuing a purchase order amendment. In other cases, especially for projects involving construction, changes are recorded on project variation orders (sometimes called simply 'project variations' or 'contract variations'), an example of which is given in Figure 11.5. Similar changes arranged by a main contractor with site construction subcontractors are often known as site variation orders.

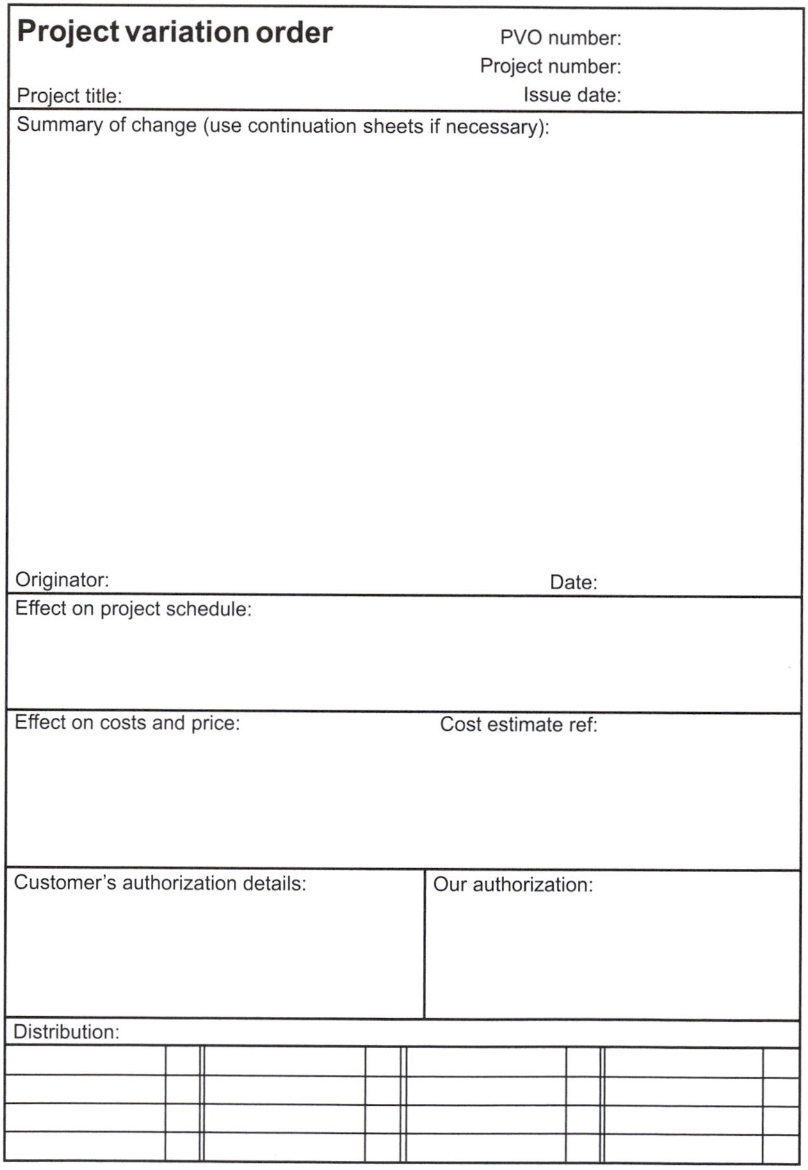
Project variation order

PVO number:
Project number:
Project title:
Issue date:

Summary of change (use continuation sheets if necessary):

Originator:
Date:

Effect on project schedule:

Effect on costs and price:
Cost estimate ref:

Customer's authorization details:
Our authorization:

Distribution:

Figure 11.5 Project variation order

A Quick Procedure For Simple, Repetitive Project Variations

In projects where a considerable number of small changes are expected, it may be possible to streamline all the change procedures, perhaps with a prearranged scale of charges. Naturally such a procedure must be restricted to changes of a routine nature, where safety and reliability cannot be affected. Provided that the scope of a change can be defined adequately, and that the work can easily be identified separately from other project work, the costs of small changes can be recovered on some agreed time and materials basis or, for construction projects, against an agreed schedule of rates per units of measured work.

Case example   A contractor was engaged on a defense contract for designing and building automatic test equipment for the electronic systems installed in military aircraft. Each complete tester was housed in a trailer which could be towed out to an aircraft, connected by cables, and left to carry out a whole range of measurements, 'go' or 'no-go' checks and diagnostic fault-finding routines.

Every time the aircraft manufacturer (the customer) wanted to change any of the test parameters a small amount of software reprogramming was necessary in the test equipment. This happened many times during many months of prototype commissioning at an airfield. Some changes also required one, two, or three wires to be re-routed as quick temporary fixes. Attempting to estimate the cost of each of these hundreds of changes and subjecting all of them to a formal change committee procedure was out of the question. Yet every change had to be recorded for incorporation into manufacturing drawings, and somehow the contractor had to recover the additional costs.

These difficulties were resolved by both companies agreeing to a set common price for all these trivial program changes. Simple, serially numbered, all-one-price, program change request forms were printed in triplicate on serially numbered no-carbon-required pads for use at the airfield. These documented the technical details of each change, were authorized by the signature of the customer's engineer, and accepted for on-the-spot action by the contractor's senior commissioning engineer. One copy of each change form was kept by the customer's engineer, and another was returned to the contractor's head office, where the relevant drawings and programming records were updated at regular intervals.

Weekly invoices were sent to the customer listing the serial numbers of all the changes in each batch. No technical details or descriptions were needed on the invoices, which were priced simply by multiplying the number of changes made each week by the standard price. The system was limited by mutual agreement to include only the simple changes to measurement parameters and test-point switching. Many hundreds of these changes were requested, actioned, and billed using these very simple pre-priced request forms. That saved valuable time at the commissioning site, with the contractor collecting a satisfying level of revenue and the customer freed from the expense of preparing, negotiating, and issuing a formal contract variation for every change.

Engineering change requests

The purpose of an engineering change request is to describe, document, and seek formal permission for a permanent design change. The change may be unfunded, or it might be the result of a project variation order and, therefore, funded. Engineering change requests of the type shown in Figure 11.6 are used widely in engineering projects, although they may be known by different titles, invariably abbreviated to sets of initials. The following are among those which may be encountered:

- ECR — Engineering Change Request
- ECO — Engineering Change Order
- MR — Modification Request

There is no reason why any person, however junior, should not be allowed to originate an engineering change request because it can have no effect until it has been authorized by the change committee. The method for completing the form should be self-evident from Figure 11.6.

```
┌─────────────────────────────────────────────────────────────────┐
│ Engineering change request              ECR number:              │
│ Project title:                          Project number:          │
├─────────────────────────────────────────────────────────────────┤
│ Details of change requested (use continuation sheets if necessary):│
│                                                                   │
│                                                                   │
│                                                                   │
│                                                                   │
├─────────────────────────────────────────────────────────────────┤
│ Drawings and other documents affected:                           │
│                                                                   │
│                                                                   │
├─────────────────────────────────────────────────────────────────┤
│ Reason for request:                                              │
│                                                                   │
│                                                                   │
│ Originator:                             Date:                     │
├─────────────────────────────────────────────────────────────────┤
│ Emergency action requested (if any):                             │
│                                                                   │
│                                                                   │
├─────────────────────────────────────────────────────────────────┤
│ Effect on costs:            Cost estimate ref:                   │
│                                                                   │
│ Will customer pay, yes ☐  no ☐   If yes, customer authorization ref:│
├─────────────────────────────────────────────────────────────────┤
│ Effect on project schedule?                                      │
│                                                                   │
├─────────────────────────────────────────────────────────────────┤
│ COMMITTEE INSTRUCTIONS: CHANGE APPROVED ☐   NOT APPROVED ☐        │
│ Point of embodiment, stocks, work in progress, units in service, special restrictions etc:│
│                                                                   │
│                                                                   │
│ Authorized by:                          Date:                    │
└─────────────────────────────────────────────────────────────────┘
```

Figure 11.6   Engineering change request

Concessions Or Production Permits

Manufacturing departments, faced with the need to keep to a budget or to accomplish work within a scheduled timescale, sometimes find that they need to depart from the specific instructions contained in the manufacturing drawings to achieve their objective. Naturally, the quality control department will keep a wary eye open to ensure that no unauthorized shortcut or botching is allowed.

Suppose, for example, that a drawing specifies the use of bolts manufactured from a specified grade of aluminium alloy, but that these are simply not available when required. The purchasing department may be able to obtain alternative screws made from a different alloy, or with slightly different length. If the production team decided to make this substitution without reference to the design engineers, there would be a danger (remote in some companies) of an inspector noticing the difference and rejecting the work because it deviated from the drawing.

But would the use of these alternative screws really matter? It all depends, of course, on the actual circumstances and whether the different alloy would have equivalent physical properties to the original specification, particularly in respect of tensile and shear strength. If longer screws are used, would the projecting threads foul any adjacent component when fitted to the aircraft? Someone has to investigate, decide, and then either authorize or reject the change.

The use of alternative materials, different adhesives,and acceptance of wider tolerances, are all reasons for originating requests for concessions. These might represent a risk to performance, reliability, safety, or interchangeability. As a general rule, therefore, concessions require the formal approval of the design authority.

Concessions (or production permits) usually fall into the classification of temporary changes. It is unlikely that the drawings will be updated to suit the change, it being assumed that the manufacturing department will either be able to adhere to the drawings in any future production, or will apply for a further concession.

Procedures for requesting concessions vary greatly from one company to another. They can range from the very informal, 'Is it all right if we do it this way instead, George?' to a rigid discipline supervised by the quality control department. In aviation projects we should assume that the latter approach will always be followed. Rigid procedures can also be expected in the defense and nuclear industries, and in any other case where safety and quality rank high as objectives. Figure 11.7 shows a suitable form.

The reasons for instituting a formal concession discipline are fairly obvious, because any departure from the instructions contained in issued drawings or specifications must be either disallowed or treated with a great deal of caution. Concession records may have less significance than other project records once a project has been finished and handed over to the customer. Nevertheless, they can prove useful in the quality and reliability control function. Concession records are part of the project records which a contractor needs to keep in order to trace the possible causes of poor performance, faults, or failures in equipment after delivery. They can be vital evidence if one of a number of identical units should fail in service, where it is essential to trace all other units containing the same concession in order to prevent further failures.

The procedures associated with the granting of concessions can exist in a variety of permutations and combinations of the methods described in this chapter. Whichever method a company decides to adopt, the concession register will be complementary to the manufacturing drawings, modification records, inspection and test records, and build schedules in defining the exact composition of the completed project.

```
┌─────────────────────────────────────────────────────────────────┐
│ Production permit/concession                                      │
├─────────────────────────────────────────────────────────────────┤
│ Drawing/spec. number:              Application number:            │
│ Revision number:                   Project or job number:         │
├───────────────────────────────────────────────┬─────────────────┤
│ Batch or product serial number(s) affected:    │ Is work held up?│
│                                                 │   Yes: □        │
│                                                 │   No:  □        │
├───────────────────────────────────────────────┴─────────────────┤
│ Application to allow non-compliance with the above drawing or     │
│ specification as follows:                                         │
│                                                                   │
│                                                                   │
│                                                                   │
│                                                                   │
│                                                                   │
│                                                                   │
├───────────────────────────────────────────────────────────────── │
│ Reason for this application:                                      │
│                                                                   │
│                                                                   │
│                                                                   │
│                                                                   │
│ Requested by:              Department:          Date:             │
├───────────────────────────────────────────────────────────────── │
│ Engineering assessment                                            │
│                                                                   │
│   Performance/reliability?                                        │
│                                                                   │
│   Health and safety?                                              │
│                                                                   │
│   Interchangeability?                                             │
│                                                                   │
│ For Engineering Department:                     Date:             │
├───────────────────────────────────────────────────────────────── │
│ Decision                                                          │
│   Granted: □    - - - - - - - - - - - - - - - -   - - - - - - - - │
│   Refused: □    For design authority              Date            │
│                 - - - - - - - - - - - - - - - -   - - - - - - - - │
│                 For quality/inspecting authority  Date            │
└─────────────────────────────────────────────────────────────────┘
```

Used for authorizing and documenting departures from drawings, specifications, or other manufacturing instructions

Figure 11.7   Production permit or concession

Engineering Query Notes

A feature of projects is that the manufacturing or construction drawings and specifications are usually completely new and untried. It is not surprising, therefore, that a higher incidence of problems in manufacture or construction is a characteristic of project work. These problems can range from design errors to difficulties in interpreting the drawing instructions. Design errors must, of course, be corrected by the issue of amended drawings, for which the full-scale engineering change procedure will usually be invoked. Simple problems associated with the interpretation of drawings can be resolved by an explanation on the spot from the appropriate engineer. Between these two extremes lie those operational difficulties that are not a direct result of design errors, but which demand more than a simple explanation to get work on the move again.

In some firms any problems that cannot be resolved on the spot are channeled into a formalized 'engineering query' procedure, which relies on the use of forms similar to that shown in Figure 11.8. The general idea is that the works supervisor who comes up against a problem explains the difficulty on one of these forms and submits it to the engineering department for investigation and reply. Naturally, this system can only operate effectively and be accepted if each query is afforded reasonably urgent consideration. The advantages provided by adopting this routine are that all queries can be registered and progressed by the coordinating clerk to ensure that none are forgotten. Regrettably, one engineering director from our past experience preferred the formal system because it kept production personnel, together with their overalls, oil, and grease, out of the nice clean engineering design offices.

Engineering query note

Drawing/spec. number: EQN number:

Revision number: Project or job number:

Other relevant drawings or specifications:

Is work held up?
Yes: ☐
No: ☐

Details of query or problem:

Query raised by: Department: Date:

Answer:

For Engineering Department: Date:

Engineering follow-up action required (if any):

Figure 11.8 Engineering query note

Case example Suppose that a specified adhesive, when used according to the appropriate process specification, failed to produce the specified bond strength, so that when the unfortunate worker removed the clamps their careful work disintegrated into its constituent parts. The supervisor would need to ask the engineers what to do, and that can be done using an engineering query note.

If this problem proved too difficult to sort out on the spot, the engineers might be forced to return the query note with a temporary solution suggested. The instruction might read: 'Clean off adhesive, and use six equally spaced pop rivets instead. Drawings will be modified and reissued.'

Conversion from engineering query to production permit If, as in the above example, an engineering query note is returned to a production department with instructions that conflict with those given in the manufacturing drawings, the query note becomes a document that carries authority to deviate from drawings. It has therefore become a concession or production permit.

Because engineering query notes are often converted into concessions in this way, companies that use them should consider combining the concession and engineering query systems into one procedure, with a single common-purpose form designed to cope with both needs.

Inspection Reports

Suppose that a block of extremely expensive raw material has been subjected to many hours of machining by highly skilled operators but, on final inspection, one of the measurements is found to be marginally outside the limits of tolerance. Too much material has been cut away; the error has resulted in the workpiece being undersized and no rectification is possible. Any inspector would have to reject the job. In most companies the inspector would fill in an inspection report ticket or form, detailing the 'non-conformance'.

The relevant design engineers, if shown the inspection report, might decide that the error was too trivial to justify scrapping such an expensive workpiece. A senior design engineer with the appropriate authority might feel able to annotate the inspection report accordingly, thus countermanding the inspector's rejection.

This is another method by which a job can be passed through an inspection stage, even though it does not conform to the issued drawings. The inspection report has been translated by the design authority into a concession or production permit.

Figure 11.9 shows an inspection report form which anticipates the possibility of subsequent conversion into a concession in appropriate cases.

VERSION CONTROL FOR MODIFIED DRAWINGS AND SPECIFICATIONS

Issue Of Incorrect Versions

It is necessary here to consider one or two pitfalls that can trap the unwary project engineering staff into issuing drawings or specifications that are not what their revision numbers would make them seem to be.

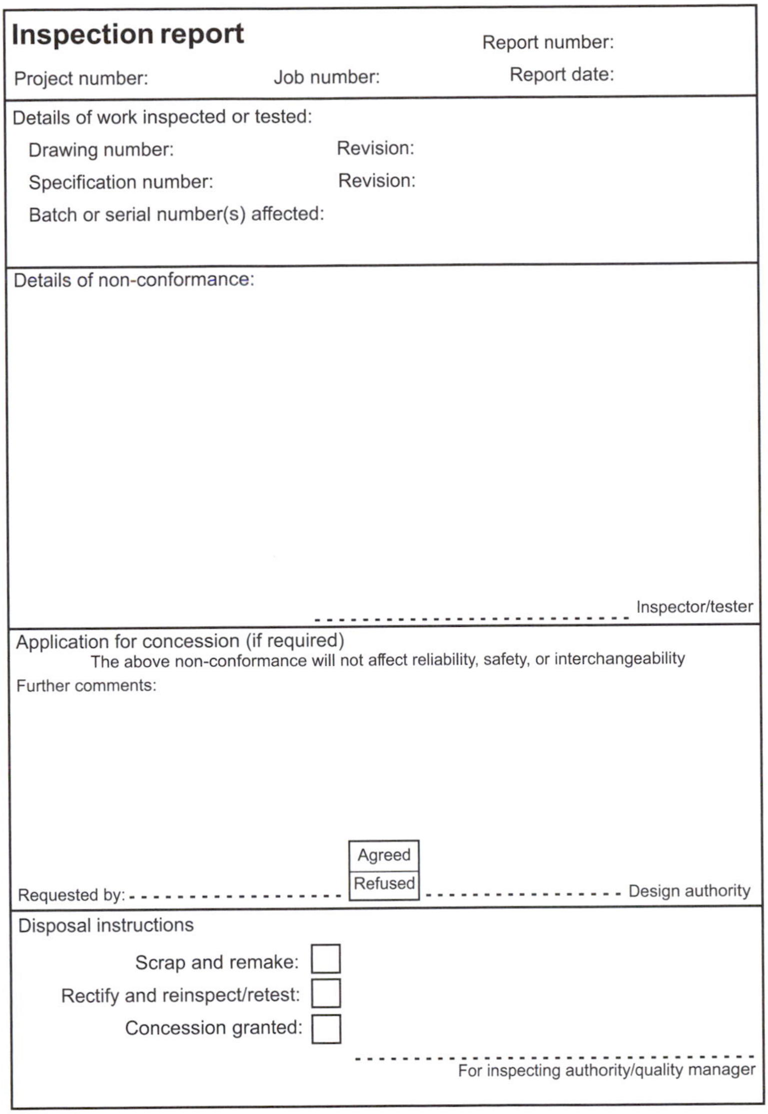

Inspection report

Report number:

Project number: Job number: Report date:

Details of work inspected or tested:

Drawing number: Revision:

Specification number: Revision:

Batch or serial number(s) affected:

Details of non-conformance:

Inspector/tester

Application for concession (if required)

The above non-conformance will not affect reliability, safety, or interchangeability

Further comments:

Requested by: Agreed / Refused Design authority

Disposal instructions

Scrap and remake:

Rectify and reinspect/retest:

Concession granted:

For inspecting authority/quality manager

Figure 11.9 Inspection report format

Diazo prints and translucent 'reproducibles' or 'submasters' are easily recognizable as copies and are thus unlikely to be confused with original documents. With today's reprographic techniques and laser printers, however, copies of drawings are indistinguishable from their originals. Drawings produced from computer files can be printed at will on film or plain paper, so that more than one apparently original version of any drawing can easily exist.

Unless rigid safeguards are introduced, any designer can alter the design information in the computer and then cause a new 'original' to be produced without making the necessary change to the drawing or revision number. Unless there is a central drawings registry for the control and issue of drawings, an independent check procedure must be devised to prevent the issue of drawings with incorrect or duplicated revision numbers.

Case example   This is an extreme example of incorrect drawing numbering from our own experience. It happened a few years ago in a large engineering company. A competent design engineer was asked to assist the company's administration manager by producing some layout drawings for a design office extension that was almost ready for occupation. The new accommodation was 5000 sq ft, all situated on one floor level, but the shape was complex and the outer walls did not form a true rectangle. The engineer visited the new accommodation area and measured it very carefully, noting the exact positions of the walls, doors, windows, and obstructing vertical support columns.

The company had just installed a brand new, very expensive, computer aided drawing (CAD) system and this engineer was the first to be given full training in its use. The new office layout was chosen as an ideal 'guinea pig' job on which to trial the CAD system.

The engineer successfully made an accurate, clear, and detailed drawing of the office shell, which he filed in the computer as a template. He was then able to overlay all the subsequent electrical, lighting, partition, and staff seating drawings on that template, all suffixed by a single letter to distinguish them from the bare template. (In an aviation design project, one can easily appreciate the value of a similar method being used, where the plan and elevations of a fuselage or wing could be set up as a template in third angle projection.)

The set of office designs was excellent, but all the drawings had to be submitted to the local authority's planning department for approval (for such things as safety and fire precautions). All of us were acutely embarrassed when the planning inspector noted that every print we had submitted bore the same drawing number, that of the original template. The engineer had forgotten to distinguish the different numbers in the drawing title boxes by adding their relevant letter suffixes.

The Interchangeability Rule

The usual practice when a drawing is changed is to reissue it with a new revision number. If, however, a change results in a manufactured component or assembly being made different from other items with which it was previously interchangeable, it is not sufficient merely to change the drawing revision number. The drawing number itself (and therefore the part number) must also be changed.

This is a golden rule to which no exception should ever be allowed, whether the item is a small component or a large assembly.

Case example   Suppose that an avionics project requires the use of 1000 small spacers, and that after 500 had been produced in brass the design was cheapened to use mild steel. These spacers are truly interchangeable, and the part number need not be changed. But the drawing for the steel spacers would be given a new revision number.

Now suppose that the spacer design had been changed from metal to moulded nylon because on later manufactured assemblies it became necessary for the spacers to be electrically insulating. The old metal spacers can no longer be used on all assemblies. The metal and nylon spacers are not interchangeable. The drawing for the nylon version of these spacers must therefore be given a new drawing number, not simply a new revision number.

EMERGENCY MODIFICATIONS

We live in an impatient age, and project time can usually be regarded as a scarce commodity. If the need for an essential modification is discovered during the active production phase of a programme, there may simply be no time available in which to issue suitably changed drawings. There are right and wrong ways of dealing with this situation and the following case is an example of the latter.

Case Example: The Kosy-Kwik Project

The project setting   Kosy-Kwik was a company which specialized in the design, supply, and installation of heating and air-conditioning systems. In 1995 it was awarded a contract, as subcontractors to a large building group, to plan and install all the heating and ventilation arrangements in a new multi-storey office block commissioned by Lox Aviation Inc., a large aircraft manufacturer who wished to use it for their headquarters. Two engineers, Clarke and Jackson, were assigned to the project. Whilst Clarke was given overall design responsibility, Jackson was detailed off to plan the central control panel and its associated controls and instrumentation.

Early difficulties   We join the project near the end of the preparation period in the Kosy-Kwik factory. By this time most deliveries of plant and equipment had been made to the Lox Aviation premises, except for the complex building heating and air-conditioning systems control panel, which was still being fabricated, later than scheduled.

Jackson was a conscientious engineer who took a great interest in his jobs as they passed through the factory. He was in the habit of making periodical tours (management by walking about) to keep a check on progress and the results of his design. During one of these tours the sheet metal shop foreman pointed out to Jackson that the almost-completed control panel was decidedly weak and wobbly.

Jackson could only agree with the foreman. The front panel was indeed decidedly flimsy, as a result of a glaring design error in specifying a gauge of steel that was far too thin. Delivery of this panel to site was already late, and threatened to delay the whole project. There was simply no time available in which to start building a new control panel. In any case, the extra cost would have been unwelcome. A simpler solution had to be found—a rescue package in fact.

Marked-up drawings   The engineer asked the foreman to weld some suitably chunky pieces of channel iron to the rear face of the panel in order to stiffen it. The foreman agreed, but was worried about getting the job past the inspection stage with the changes. 'No problem!' said Jackson, who took a pen from his pocket, marked up the foreman's copy of the drawing with the channel iron additions, and signed it to authorize the alteration.

The modification was successful. Everyone concerned was very relieved, not least Jackson, whose reputation had been likely to suffer. Only a few hours were lost, and the panel was duly delivered. The remainder of the project went ahead without further mishap, and Lox Aviation joined the long list of Kosy-Kwik's satisfied customers.

The follow-up project   In the summer of 2005 Kosy-Kwik were awarded a follow-up contract by Lox Aviation. This company's offices were to be extended, with a new wing to house an aircrew training and retraining center for all companies that acquired and operated its aircraft. This center would be complete with lecture rooms, cinema, flight simulators, and all the other facilities needed for initial training of customers' aircrew and for regular refresher courses.

Lox Aviation were working to a well-planned but tight schedule, which demanded that the new training center should be opened on the first working day of 2006. Indeed, Lox Aviation had planned a grand opening ceremony in the presence of several VIP visitors.

Because of the rigid timescale restrictions, special contract conditions were imposed on Kosy-Kwik. In particular, the only complete shut-down period allowed for the existing heating and ventilating plant (for connecting and testing the additional circuits and controls) was to be during December 2005 Christmas break. Otherwise Lox Aviation Inc. would suffer loss of work by their office staff, and there would be inconvenience to the trainee aircrew of its customers. There was to be a penalty payment of $5000 for every week or part of a week by which Kosy-Kwik failed to meet the scheduled completion date.

During the 10 years which separated these two projects several changes had occurred in the Kosy-Kwik organization. Clarke received well-deserved promotion to a remote branch office, where he became area manager. Jackson retired to enjoy his pension. The engineering department expanded, and attracted several new recruits. Among these was Stevens, an experienced contract engineer. He had no means of contact with Clarke or Jackson, and would never meet either of them.

Preparation for the Kosy-Kwik project at Lox Aviation Inc.   Stevens was appointed as engineer in charge of the new Lox Aviation project. He knew that the best policy would be to prefabricate as many parts of the project as possible in the factory. This would reduce the amount of work to be done on site, and ensure that the final link-up and testing could be accomplished during the Christmas break. Stevens found a roll of drawings labeled 'Lox Aviation Project' in a dead file drawer, dusted them off and set to work.

Most of the system was found to be straightforward, and the final tying-in with the existing installation was to be achieved by providing the installation engineers with a bolt-on package that could be fitted to the original control panel. This package was duly designed, manufactured, and delivered to site along with all the other essential materials. By the time Christmas arrived, all equipment, pipes, and ducts were in place in the new part of the building. All that remained was for the final installation team to arrive, shut down the plant, modify the control panel with the kit provided, and then test and set up the whole system.

The installation attempt   Early on Christmas Eve, two Kosy-Kwik fitters were sent to shut down the plant and start work on the control panel. Their first job was to cut a large rectangular hole in an unused part of the original panel in order to fit the new package. A template had been provided for this purpose, which they now placed in position. When they started cutting, the engineers met unexpected resistance in the shape of several large channel iron ribs welded to the rear face of the panel. The engineers had come prepared only to tackle the thin sheet shown on the old drawings. It took them over 2 hours and many saw blades before the hole was finished. Then they found that the connections to the new control package were fouled by what remained of the channel iron. Worse still, the panel was now weak and wobbly again.

The two engineers were experienced and trained as skilled installation fitters, but were equipped neither materially nor mentally to deal with problems of this magnitude without help. They suffered an acute sense of frustration and isolation, although they found different (much shorter) words with which to express their feelings.

A cry for help was indicated. Unfortunately, however, the response to their impassioned telephone call to Kosy-Kwik headquarters was less than satisfactory. Against the background noise of a lively office party they learned that all the senior engineering and management staff had left to begin their Christmas holidays. The telephone operator wished the fitters a 'merry Christmas' and suggested that they 'have a nice day'. The two engineers interpreted these greetings as good advice, gave up, and went home to start their unexpected holidays.

The extra cost   There is no real need to dwell at length on the consequences of this case, or to describe the scenes of anguish and recriminations back at headquarters in the New Year. A short summary of the additional cost items follows:

		$
1.	Design and manufacture new control panel modification kit	7000
2.	Cost of time wasted time during first visit of the two fitters	2000
3.	Cost of repairing weakened panel, on site	400
4.	Contract penalty clause, 4 weeks at $5000 per week	20 000
	Total additional costs, directly attributable	29 400

Post mortem   A retrospective glance at the circumstances leading to the disastrous consequences of the project at Lox Aviation provides a useful basis for describing a more reliable method of dealing with very urgent modifications.

In this example, all troubles can be traced back to the use of a marked-up drawing on the sheet metal shop floor, the details of which were not incorporated in the filed project drawings. The use of marked-up drawings is generally to be deplored, but we have to be realistic and accept that there will be occasions when they are unavoidable, when there is simply no time in which to update the master drawings or computer file and issue new copies of the drawing. Under these circumstances, some sort of temporary documentation must suffice, but only where safeguards are in place to ensure that the original drawings do get changed to show the true 'as-built' condition of the project.

Safeguards

One way in which the updating of final drawings can be safeguarded in the event of emergency changes relies on a streamlined version of the formal modification procedure, which does not bypass any of the essential control points.

The originator of an emergency modification must write out an engineering change request in the usual way and get it registered by the change coordinator. After seeking the immediate approval of the chief engineer (or the nominated deputy), the originator must pass one copy to the design office in order that the change will eventually be incorporated in the drawings. Another copy of the change request is kept by the coordinating clerk, who must make certain that it is seen at the next change committee meeting.

The original change request form is passed to the production department for action, where it becomes part of the issued manufacturing instructions, so that there is no need to wait for the official issue of revised drawings.

If a working copy of a drawing does have to be marked up, which may be inevitable if there is insufficient space to show all the details on the change request form, an *identical* marked-up copy must be deposited in the design office, together with their copy of the change request. The original change request must accompany the job right through all its production stages, particularly until it reaches final inspection and testing.

VERSION CONTROL, BUILD SCHEDULES, AND TRACEABILITY IN AEROSPACE PROJECTS

Version Control

By version control we mean implementing the procedures necessary to ensure that the build status of every aircraft and every component in that aircraft is known. We need to know not only all the drawings and specifications that were used in manufacture and assembly, but also the revision status of each of those documents. From that information we should be able to track back over all the authorized engineering changes, manufacturing concessions, and production permits that applied.

At the component level, airlines would be seriously inconvenienced if they found that spares ordered for an aircraft in service did not fit or did not function correctly when the time came to use them as replacements because their modification status did not match the requirement for the particular aircraft.

To give an everyday analogy, every automobile owner knows that when spares have to be purchased the repair shop will consult records made by the manufacturer so that the correct parts can be supplied. For that, either the chassis or engine number of the vehicle will track the repair shop back to the correct parts list. The automobile industry also operates traceability systems so that all vehicles with a certain range of chassis numbers can be recalled for modification if design or manufacturing faults are discovered after a particular model has been launched for sale. If that is important for automobiles, just consider how much more vital it is in aviation, where the potential for disaster is so much greater.

Remember that software changes require the same degree of version control and traceability. Software here means not only the many code-controlled programs used in aircraft systems, air traffic control, and maintenance equipment, but it also applies to operating, maintenance, and instruction manuals, whether these are for ground or flight purposes.

In theory, all that is necessary to identify the as-built status of an aircraft is to list every drawing, specification, and other document describing the project design, configuration, and content (not forgetting to include the serial and correct revision numbers of all these documents). All engineering changes should have been incorporated, so that every document is in its final condition. Remember here that the latest revision of a document may not be the correct revision for a particular component or aircraft.

This document listing becomes more complicated when, over time, a number of aircraft are manufactured that, although they share the same basic airframe and aircraft type numbers, they differ from each other in accordance with design modifications and specific customer requirements.

This difficulty is overcome using a document called a build schedule. Invariably build schedules will be set up in a computer system, where it is very important that backup files are made and securely stored. We illustrate the concept in Figure 11.10, which is a form intended for clerical use.

Build schedule			Product number:		
Product or assembly:			Issue date:		
Batch/serial numbers covered:			Sheet # of sheets		

Drawing or spec. number	Sheet	Rev	Drawing or spec. number	Sheet	Rev

The following modification numbers are incorporated in this build schedule issue

LOX AVIATION INC.

A build schedule defines without ambiguity the build content and modification status of a manufactured product or a project. It is used particularly to define the content of a unit (or batch of units) that is produced in more than one version. Definition is achieved by listing all drawings and associated documents together with the revision numbers that apply to a particular unit.

Figure 11.10   A build schedule sheet

Build schedule records should be assembled in hierarchical fashion, to agree with the physical work breakdown (or goes into chart) for the complete aircraft. Every document should be listed, giving at least its serial number and relevant revision number.

One complete build schedule document will usually refer to a single aircraft, or to a batch of aircraft made to exactly the same build status.

Build schedule records should list not only drawings and other manufacturing documents, but also the document serials numbers and correct revision numbers of operating and maintenance instructions.

Sufficient information must be given in the build schedule to identify not only documents produced within the project organization, but also drawings and specifications received from the suppliers of parts and components.

Traceability

In the event of an in-flight malfunction, whether or not an accident results, it is vital to be able to trace all other aircraft in service with the same build, so that faults found in the malfunctioning aircraft can be prevented in all other aircraft in service that have the same build status. The same argument applies, but with greater emphasis, to faults found after an accident.

Prompt traceability is even more important when information from the flight data recorder, cockpit voice recorder, and accident investigation reports has to be acted upon promptly to prevent repeat further tragedies in similar aircraft still in service. Build records need to show not only the build status of the airplane and, in turn, all of its components, but also the source of every component (who made or supplied it). For example, if a bolt fractures because of a flaw in the raw material from which it was made, the investigators must be able to trace back at least to the name of the company that manufactured these bolts so that all other aircraft fitted with them can be identified, grounded, inspected and, if necessary, modified.

Clear marking on every assembly of its part number and serial number is another essential part of the traceability process.

CASE EXAMPLE: A VERSION CONTROL PROBLEM AND ITS NOVEL SOLUTION

This case example concerns the same project for the supply of automatic test equipments mentioned earlier in this chapter in the context of a simple change pricing procedure.

At the time of this case, six trailers were parked in the assembly bay undergoing final commissioning before dispatch to the airfield. All trailers were of identical build, but each contained a large number of electronic modules, all individually serial numbered. It was essential for subsequent version control and traceability that the company kept a record of every trailer when it was shipped, with a complete build schedule listing not only the individual module part numbers but also their serial numbers.

Commissioning on these ATE trailers was a continuous process, running through nights and weekends over several weeks, including times when all the main design staff and managers were asleep or at leisure. Unfortunately the commissioning engineers, driven by urgency, developed a habit of exchanging modules between different trailers in attempts to identify faults. Thus build schedule integrity was quickly becoming lost.

The engineering manager solved the problem by purchasing six clock card racks, of the type once common on factory walls just inside the staff entrance. The slots in these racks were labeled so that, for each trailer, one slot corresponded to a module in the trailer. There were sufficient slots to cover all the modules, and each rack was wall mounted adjacent to one of the six trailers. The slot labels were located in a pattern equivalent to the 'goes into chart' for each trailer.

Next, all the inspection tickets were removed from all the modules in all the trailers, and these tickets were placed in their relevant slots in the clock card racks. Now each clock card rack was effectively a model of the build schedule for the trailer which it represented.

Then, the commissioning engineers were warned, under threat of dire penalty, that every time they swapped two modules between trailers, the relevant final inspection labels must simultaneously be exchanged in the corresponding clock card racks.

Commissioning engineers working late at night, and on long shifts, do not take kindly to clerical tasks. However, they had no excuse for failing to observe the simple system that was asked of them, and the integrity of the build schedules (and version control) was restored.

12

Managing Project Costs

Many things can happen during the life of a project to distort the expected rate and magnitude of expenditure or to delay expected revenues. Whereas this is true for any project in any industry, it is especially true in the aviation industry where profit margins tend to be traditionally low and the ability to control costs, especially in non-value added activities, can make the difference between an organization's profit and loss. The direction of change is usually disadvantageous. Some of the reasons may be unavoidable or unforeseen but, in many cases, the fault will lie somewhere within the project organization. The principal purpose of cost control is to ensure that no preventable wastage of money or unauthorized increase in expenditure is allowed to happen.

Strictly, cost management means far more than the control of expenditure. It also includes the control of revenue, making sure that all possible and justifiable income is recovered from the customer or other possible sources. Cost management involves ensuring not only that the amounts of money spent and received are in accordance with budgets, but also that the timing of each transaction is appropriate and in line with the scheduled cash flows.

Cost management is not a separate function of project management. While it is true that some people specialize in the cost aspects of project management, possibly holding titles such as 'cost and planning engineer' or even the more specialized 'cost engineer', their roles are part of a far wider framework of project cost control, which must involve many people working throughout the project organization.

A common misconception is to confuse cost reporting with cost control. Accurate and timely cost reporting is essential but cost *reporting* is not the same as cost *control*. By the time overspending has been measured and reported, damage has already been done. Cost accountants (although they might be called cost and management accountants) spend most of their time in measuring, analyzing, and reporting costs, revenues, and trends, but not in actually controlling expenditure.

This chapter begins with a section on cost (expenditure) control principles, but much of what follows is necessarily concerned more with methods for measuring, analyzing, and reporting project costs. In fact most so-called cost management methods actually add costs themselves, without adding value to the project.

PRINCIPLES OF COST CONTROL

Understanding The Main Elements Of Project Costs

Cost control methods depend to a very large extent on the nature of the costs, so it is first necessary that project managers understand the different categories of costs they will have to deal with. Some of these issues were discussed in Chapter 3, in the context of cost estimating, and the definitions given in the beginning of Chapter 3 are also relevant here. It is convenient to repeat some of these definitions in the following paragraphs.

Figure 12.1 illustrates the main cost elements that make up the costs of a typical project. These split into two main groups, as follows:

1. **Variable costs**: Costs that are incurred at a rate which is proportional to the rate of working on the project: these are generally the same as the *direct* costs. 'Direct' means that these costs can be measured and associated directly with, and only with, a particular job or project.

2. **Fixed costs**: Costs that with few exceptions constitute the company's overhead or *indirect* costs. 'Indirect' means that these are costs incurred generally in running the business, so that they cannot be directly associated with any one of several projects that might be in progress. The only exception to this rule is where the company has been specially created to conduct only one project, in which case of course all the company's costs can be directly associated with that project.

CONTROLLING VARIABLE COSTS

Figure 12.1 shows that the variable costs of a project split into two additional subcategories, namely:

- the costs of purchasing direct materials, services and hired tools, plant, and equipment;
- the direct labor costs (wages, salaries, and related employer's expenses).

Materials, bought services, and expenses

Materials, bought services, and expenses usually constitute more than half the costs of a project, and controlling these costs is thus particularly important. Cost control is exercised

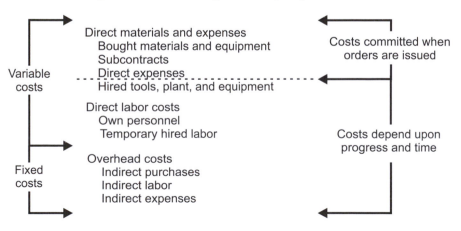

Figure 12.1   Project cost elements in the context of cost control

by following sensible purchasing procedures (as described in Chapter 10) and by using every possible design and management method to avoid making subsequent changes. By far the most important act of materials cost control is exercised at the point of commitment, which means when the purchase order is issued or a contract is signed.

Once a contract has been made with a supplier, the buyer's competitive advantage has gone and the seller has a one-to-one monopoly when fixing the price of subsequent order amendments or cancellation costs. It is generally important to avoid purchase order amendments as far as possible because these can push costs over budget.

The hire of plant and machinery is a special case, because the costs of these items depend not only on the initial contract terms, but also upon the length of time for which the hire continues. To some extent these hirings combine the characteristics of both variable and fixed costs. Thus progress management is a principal factor in controlling hire costs.

Direct Labor Costs

A job that finishes on time will generally incur only the budgeted labor costs, which should be derived from the original cost estimate. Obviously that depends on using only the amount of labor resources (people) intended and listed in the project resource schedules or work-to lists. Conversely, jobs that run late tend also to overrun their budgets. The exception here would be a job into which extra resources and overtime have been injected to accelerate a critical task to prevent it from running late. Although this job might then finish on time, it will incur additional costs as a direct result of the additional resources used. However, those additional costs will usually be more than compensated by the time (and therefore costs) saved for the whole project.

The conclusion to these remarks is obvious, namely that if you can control progress using only the budgeted resources you will automatically control the costs of labor. It follows that good leadership and the ability to motivate people are important attributes of the successful manager.

CONTROLLING FIXED COSTS (OVERHEADS)

Management must always strive to keep the fixed (indirect or overhead) costs as low as possible in relation to the variable (direct) costs, because high overheads can kill a company's chances of being competitive in the marketplace.

Project Manager's Control Of Fixed Costs

Most project managers work in premises or environments where they can have no substantive influence on the organization's fixed costs. The project manager is not usually responsible for the periodic costs of accommodation, heat and light, sales and marketing, accounting, communications, or the salaries and other expenses of general management.

However, as Figure 12.2 indicates, these fixed (overhead) costs are incurred by the organization every day, without fail, whether or not any work takes place on the project. A feature of fixed costs is that they continue to accrue, in the background, for as long as the project is active, taking up space, and using the company's infrastructure services. Thus, if a project runs late, it will most likely use more indirect costs than expected or budgeted. Figure 12.2 illustrates this condition.

Thus the principal control that the project manager can exercise over fixed costs is to make sure that the project will be finished on time.

Cases where the project manager can exercise limited control over the rate of overhead expenditure   The boundary between fixed costs and variable costs is not always precise. For example, overhead costs, although they are predominately fixed, often contain a variable element. Communications, printing, and photocopying are all activities which are often regarded as indirect or overheads, because they are costs incurred in running the business that cannot easily be identified with particular jobs. But these are variable costs, because they will increase or decrease with the level of business activity. It is in this variable portion of the overhead costs where the easiest and quickest savings can be made by the project manager.

Some contracts allow the contractor to claim reimbursement of sundry expenses such as telephone calls, printing, photocopying, and some clerical tasks, provided that these can be identified directly with the project. This is sometimes the case with companies in the mining and petrochemical industries, and for some professional organizations such as architects and legal partnerships.

In organizations carrying out several projects simultaneously it can be awkward to isolate the costs associated with one customer or one project but the effort should be made if possible. Although it is unlikely that the sums involved will be large compared with mainstream project activities, they are usually significant and worth recovering. Every expense that can be charged directly against a project should be so charged. Otherwise these expenses will simply inflate the general overhead costs, which must always be kept as low as possible if the contractor is to remain competitive in the market.

Suggested collection methods include:

- the use of a simple requisition system for all bulk photocopying and other reprographics services, with mandatory use of client or cost codes;
- mandatory use of cost codes on petty cash vouchers and all expense claims forms;
- the installation and proper day-to-day management of an automatic call logging system covering all telephone, and facsimile lines.

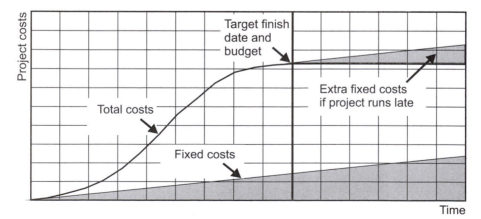

Figure 12.2   Typical project cost/time patterns and the impact of fixed costs

In one case from our experience this last measure reduced a company's total annual communications bill from $200 000 to $100 000 by preventing fraudulent use and by the recovery from staff of the costs of their private calls. Also, $50 000 of the remaining legitimate $100 000 costs were identified, allocated to their projects, and recovered from customers (where the individual contracts allowed). So, $150 000 was removed from the company's overhead account for very little expense and effort.

Recovering Overhead Costs

Most project costing systems work on the basis of charging direct labor costs (including the labor burden) as time recorded on the job multiplied by the standard hourly cost applicable to the grade. An amount is then be added to this labor cost (usually as a rate per cent) to recover a part of the company's indirect, overhead costs.

This method of recovering overheads as a 'levy' on direct labor costs is called *absorption costing*. Setting the percentage overhead rate is a task demanding perception and skill from the organization's cost and management accountants. Getting the answer right depends on accurate workload forecasts and effective overhead cost estimating, budgeting, and control.

The overhead rate charged will vary enormously from one company to another, and even from one project to another (because customers sometimes wish to negotiate the amount of a company's fixed costs that they are prepared to fund). Companies with a high level of research and development to fund will probably have very high overhead costs, which might be charged at well over 200 per cent. In labor intensive industries, with little research and development and no high-grade premises, the overhead rate might be 50 per cent or even less. It is not possible to indicate norms, because the circumstances of companies vary considerably from one to another (even where they are carrying out similar work).

The company which manages to keep its indirect costs (and overhead rate) to a minimum enjoys a competitive cost and pricing advantage.

Clients for large capital projects wield considerable power, and can be very critical of proposed overhead rates chargeable to their projects. They might ask for detailed explanations of what the overhead costs are intended to include. The overhead rate used for a large project might have to be negotiated with the client before a contract can be made.

Overhead under-recovery   If the planned direct workload should fail to materialize for any reason (perhaps through cancelled orders or over-optimistic sales forecasts), the amount of direct labor costs that can be allocated to jobs and charged out in invoices will be less than the forecast. Because overheads have been estimated as a fixed percentage of the direct labor costs, the amount of revenue received to pay for the overheads will also fall below plan. This condition is called overhead under-recovery. The principal remedies to consider include the following:

- Increase the overhead rate (thus increasing prices, which might reduce the quantity of products or project work sold).
- Increase sales by a marketing drive to sell more products or project work.
- Persuade each new project client to agree to pay for some jobs previously regarded as indirect. This will depend on being able to identify those jobs and

record their costs in a way that would satisfy subsequent audit. Examples of such costs are special printing and copying of project drawings and other documents, telephone calls, travel expenses, and so on.

- Make economies to reduce the overhead costs. That can lead to painful actions, even to the extent of dismissing administrative staff and managers.

Overhead over-recovery   Overhead over-recovery will occur if workload and direct labor billings exceed expectations, so that the per cent rate set proves to be too high. Although this can increase profitability in the short term, it may not be desirable because it can imply that the company's pricing is not sufficiently competitive, with damaging consequences for future order prospects.

A CHECKLIST OF COST MANAGEMENT FACTORS

1. Cost awareness by those responsible for design and engineering.
2. Cost awareness by all other project participants throughout the life of the project.
3. A project work breakdown which yields work packages of manageable size.
4. Cost budgets, divided so that each work package is given its own share of the total budget.
5. A code of accounts system which can be aligned with the work breakdown structure.
6. A cost accounting system that can collect and analyze costs as they are incurred and allocate them with minimum delay to their relevant cost codes.
7. A practicable work schedule.
8. Effective management of well-motivated staff, to ensure that progress meets or beats the work schedule.
9. A method for comparing expenditure with that planned for the work actually done.
10. Effective supervision and quality control of all activities to aim at getting things right first time.
11. Proper drafting of specifications and contracts.
12. Discreet investigation to ensure that the customer is of sound financial standing, with sufficient funds available to make all contracted payments.
13. Similar investigation, not necessarily so discreet, of all significant suppliers and subcontractors new to the contractor's experience.
14. Effective use of competitive tendering for all purchases and subcontractors to ensure the lowest costs commensurate with quality and to avoid committing costs that would exceed estimates and budgets.
15. Appropriate consideration and control of modifications and contract variations, including the passing of justifiable claims for price increases on to the customer.
16. Avoidance, where possible, of unbudgeted dayworks on construction contracts.
17. Where dayworks are unavoidable, proper authorization, retention, and administration of dayworks sheets.
18. Strict control of payments to suppliers and subcontractors, to ensure that all invoices and claims for progress payments are neither overpaid nor paid too soon.
19. Recovery from the customer of all incidental expenses allowed for in the contract charging structure (for example, expensive telephone calls, printing, travel, and accommodation).

20. Proper invoicing to the customer, especially ensuring that claims for progress payments or cost reimbursement are made at the appropriate times and at the correct levels, so that disputes do not justify the customer delaying payments.
21. Effective credit control to expedite overdue payments from the customer.
22. Occasional internal security audits to prevent losses through theft or fraud.
23. Effective and regular reports of progress and costs to senior management, highlighting potential schedule or budget overruns in time for corrective action to be taken.

ADDITIONAL COST CONTROL FACTORS

Adherence To Cost Budgets

Taking the narrowest view, a project contractor should be concerned (for many obvious reasons) that the project is completed successfully without exceeding the planned costs (authorized budgets). In many cases, this is the only cost objective set for the project manager. Most of the conventional cost reporting and control procedures, including those described in this and the following chapter, aim to achieve that objective.

In some cases (for example in internal management change and IT projects) budgets are the only cost consideration. There is no external customer and no profit to be safeguarded: simply the need to contain spending within the amounts previously authorized by the organization's senior management against the business plan.

Where there is a profit objective, it has to be remembered that profits are fragile and easily destroyed by overspending. When a company is operating in a highly competitive market, margins might have to be kept low. If the project is very keenly priced, say for a 10 per cent profit, a budget overspend of only 5 per will halve that profit.

Contractor's Responsibility To The Customer Or Project Owner

The contractor usually has some degree of responsibility for ensuring that the customer's cost objectives are also satisfied. The most obvious manifestation of this is the firm price contract, in which the contractor's firm *price* is the customer's firm *cost*. Unless the customer rocks the boat by asking for changes, or the contractor goes bankrupt or is otherwise unable to finish the project successfully, the customer can plan capital expenditure with confidence against a fixed budget.

In cost-plus projects, where the contractor is able to mark up costs and pass them on to the client with no fixed price limit, there is less incentive for the contractor to limit costs. In fact, the converse can be true: the greater the amount spent, the greater will be the 'plus' or profit. A long running cost-plus service contract or an ill-defined reimbursable cost project can be regarded as a gravy train. Then the contractor has an ethical, but difficult, duty to ensure that:

- only legitimate costs are claimed;
- work is carried out as efficiently as if the contractor were spending its own money.

Where large capital investments are involved, the managing contractor's project manager can have a specific cost management duty to the client, which broadens the cost objective further. The project cost management function then extends to predicting and reporting costs to the client, working with the client to help schedule and control expenditure and marshal the necessary funds.

THE TOTAL COST APPROACH

The total cost approach is a way of regarding costs holistically, solving logistical problems, or otherwise planning to achieve the lowest overall cost. This approach can be used in a wide variety of situations. It has been used, for example, in distribution logistics where decisions have to be made about the location of warehouses and designation of transport methods so as to achieve the lowest possible total distribution costs of retail goods.

Total Costs In Project Management

In the context of project management, total cost considerations mean that managers in the project organization work together, each considering unselfishly how the work contribution of their department is likely to affect the costs incurred by other departments. One example is where a suggested change in design approach, although resulting in greater design difficulties and costs, might save considerable time and money in the resulting production or construction methods. The total cost approach can, therefore, mean increasing the planned expenditure in one department in order to generate greater cost savings in the rest of the organization.

Example   One of us was once privileged, in the role of planning consultant, to witness a convincing demonstration of the total cost approach in action. The scene was a project planning meeting in the engineering director's office of a company in the USA. The company was about to start three new projects, each for an external customer. The engineering director was in the chair. Also present at the meeting were the chief engineer and other senior engineers, and (significantly) the manufacturing manager and his senior production engineers.

Various design proposals were passed back and forwards between the design engineers and the production people and, one by one, design approaches were agreed that would lead to the lowest total company cost, while maintaining the highest quality and reliability standards. A high level of enthusiasm, motivation, and cooperation was generated from the start.

The three projects, planned with multi-project resource allocation and given effective project management, were all subsequently completed on or before time and well below their originally budgeted costs (which also meant below the total cost levels previously experienced by the company for comparable projects).

SETTING AND RESETTING COST BUDGETS

Plainly the initial project cost budgets should be derived from the cost estimates used when the commercial tender or internal business plan was prepared. That means the budgets before the addition of below-the-line allowances and indirect costs. If the target financial benefits are not to be eroded, these budgets must become the maximum authorized levels of expenditure.

The work breakdown and organization structures described in earlier chapters will allow this control budget to be distributed among the various departmental and functional managers responsible for carrying out all the project tasks.

It is not only the top budget limits that are important, but also the rate at which expenditure is scheduled to take place. That will be discussed later in this chapter in the context of cash flow scheduling.

Labor Budgets

Use of labor-hours   It is often said, with good reason, that managers and supervisors should be given their work budgets in terms of labor-hours rather than as the resulting costs of wages and overheads. The argument is that a manager should never be held accountable for meeting targets where they have no authority to control the causal factors. Project managers are rarely responsible for wage and salary levels, increases in wages and salaries, and company overhead expenses. They are, however, responsible for progress and (through supervision) for the time taken to complete each work package.

In this chapter, therefore, it is assumed that each manager with budget responsibility will be given, and will be expected to observe, the labor-hour budget for every work package under their control.

Resetting Budgets To Cope With Project Changes

Budgets on most projects are not static. They increase each time a contract variation order results in an agreed increase in the project price. At any time it should be possible for the budget to be stated in terms of its initial amount, additions subsequently approved by the client and, therefore, the total current budget. If possible, these changes to the budgets should be made at work package level so that all parts of the budget remain up to date and valid.

Taking authorized budget changes into account, as time proceeds the typical project budget graph should resemble an S curve on to which a stepped rise has been grafted for every significant addition to the budget.

Budget adjustments for below-the-line allowances   If the project spreads over more than a few months, cost escalation and (for international projects) foreign exchange rate fluctuations will probably have to be taken into account. Any relevant below-the-line provisions for such changes made in the original project estimate, provided they have been built into the pricing or charging structure, can be regarded as 'reserve budgets'. Appropriate sums can be 'drawn down' from these reserves from time to time as necessary to augment the active control budget.

Currency Units For Foreign Transactions

The currency units used in cost estimates, budgets, cost reports, and in other project documents are obviously important. For projects conducted entirely within the borders of one country there should be no problem and the national currency is the natural choice for all budgeting and reporting purposes. If the project is to use imported services or materials, the logical method for expressing both the budget and the expenditure is to convert all sums into the 'home' currency, being careful to state the exchange rate used in each case.

When a project involves working for a foreign client, the contractor may be obliged by the terms of the contract or the agreed project procedures to prepare budgets and report all expenditure in the currency of the client's country, or in some other international currency (such as Euros or US dollars). The currency chosen may then have to become the control currency for the project.

Purchased Materials, Equipment, And Services

The costs of bought-out supplies and services are decided when the purchase orders are issued and accepted by the suppliers (thus creating legal contracts). Purchasing cost control can only be exercised, therefore, when each order is being placed. Once an order has been issued, the costs are committed. If the total price agreed exceeds the amount budgeted for the particular item, it is then too late to do anything about it.

Any subsequent purchasing cost control procedures can only contribute to cost control by giving early warning of adverse trends. If poor purchasing performance has been experienced early in the project, the best that can be done is to ensure that an improvement takes place before or when the remaining orders are committed.

COST COLLECTION METHODS

It can be assumed that every established company will have procedures in place for collecting, analyzing, and recording project costs. It is important that this analysis and reporting, of both incurred and committed costs, is carried out promptly. If the figures are a month or more old when they reach the project manager, what chance do they have of taking action in time to reverse any bad trend?

Most of the procedures for collecting costs and allocating them to the project cost codes are the responsibility of the company's cost accountants but cooperation from the project manager and other operational managers is usually essential to prevent delays and mistakes.

Collecting The Costs Of Bought-in Materials And Equipment

It can be assumed that the organization's purchasing, accounting, and stores procedures will ensure that the costs of materials and bought-in equipment are always collected and recorded. The routine cost accounting systems would normally cover costs associated with the payment of invoices, and the later job costs when materials are issued from stores for manufacturing jobs. The three options are as follows:

1. The dates when orders are placed (the committed costs). This is the earliest possible time for monitoring the costs of materials and the most useful for assessing performance against budget.
2. The dates when invoices from the suppliers of goods and services are due to be paid (the actual costs).

3. Particularly for manufacturing projects, job costing that depends on the evaluation of stores requisitions (when the materials are withdrawn from stores for use on the project). That can often be after the suppliers' invoices have been paid.

Figure 12.3 is a graphical representation of these three different methods, each of which has its own advantages and disadvantages. All the curves have one thing in common. Each has been drawn by adding together the materials expenditure on a month-by-month basis as soon as the data are known. The main difference between these curves is the information route through which the cost data have been obtained.

Cost data from committed purchase costs   Whenever the project is of the kind where equipment, materials, or subcontracts are ordered specifically for use on the project, the project manager should be concerned particularly to see that a system is in place for recording and tabulating the values of purchase orders as they are placed. This information, at the time of commitment, will give the earliest possible indication of cost trends against the budget (see curve (A) of Figure 12.3. It is unlikely that the purchasing organization or the company's cost accounting procedures will be set up to record committed costs in this way, and cooperation between the project manager and the purchasing organization is essential if this form of communication is to be established and maintained.

Any items already available from general stocks, and which are not to be ordered specially for the project, must of course be allowed for and included in the total commitment. This is easily accomplished: all that is necessary is to withdraw these stocks from general stock and pre-allocate them by transfer into the project stores. The requisitions used to withdraw these materials from production stores can be costed at their standard cost, and the costs added to the total project commitment.

Cost data from stores issues   Curve (B) in Figure 12.3 is the only graph which could be derived in all circumstances, whether stock or project purchasing had been adopted.

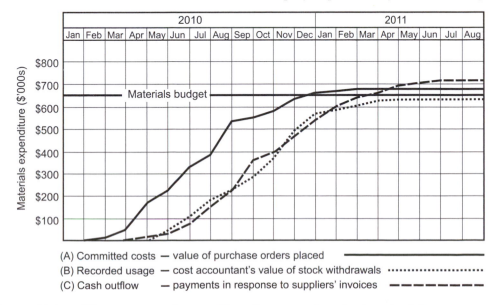

Figure 12.3   Three ways of recording the cost of project materials

In this case, the materials costs have been found by valuing all the items listed on stores requisitions or similar paperwork (usually at standard cost) as the items have been withdrawn from stores for use on the project. This method is particularly applicable to manufacturing projects.

Errors can arise owing to discrepancies between the amounts listed and the amounts actually issued or used. Valuations can also be inaccurate if outdated standard costs have been applied. These errors ought not to be significant, however, unless there are serious shortcomings in the stores or costing administration. The real disadvantage of this most usual form of costing only becomes apparent when the results are compared with those obtained from alternative methods. It is not called 'historic costing' for nothing. The project manager would have to wait until after the materials had actually been used before any under- or overspending trend became apparent. Thus the data obtained from this method will be of no help in controlling project costs.

Cost data from suppliers' invoices   Payments made against suppliers' invoices provide the most accurate account of purchased materials costs for a contract. Project purchasing is an essential condition; otherwise all invoices cannot easily be related to the project being costed. Curve (C) in Figure 12.3 shows how this kind of cost information might build up as the project progresses.

Note that Curve (C) lags behind both the other two curves by an appreciable period. Most invoices will be paid only after the goods have been received or, in many cases, after they have actually been built into the project.

The significant fact which emerges here is that information derived from suppliers' invoices is far too late to be of any use whatsoever in budgetary control. By the time the facts are known, the money has long since been committed and nothing can be done. This emphasizes the importance of measuring and controlling project purchase costs at the point of commitment, which means when the purchase orders are issued.

Comparative accuracy   Before leaving Figure 12.3, observe that all three curves attain different final levels. In this example the differences have been exaggerated deliberately, and in practice no more than about 5 per cent of the total material costs should separate the highest and lowest asymptotes.

The curve of committed costs (Curve (A)), did not quite reach the true final cost value (Curve (C)) owing to slight differences between suppliers' quotations (the amounts shown on the purchase orders and used to compile Curve (A)) and the final prices actually invoiced. These extra costs arose because one or two purchase orders were placed after the suppliers' quotations were time-expired, and because of incidental expenses, such as freight, packing, insurance, and port and customs duties that were not originally taken into account.

Curve (B) (materials actually withdrawn from project stores) also fell slightly short of the real total as shown by Curve (C). This could imply that some over-ordering took place (leaving some goods in stock at the end of the project). Changes to the scope or specification of the project during its execution might also have led to materials being left unused in stores. When surpluses are accumulated in this way these should really be written off as a charge against project profits, unless they can be returned to the suppliers for full credit or used elsewhere on other projects. Otherwise the surplus materials will only have to be written off at a later date.

Collecting Labor Costs

General timesheets   A common method for recording and collecting the time spent on projects by professional and other direct office staff on projects is to ask each individual to complete timesheets at regular intervals. Timesheets are usually compiled weekly and require each person to enter the time spent against each relevant cost code or job number, probably expressed to the nearest half-hour. An example of a weekly timesheet is shown in Figure 12.4.

An important part of the timesheet procedure is that the person's supervisor should check and verify the entries before adding an approval signature.

Whatever the method used for collecting labor costs, the time records should be as accurate as possible. If the project is organized as a team, so that everyone works on the project all the time, the only errors to be expected would be in allocations to subcodes within the project. If, however, the organization is a matrix, people might be working on more that one project during a week, or even on the same day, and the apportionment of time between projects becomes more subjective and open to error or abuse.

Staff often have times when they work less efficiently or actually waste time, and there is always a risk that such time will be booked wrongly to the most convenient number available. People should be encouraged to fill in the entries on their timesheets every day. If this chore is left until collection of timesheets at the end of the week, mistakes will inevitably be made as individuals strive in vain to remember what they were doing earlier in the week.

Timesheet errors on firm price contracts can throw up false profit and loss assessments and reduce the value of historical cost records for future analysis and comparative cost

Timesheet											For accounts department use only

Name: _____   Staff number: _____

Department: For week ending:

Job number	Sat'day	Sunday	Monday		Tuesday		Wednesday		Thursday		Friday	
			Normal	O'time	Normal	O'time	Normal	O'time	Normal	O'time	Normal	O'time
	.	.	.	.	.	.	.	.	.	.	.	.
	.	.	.	.	.	.	.	.	.	.	.	.
	.	.	.	.	.	.	.	.	.	.	.	.
	.	.	.	.	.	.	.	.	.	.	.	.
	.	.	.	.	.	.	.	.	.	.	.	.
	.	.	.	.	.	.	.	.	.	.	.	.
	.	.	.	.	.	.	.	.	.	.	.	.
	.	.	.	.	.	.	.	.	.	.	.	.
	.	.	.	.	.	.	.	.	.	.	.	.

Enter times to nearest half-hour. For holidays use 0096 sickness 0097; special leave 0098; waiting time 0099

Signature: _____   Approved: _____

Figure 12.4   A weekly time sheet

estimating. In cost-plus contracts, timesheet mistakes will result in billing errors to the customer, which could be at best unethical and, at worst, fraudulent.

Timesheets should, therefore, only be signed as approved by those nominated as being authorized to do so. It may be necessary to introduce a higher-level check by arranging for a suitable independent person to carry out an occasional timesheet audit. In cost-plus contracts the customers will probably insist on some such safeguard.

Timesheets for agency staff   Staff supplied by external agencies to work in the contractor's offices will be provided with their own agency timesheets, which the project contractor is expected to sign to show that the company agrees with the hours for which the temporary employee will be paid by the agency, and which will eventually appear on the agencies' invoices. These timesheets are rarely suitable as project cost records, and it will probably be necessary to ask the agency staff also to fill in the contractor's own timesheets (which can be color coded if required to distinguish them from the timesheets used by permanent staff).

The time spent by agency staff working in agency offices will usually be charged for weekly, supported by detailed timesheets from the agency. The contractor may wish to specify and supply the timesheets that are to be used. Checking and correct authorization are obviously important, and the contractor may decide to arrange random, unannounced inspection visits to the external office as a precaution against fraud.

Direct input of timesheet data to the computer   Some of the more powerful project management software systems, when networked, allow staff to key in their timesheet data directly. This procedure can save considerable time but the following must be borne in mind:

- checking, auditing, and approval are more difficult to arrange and errors can be expected;
- the system will not work unless everyone is clear about the cost codes to be used, and how these compare with the task information on file;
- there will be additional system costs, which can be considerable and might even be a multiple of the number of staff who will enter data.

AUDITS AND FRAUD PREVENTION MEASURES

The need for timesheet entries to be checked and approved by managers and supervisors has already been mentioned. This is, in effect, a form of auditing. It helps to protect the client of a cost-plus project from being overcharged. Incidentally, it also helps to ensure that archived records of fixed-price projects will be relatively free from errors, and therefore of more use when making comparative estimates for future projects.

Any company must always be aware of the possible risks when any manager or other member of staff has authority to commit expenditure or authorize payments on its behalf. Even where complete trust exists between senior management and their subordinates, the procedures should be audited and, where necessary, amended to reduce the possibility of fraud.

A company should set financial limits above which any manager must seek superior approval before authorizing any particular item of expenditure (for example a purchase requisition).

Payment of suppliers' invoices should be authorized by a responsible person who is not the same person who signed the associated purchase orders. That will provide an independent check and reduce any temptation for a buyer to order goods or services for their own use.

Rules should be laid down as to the levels of hospitality or gifts that those with purchasing authority may accept from suppliers and subcontractors. These should be drafted carefully so that they do not destroy normal goodwill and accepted moderate practices, but instead deter managers from receiving pecuniary benefits that might tend to corrupt, distort judgement, or generate feelings of obligation to one source of supply.

Petty cash vouchers are open to misuse. In one UK company, a highly regarded member of the purchasing department regularly made small purchases of sundry stationery items, claiming reimbursement against petty vouchers. All would have been well if they had not made a common practice of adding considerable amounts to each petty cash claim voucher for fictitious purchases that were not on the original requisitions. A great deal of money and the subsequent criminal court case could have been saved if regular procedures audits had been carried out.

MANAGING CASH FLOW

Cash is the lifeblood of businesses and their projects. Without money to pay the people, suppliers and subcontractors, all work must stop and even the most promising project will fail.

The subject of project cash flow is often misunderstood. Two common mistakes are:

1. confusing cash *outflow* schedules with *net* cash flow schedules;
2. regarding a predicted final project profit and loss statement as being completely satisfactory if it forecasts a good end result, but giving no thought to the cash flows that must take place before the project can be finished.

The easiest way to appreciate cash flow management is to imagine yourself as the project contractor, and picture the cash payments flowing into and out of the project as if they were flowing in and out of your personal bank balance. Thus you must manage cash inflows and outflows so that the account does not go into an unauthorized level of borrowing.

Cash flow management means getting all payments into the project on or very soon after their due dates. These typically include stage payments (progress payments) that are linked to project milestones or invoices certified by an independent authority to prove that the amount of work claimed for has, in fact, been done. If a project runs late, such payments cannot be claimed from the customer, and cash flow difficulties might result.

Credit control is important. That means ensuring that customers are not allowed to default on legitimate claims for payment.

The project manager might be asked to advise the financial department of predicted cash requirements by preparing a cash flow schedule before the project begins. Because cash is a vital project resource, we discussed the principles of net cash flow scheduling in Chapter 8, which dealt generally with scheduling techniques for all project resources. We demonstrated in Figure 8.9 that cash flow scheduling means following a series of logical steps in sequence. Note how often that word 'logical' appears in project management!

Cost item	Quarterly periods - all figures $1,000s*																	Total budget
PROJECTS UNLIMITED LTD / **Tulsa MRO facility for AA** / Project number P21900 / Issue date March 2010	2011				2012				2013				2014				2015	
	1	2	3	4	1	2	3	4	1	2	3	4	1	2	3	4	1	
INFLOWS																		
Agreed loans	50				150													200
Client's payments	10		50	100	200	500	1500	1000	1000	1750	1000	1000	1000	3000	1000	1000	1000	15110
Total inflows	60		50	100	350	500	1500	1000	1000	1750	1000	1000	1000	3000	1000	1000	1000	15310
OUTFLOWS																		
Engineering	14	25	59	80	85	63	43	23	12	11	9	6	7	10	14	14		475
Purchasing		5	45	5	550	310	745	295	750	665	215	457	2242	76	2	470		6832
Construction				17	35	97	245	393	436	654	382	241	186	45	30			2761
Contingency					10	20	25	25	30	30	35	35	45	45	50	50		400
Escalation					35	29	74	59	110	136	70	88	322	30	32	85		1070
Total outflows	14	30	104	102	715	519	1132	795	1338	1496	711	827	2802	206	128	619		11538
NET FLOWS																		
Periodic	46	(30)	(54)	(2)	(365)	(19)	368	205	(338)	254	289	173	(1802)	2794	872	381	1000	
Cumulative	46	16	(38)	(40)	(405)	(424)	(56)	149	(189)	65	354	527	(1275)	1519	2391	2772	3772	3772

This spreadsheet is for method illustration only and all the dates and numbers are fictitious.

Figure 12.5   Format for a net cash flow schedule spreadsheet

An outline example of a net cash flow schedule tabulation was given in Figure 8.10, but we have included another here as Figure 12.5 to show in more detail how a cash flow schedule should be laid out in spreadsheet style.

Main contractors and other managers of large capital projects may be asked to predict cash flows as a service to their clients. Those clients need to know when to expect claims for payment from the contractor. In some very large capital projects, customers set up accounts from which to pay for project equipment themselves, relying on advice from the main project contractor for release of instructions to pay. This is another case where clients need to be advised in advance of the likely amounts and timings of their commitments.

So project cash flow schedules can serve a dual purpose, helping both the contractor and the customer to make the necessary funds available to keep the project afloat and financially viable.

COMPARING PROJECT COSTS WITH ACHIEVEMENT

All effective managers have questioning minds. In cost control matters this curiosity leads to the questions, 'For all the dollars spent on this project so far, how much has actually been achieved?' and, 'Have we obtained value for the money spent?' Those questions lead to the subject of earned value measurement, which is dealt with in the following chapter.

13

Earned Value Analysis and Cost Reporting

All effective managers have questioning minds. In cost control matters this curiosity leads to the following questions:

- For all the money spent on this project so far, how much has actually been achieved?
- Have we obtained value for the money spent?
- If we go on as we are, how much more shall we spend before this project is finished?

Answers to these questions, or at least approximations to them, can usually be found using one or other of the techniques of earned value analysis.

MILESTONE ANALYSIS

Milestone analysis is one of the simpler methods which managers can use throughout the project life cycle to compare the actual costs and progress experienced with the costs and progress planned. The method is less effective and less detailed than others described later in this chapter, but it has the merit of needing a relatively modest amount of management effort to set up and maintain. It also requires less sophisticated cost accounting than other methods and can be used when project schedules are not particularly detailed.

Perhaps the best way to demonstrate the benefits of milestone analysis would be to begin by considering what happens when actual costs are compared against cost budgets when there are no milestones or other relevant information about the progress achieved.

Cost Monitoring Without Milestones

Figure 13.1 shows the kinds of curves that might result if total project costs are recorded regularly and plotted on a graph against time and the budget.

The practice depends on first plotting a graph of expected costs against time. Such graphs are sometimes known as time-scaled budgets. The time-scaled budget in Figure 13.1 is represented by the dotted curve. This curve was plotted by combining information from the cost estimates and the project plan, so that the estimated costs for all work packages are included in the curve at their scheduled times. The project

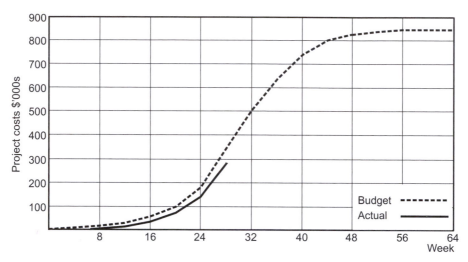

Comparisons like this mean little unless the corresponding achievement is measured.

Figure 13.1   Comparison of actual costs against a time-scaled budget

manager should, therefore, be able to consult the graph at any time during the execution of the project to find the amount of total project costs that should have been reached if all is going to plan.

In the absence of a suitable work breakdown with budgets it would not, of course, be possible to draw a time-scaled budget curve. In that case, the best that could be done would be to draw the budget as a straight line joining two points, starting from zero cost at the graph's origin and reaching the total estimated cost at the planned completion date. That approach can be dismissed as being of no use whatever.

The actual cumulative project costs can be plotted at suitable intervals on the same axes as the time-scaled budget. If the costing system is at all reasonable, it will be possible to plot these costs fairly accurately. This has been done in Figure 13.1, where it can be seen that actual costs have been recorded up to the end of week 28.

Interpreting the result where there are no milestones   Graphs that attempt to compare actual costs with the time-scaled budget, even when they are plotted with great care, are of very limited management use as they stand. The missing piece of information in Figure 13.1 is the corresponding measure of progress or achievement.

At one extreme, if no money is being spent at all, then it is a fair assumption that no progress is being made either. It is also true and easily understood that a significantly low rate of expenditure usually indicates an inadequate rate of progress and achievement. Unfortunately, some managers then proceed to make the less acceptable assumption that if expenditure is being incurred at the planned rate, then progress and achievement must also be either on plan or 'about right'. This is a very rough and ready guide that can lead to dangerously wrong conclusions.

Suppose that the project illustrated in Figure 13.1 has been running for 32 weeks, when the planned expenditure should then be $500 000. There are people who would be well satisfied on being told that the reported expenditure is at or just below $500 000. But those people fail to ask all the vital questions which should be considered by any project manager, namely:

- How much have we spent to date?
- What should we have spent to date?
- What have we achieved so far?
- What should we have achieved by this time?
- What are the final cost and delivery prospects for the project if our performance continues at the current level?

Milestone monitoring, although not a perfect method, can help to answer these questions.

Explanation Of The Milestone Method

Identifying milestones   The first requirement in milestone analysis is to understand what is meant by a milestone. A milestone denotes a particular, easily identifiable, stage in the progress of a project towards completion. It might be acceptance by the customer of a final design concept or layout drawing, the issue of a package of drawings for work to begin, the day when a building is made watertight so that internal trades can start, the date when electrical power is first switched on to a new installation, or any other such occasion. In an aircraft development project, each stage of approval from the relevant regulatory body would be a milestone, as would be other significant events like the issue of final designs from the drawing office, the receipt of engines from an outside supplier, or completion of the first test flight.

All good project management software allows the user to designate appropriate critical path network activities as milestones. Each milestone is then achieved when the relevant milestone activity is reported as finished. This becomes a little complicated when a true project milestone depends on completion of more than one parallel activity. Precedence notation, however, is very adaptable and it is easy to solve this problem by creating milestone events artificially. All that is necessary is to insert milestone activities with zero or unit duration at the appropriate network intersections. This is rather similar to the creation of artificial dummies that was shown earlier, in Figure 7.13.

Milestone analysis starts, therefore, by choosing and naming the achievements that can most effectively be used as project milestones. Ideally, milestones should coincide with the completion of packages from the WBS or events marking other significant stages in progress.

Plotting the budget/milestone plan   For each milestone, two pieces of data are required. These are:

1. the date on which the milestone is scheduled to be achieved;
2. the estimated cost or budget for the associated work package (or, alternatively, the expected cost of all the work needed to achieve the milestone).

When all milestone data are available the milestone/budget curve can be plotted. This process starts by sketching the time-scaled budget curve. The position of each point is determined by matching the cumulative cost estimates for the project work packages against the planned achievement dates for those work packages. It might be necessary to use all the constituent tasks, rather than complete work packages, to produce sufficient points on the graph. Care must be taken to ensure that no estimated costs are left out, so that the budget curve will reach the cost estimated for the project. So far this is similar to the process used to produce the time-scaled budget curve in Figure 13.1.

To complete the budget/milestone graph, symbols must be added to the budget curve to represent all the milestones. Each milestone must be positioned on the budget curve at the date scheduled for its completion.

Plotting the graph of actual expenditure and milestone achievement   To be able to plot the graph of actual expenditure for comparison against the plan, two further items of information must be collected:

1.   the date on which each milestone was actually achieved;
2.   the project costs actually incurred (including committed costs of relevant purchased items) at the end of each cost monitoring period.

It must therefore be assumed that a procedure exists for recording the total costs actually incurred and committed for the project at suitable intervals. These intervals might be weekly or monthly, and will depend to some extent on the life cycle time for the project.

The actual costs can be plotted as a graph on the same axes as the time-scaled budget. Points on the graph should be highlighted by symbols that indicate the actual completion date for each milestone. To be able to compare the planned and actual graphs sensibly, it helps enormously if all the milestones can be given simple numbers. If the milestones marked on the budget curve are, for example, numbered 1, 2, 3, 4, and so on, the corresponding points on the actual cost graph can carry the same numbers to make comparison easy.

A Milestone Analysis Example

A construction project lasting just over one year is the basis for this example and Figure 13.2 displays the relevant graphs. This might be for a small building on an airport. A similar approach can be followed for any project in aviation or any almost any other industry.

The dotted curve in Figure 13.2 shows the time-scaled budget for the project, drawn by combining data from the project schedule and the authorized cost estimates. Thirteen milestones have been identified for the project, and the schedule and cost data for these are tabulated in Figure 13.3.

Each milestone has been indicated on the planned curve by placing a circle at the time when it should be achieved. The numbers within the circles identify the particular milestones.

Monitoring method   Actual cost and progress data have been gathered up to the end of week 30 for this project and these are included in the tabulated data shown in Figure

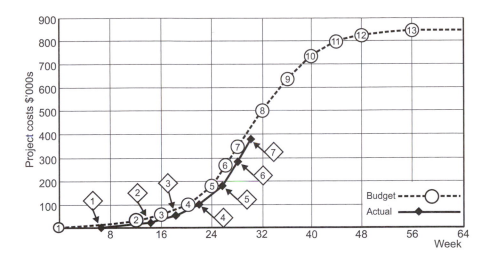

Figure 13.2   Project cost and achievement comparison using milestones

Milestone description	Schedule (week number)		Cumulative cost $(1000s)	
	Plan	Actual	Budget	Actual
1 Project start authorized	0	6	0	0
2 Design approved	12	14	25	20
3 Drawings issued for building	16	18	60	55
4 Foundations completed	20	22	100	100
5 Drawings issued for services	24	26	180	180
6 All equipment for services ordered	26	28	275	290
7 Walls built to eaves	28	30	345	385
8 Windows and doors finished	32		500	
9 Roof on, building watertight	36		630	
10 Wiring and plumbing finished	40		730	
11 Services installed and tested	44		795	
12 Internal finishes completed	48		825	
13 Site and building handover to airport	56		845	

These data were used to compile the chart shown in Figure 13.2.

Figure 13.3   Data for a milestone chart

13.3. The results have been plotted, at 2-weekly intervals, as the solid line curve in Figure 13.2. Any milestone passed during each 2-weekly period has been indicated on the actual cost curve by means of a diamond containing the milestone's identification number.

Interpreting the results of milestone analysis   Of course, if all is going exactly according to plan, the budget and actual graphs should lie together on the same path and the milestone points should coincide. When they do not, investigation should give some indication of the project cost and achievement performance to date.

Imagine that you are the general manager of the construction company responsible for this project and that it has been running for just over 8 weeks. If you look at week 8 on Figure 13.2 you will see that milestone 1, project start, has been achieved 6 weeks late, as indicated by the position of the diamond compared with the circle. The very low costs recorded at week 8 indicate that little or no activity is taking place. So, you can easily see that the project has started late and that more effort is needed urgently if progress is to catch up with the plan.

When you receive your updated milestone chart at the end of week 14 it tells you that milestone 2 has been reached. It should have happened at week 12, but the project has now been pulled up from being 6 weeks late to only 2 weeks late. Costs recorded up to week 14 are $20 000. These costs compare against a budget of $25 000 for achieving milestone 2.

Expenditure at week 14 should have reached about $45 000 (the dotted curve). So you conclude that the project is still running slightly late and that the rate of expenditure is lower than plan, so extra effort is needed. You are, however, getting value for the money spent because milestone 2 was achieved for $5000 less than its estimated cost.

If you continue to observe the chart at consecutive 2-weekly intervals, you can see how it depicts the changing trend. In particular, the cost performance gradually deteriorates. One significant report from the project manager is the milestone chart updated to the end of week 28. The graphs indicate that milestone 6 should have been achieved at week 26 for a project cost of $275 000. You can see from the graphs, however, that milestone 6 has only just been reached at week 28 at a cost of $290 000. So the project is not only still running 2 weeks late but is now also $15 000 over budget.

By week 30, it is apparent that the project programme, as indicated by milestone 7, continues to run 2 weeks late, and the costs at $385 000 have risen to $40 000 over the corresponding budget for this milestone

Without the milestones as measuring points, none of this analysis would have been possible.

Need for replotting   If a change in project scope or any other reason causes rescheduling of work or costs, then the data for future milestones will obviously change too. The curve of predicted expenditure and milestones will have to be amended at each significant authorized change so that it remains up to date and a true basis for comparison of actual costs against plan.

Disadvantages Of The Milestone Method

The milestone method suffers from a few disadvantages. These include the following:

- The information that can be extracted for management use in controlling the project is often obtained after the damage has been done, and certainly much later than the predictions possible with more detailed earned value analysis (described below).
- If programme slippages are going to occur very often, the curves may have to be redrawn frequently, unless a computer can be used or some very flexible charting method is devised.
- The method takes only an approximate account of work in progress (work packages which have been started, but where the milestones have yet to be achieved).
- The method only shows coarse trends rather than the more detailed measurements obtainable with earned value analysis.

- It is not easy to use the results of milestone analysis to predict the probable final outcome for the project.

However, the method involves comparatively little effort, is a considerable improvement on simple cost versus budget comparison, and may therefore commend itself to the busy project manager.

EARNED VALUE ANALYSIS

Earned value analysis can be regarded as the missing link between cost reporting and cost control. It depends on the existence of a sound framework of planning and control, including the following:

- a detailed WBS;
- a correspondingly detailed cost coding system;
- timely and accurate collection and reporting of cost data;
- a method for monitoring and quantifying the amount of work done, including work in progress.

The earned value process aims to compare the costs incurred for an accurately identified amount of work with the costs budgeted for that same work. It can be applied at the level of individual tasks or complete work packages and the data are usually rolled up for the whole project. The procedure uses the results to produce a cost performance index. If everything is going exactly according to plan the cost performance index will be 1.0. An index less than 1.0 indicates that the value earned for the money being spent is less than that expected.

Importance Of WBS

The first stage in establishing an effective procedure for assessing achievement is to decide which work elements are to be subjected to measurement, analysis, and reporting. In fact, this choice should be clear; the work packages from the project work breakdown, together with their cost estimates or budgets must provide the framework. It is important to carry this breakdown through to the level of activities performed by individual departments or work groups, so that each responsible manager or supervisor can be given quantified objectives that can be monitored by the earned value process.

Earned Value Nomenclature And Definitions

The following are a few of the names and abbreviations used in earned value analysis. The list is not complete but includes the most commonly used quantities.

Abbreviation	What it means
ACWP	Actual Cost of the Work Performed at the measurement date.
BCWP	Budgeted Cost of Work Performed—this is the amount of money or labor time that the amount of work actually

	performed at the measurement date should have cost to be in line with the budget or cost estimate. It is usually necessary to take into account work that is in progress in addition to tasks actually completed.
BCWS	Budgeted Cost of Work Scheduled—this is the budget or cost estimate for work scheduled to be complete at the measurement date. It corresponds with the time-scaled budget.
CPI	Cost Performance Index—this factor indicates the measure of success in achieving results against budget. Anything less than unity indicates that the value earned from money spent is less than that intended.
SPI	Schedule Performance Index—this can be used as a measure of progress performance against plan, but is less commonly used than the CPI. Anything less than unity shows progress slower than that planned.

These quantities can be used in the following expressions:

$$CPI = \frac{BCWP}{ACWP}$$

$$SPI = \frac{BCWP}{BCWS}$$

CASE EXAMPLE: USING EARNED VALUE ANALYSIS ON A PROJECT TO RENEW PERIMETER FENCING AT AN AIRPORT

For this example of earned value analysis we have chosen a project comprising one main activity for which progress can be measured quantitatively without difficulty or ambiguity.

The perimeter of an airport has been safeguarded for many years by a chain link fence some 8 feet high but, in view of the need for better security following the terrorist atrocities of 9/11, the airport authority has decided to install electronic sensors around the perimeter and to replace the old rusting fence with a new heavier gauge fence, topped with razor wire.

Two different subcontractors have been employed. One of these will be responsible for the electronic alarms, which the airport authority is managing as a second, subsequent project. We are concerned here only with the other subcontractor, whose task will be to replace the old fence.

The total length of fencing is about 8.5 miles, which we have approximated to 15 000 yards. The fencing project contract stipulates that the removal of the old fence and installation of the new shall take place continuously, working day and night (with portable gas powered floodlights during the hours of darkness). This is, therefore, almost a single continuous task project. The task will require two work gangs, working in partnership, so that as one gang removes a short section of the old fence, the other gang follows and, immediately, sinks new steel posts and fills the gap. Thus these two gangs will follow each other around the airport perimeter until the whole 15 000 yards of fence have been renewed and improved. Continuous working will ensure that at no time will unattended gaps be left in the fence that could threaten airport security. The scope, budget, and schedule for this fencing project have been defined by the following data:

- total length of fencing to be renewed is 15 000 yards;
- estimated contractor's cost of labor and materials before mark-up for profit is $750 000;
- time allowed for the project from the first working day at the airport site is 200 days (which is about 6.6 months);
- the rate of progress is expected to be uninterrupted and linear.

When the above data are considered, the following additional facts emerge:

- budget cost per day = $750 000 divided by 200, which is $3750 per day;
- planned rate of building = 15 000 yards divided by 200, which is 75 yards per day;
- the budget cost for each yard of fence is $750 000 divided by 15 000, which is $50 per yard.

At the end of the second month, on day 35, the project manager has been asked to carry out an earned value analysis. The planned progress for the end of day 35, at a scheduled 75 yards per day, should mean that 2625 yards have been completed.

Now suppose that the fencing contractor and their quantity surveyor report the following measured performance data:

- length of fence completed at day 35 is 2250 yards;
- contractor's costs for those 2250 yards has been $120 000.

Earned Value Analysis Of The Airport Fencing Renewal Project

From the project schedule, the project budget, and the measurements at day 35 we can deduce the following data for the purposes of earned value analysis:

- the ACWP is $120 000;
- the BCWP is $(2250 x 50) = $112 500;
- at day 35 the scheduled amount of work is 75 x 35 which is 2625 yards;
- the BCWS would be $(2625 x 50) = $131 250.

Now we can substitute these values in the earned value formulae to derive the cost and schedule performance indices, as follows.

Cost performance   The cost implications of these data can be analyzed using earned value analysis as follows:

$$\text{The cost performance index (CPI)} = \frac{\text{BCWP}}{\text{ACWP}} = \frac{112\,500}{120\,000} = 0.9375$$

The implication of this for final project cost can be viewed in at least two ways:

1. We could divide the original estimate of $750 000 by the cost performance index of 0.9375 and say that the predicted total project cost has risen to $800 000, which gives a predicted forecast cost overspend (variance) of $50 000 for the project at completion.
2. Alternatively, we can say that $120 000 has been spent to date to build 2250 yards of fence, so that each yard is actually costing $53.33. Thus the total 15 000 yards, if this level of performance continues, will cost $(53.33 x 15 000) which is $799 950, or a predicted overspend at completion of $49 950.

The apparent $50 difference in these results occurs because we expressed the actual cost of $53.33 in the second calculation to only two decimal places.

Schedule performance   Earned value data can be used to predict the likely completion date for an activity or a project, although a straightforward comparison of progress against the plan is probably an easier and more effective method. If the earned value method is used, the first step is to calculate the schedule performance index. For the airport fence at day 35 the SPI is found by:

$$SPI = \frac{BCWP}{BCWS} = \frac{112\ 500}{131\ 250} = 0.86$$

The original estimate for the duration of this project was 200 days. Dividing by the SPI gives a revised total project duration of about 233 days. So if this work continues at the present rate, the project can be expected to finish about 33 days late.

Methods For Assessing Progress In Earned Value Calculations

Most earned value analysis must be performed not just on one activity, as in the airport fence project just described, but on many project activities. At any given measurement time in a large project, three stages of progress can apply to all the activities. These stages are as follows:

1. Activity not started—earned value is therefore zero.
2. Activity completed—earned value is therefore equal to the activity's cost estimate or budget.
3. Activity in progress or interrupted—for construction projects, as in the case of the airport fence project, earned value for work in progress can often be assessed by measuring actual quantities of work done. For other, less tangible tasks, it is necessary to estimate the proportion or percentage of work done, and then take the same proportion of the current authorized cost estimate as the actual value of work performed.

Earned Value Analysis Prediction Reliability And Implications

Early predictions of final costs always tend to be unreliable. There are at least four principal reasons for this:

1. Estimates of progress, or of work remaining to completion are usually only judgements, and people tend to err on the side of optimism.
2. During the first few weeks or even months of a large project, the sample of work analyzed in earned value calculations is too small to produce valid indications of later trends.
3. There is no guarantee that the performance levels early in a project, even when they have been accurately assessed, will remain at those same levels throughout the remainder of the project.
4. Although many activities, especially in design, might be declared as 100 per cent completed, it is inevitable that further work will be needed when questions arise as drawings and specifications are put to use in manufacturing or construction. It is quite likely that some drawings will have to be reissued with corrections or modifications. Unless due allowance has been made elsewhere for this 'after issue' work, the project budget might eventually be exceeded.

Now it is time to introduce some words of severe caution concerning all earned value analysis methods. The first point to note is that these calculations are usually based not on concrete facts, but upon estimated progress. Whilst some tasks are capable of being judged according to physical measurement of work actually done, many other tasks are not and estimated progress can only be a matter for judgement, which will not always be accurate.

Earned value analysis performed soon after the beginning of a project can throw up some very spurious results because the quantity of work sampled is too small, in statistical terms.

Some people without scientific or statistical training are not familiar with the rule that any mathematical result should not be expressed to more places of decimals, or to more significant figures than the input data accuracy justifies. Thus to declare that a project will be overspent on its original budget of $1m dollars by $50.35 would be plain daft, but we have both seen similar gaffes.

The earned value analysis method depends on good communications and upon everyone responsible supplying progress and cost data when required. It can be incredibly difficult to arrange that every project participant supplies data in time for each scheduled recalculation of earned value.

The project support office is often a good home for managing earned value analysis, and its staff should be able to assist in solving the communications problem by issuing reminders and pursuing defaulters to gather in every last bit of data required.

It sometimes happens that a task incurs expenditure before any progress is made. If expenditure of only one dollar is reported for a task with zero performance, the cost performance index for that task is zero. Then the computer will predict the final cost of that task (and therefore of the entire project) as infinity, unless the software is particularly 'intelligent'.

Earned value analysis is labor intensive. It involves input from many people, most of whom are fairly senior and earn significant salaries. It therefore comes at a cost. And that cost does not add value to the project.

WHAT IF THE EARNED VALUE ANALYSIS PREDICTION IS BAD?

Suppose the cost performance index is less than the ideal value of 1.0 or that the schedule performance is similarly less than unity. The first thing to be noted is that the project manager should be grateful to this method for producing the earliest possible warning. Escape may be possible even from an apparently hopeless situation, provided that suitable action can be taken in time.

Stricter control of modifications should help to curb unnecessary expenditure and conserve budgets. While changes requested by a customer will be paid for, and so should augment the budget, all other requests for changes must be thoroughly scrutinized before authorization. Only essential unfunded changes should be allowed. Change control, a very important aspect of project management, was described in Chapter 11.

In the face of vanishing budgets, the demands made on individuals will have to be more stringent, but this can only be achieved through good communications, by letting all the participants know what the position is, what is expected of them, and why. It is important to gain their full cooperation. The project manager will find this easiest to achieve within a project team organization. If a matrix organization exists, the project manager must work through all the departmental managers involved to achieve good communications and motivation.

The performance of individuals can often be improved considerably by setting short- and medium-term goals or objectives. These must always be quantifiable, so that the results can be measured objectively, removing any question of favoritism or bias in performance assessment, and helping each individual to monitor their own performance.

In the project context, these personal objectives must be equated (by means of the WBS) with the objectives of time, cost, and performance for the project as a whole. The three objectives go hand-in-hand and, if work is done on time, the cost objective should be met. Although all the objectives should have been set at the start of a project, they can be reviewed if things are going wrong and budgets appear to be at risk. However, care must be taken not to set objectives that cannot possibly be met.

If, in spite of all efforts, a serious overspend still threatens, there remains the possibility of replenishing the project coffers from their original source—the customer. This feat can sometimes be accomplished by reopening the fixed-price negotiation whenever a suitable opportunity presents itself. An excuse to renegotiate may be provided, for example, if the customer should ask for a substantial change, or as a result of economic factors that are beyond the contractor's control. Failing this step, smaller modifications or project spares can be priced generously to offset the areas of loss or low profitability. Care must also be taken to ensure that every item that the contract allows to be charged as an expense to the customer is so charged.

Remember that, without earned value analysis, forewarning of possible overspending may not be received in time to allow any corrective action at all. The project manager must always be examining cost trends, rather than simple historical cost reports. When the predictions are bad, despair is the wrong philosophy. It is far better to carry out a careful reappraisal of the remaining project activities and explore all possible avenues that might lead to a restoration of the original financial targets.

EFFECT OF PROJECT CHANGES ON EARNED VALUE ANALYSIS

Every change introduced into a project can be expected to have some effect on the level of achievement attained by the departments involved. Before this effect can be measured, one significant question must always be answered, namely: can the customer be held liable for any additional costs, or must the additional work be paid for out of the existing budget (and, therefore, out of the potential profits)?

Control of project changes was dealt with in Chapter 11. It can be assumed that, long before any modification reaches the stage of implementation, the change committee or other designated authority will have ensured that every approved change is clearly defined as 'customer funded' or 'unfunded'.

Unfunded Changes

Each unfunded change will affect the total workload remaining, usually with no corresponding change to the authorized budgets. In most cases changes increase the remaining workload, so that the proportion of earned value achieved is depressed in all the departments affected.

It should be possible to make an appropriate correction to the achievement measurement for each department to allow for unfunded changes. Each modification would have to be added to the project task list or WBS, along with a cost estimate for the additional work needed. Change costs are, however, often extremely difficult to estimate and record, because of the way in which the work is intermingled with the original task affected.

There can, of course, be no corresponding increase in the authorized budget. But for practical purposes, such adjustments are unnecessary, and unfunded modifications can be ignored provided that:

- they are not too numerous or horrendous;
- they do not cancel out work already reported as achieved.

Work on unfunded modifications will therefore show up as apparent overspending—which is of course exactly what it is. Earned value predictions will be self-correcting as these overspends are picked up, even if they are not immediately identifiable as being expressly due to unfunded modifications.

Completed work rendered void by unfunded changes   Unfunded changes that nullify work already carried out must always be taken into account by erasure of the relevant earned value elements from the records. This should be done for every department affected, and either whole tasks or parts of them may have to be reinstated into the remaining workload. In this way, the earned value calculations can be kept on a true course.

Customer-Funded Changes

Funded changes can be considered as new tasks, for addition both to the task list and its authorized budgets. The customer should be asked to pay for any work which is scrapped as a result of the change, in which case that work can be considered as having been sold and, therefore, achieved. It need not be subtracted from the achievement tally.

PREDICTING PROFITABILITY FOR A WHOLE PROJECT

Once a basis has been established for the collection of earned value statistics from all parts of the project organization, it is a logical and progressive step to put all these results together into a composite prediction of total project costs.

Of course, the first such prediction is that made before the start of the project, when the initial cost estimates and budgets are prepared and when progress can confidently be declared as zero.

Subsequent analysis and cost predictions can be regarded as a continuous process by which the original estimate is steadily refined. As more work is completed, the total estimate to completion contains an increasing proportion of actual cost data, so that the predictions should become more accurate.

For cost-control purposes, it is necessary that these data are presented in a way that shows unwanted trends as early as possible, before it becomes too late for anything to be done.

Graphical Prediction Method

Cost predictions can be plotted on a graph against project time for direct comparison with the budget, so that any upward or downward trends can be seen clearly and early.

Before the cost data for all the various departments or groups can be brought together and combined with the cost of purchased equipment and materials, they must all be expressed in terms of one common denominator, which must be the control currency for the project. The labor-hour units that were appropriate for scheduling and supervisory control must now be converted into costs, using the appropriate rate for each labor grade. The labor-hour records must, however, be kept because these will provide the stable and reliable yardsticks (unaffected by cost inflation) when comparative cost estimates for future projects are made.

Cost monitoring and prediction are aimed primarily at containing costs within budgets but, when a project has been sold commercially for profit, the profit becomes the end objective. Accordingly, the final prediction graphs should relate the cost and budget levels to the effective net selling price. Both the targeted and predicted gross margins will be displayed so that, as time passes, a wary eye can be kept on the likely outcome. The budget and price levels will have to be readjusted whenever a variation order or other change is introduced that affects the contract price.

Figure 13.4 shows the type of curves that can result from the regular plotting of cost predictions for the whole project. This contains the following two curves:

1. A curve of cumulative recorded expenditure for the whole project, plotted at 4-weekly intervals. The materials and bought-out equipment costs have been included at the

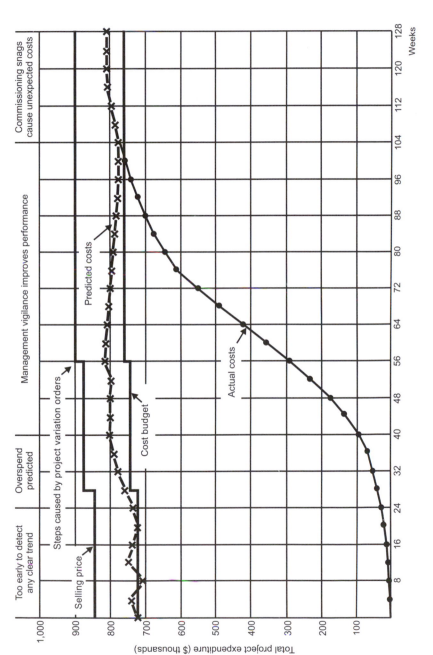

A graph of predicted costs based on earned value analysis gives early warning of possible overspending. It is more valuable than a simple curve of actual costs.

Figure 13.4   A cost/profit prediction graph

time of commitment, and not at the time of invoice payment (which would be too late for control purposes).
2. A curve showing the final cost prediction from earned value analysis calculations made at 4-weekly intervals.

In this example, the project has been finished. It is possible to recapture some of the sense of occasion that would have existed during the active stages of the project by placing a piece of card over the diagram and moving it from left to right to expose the graphs in 4-weekly steps.

The first point plotted on the prediction graph, taken at zero project time, is the initial prediction for project expenditure before it has been influenced by actual experience. In other words, this is the original estimate and budget taken straight from the total task list and work breakdown.

The next three or four points on the prediction graph display rather startling variations because they are based, in statistical parlance, on samples that are too small. These early results also contain a high proportion of assessed progress rather than activities that have definitely been completed. As time proceeds and the tally of completed work begins to mount up it is not very long before a more consistent trend shows so that, after a few months, the results carry sufficient weight to be taken seriously in determining any need for corrective action.

At about the 24th week, a fairly consistent overspending condition begins to show. Any manager faced with the prospect of overrunning budgets must take some action, and a degree of success in holding down the rate of expenditure was obviously gained in this case. The rate of overspending is seen to decline, to be followed by a long period in which the cost performance steadily improves.

In most projects a danger exists that expenditure will not be cut off immediately when the last scheduled task has been finished. Clean-up operations, other finishing jobs, drawing corrections, and commissioning problems are all possible causes of last-minute additions to costs. Sometimes feverish activity takes place during the final phases of a project in order to get it finished on time, and this too can give rise to unexpected expenditure. Something of this nature has obviously happened over the last weeks of the project in Figure 13.4.

Now compare the graph showing predicted expenditure with that drawn to record actual costs. The curve of actual costs is cumulative, showing the total build-up of costs rather than just the costs incurred during each period of measurement. Notice how much more information can be gleaned from one glance at the prediction curve than can be derived from the cumulative cost curve, especially during the early and middle parts of the project. The overspending danger is simply not shown up at all by the actual cost curve until very late in the project, at which time it is far too late to take any corrective action.

Spreadsheet Presentation

Project cost summaries and predictions are commonly presented in tabular or spreadsheet form. Figure 13.5 shows a widely used arrangement, suitable for preparation from purely clerical methods or from computer systems. Tables such as this are typically bound into regular cost and progress reports, often produced at monthly intervals. A description of this format on a column-by-column basis will serve to round off this chapter with a reiteration of the principles embodied in the interpretation of cost and progress data. The spreadsheet columns have been labeled A, B, C, and so on, for ease of reference.

The report form is headed with the project title and project number information. The report date is important, being the effective common reference date for all measurements and progress assessments.

The time lag between the effective report date and the actual report issue date depends on the size and complexity of the project to a great extent: it obviously takes more time to collect results from a project spread over a large, geographically scattered organization than it would where the whole project is conducted within one office or factory. Nevertheless, all possible steps must be taken to produce these reports before they become outdated and too late to provoke constructive management response.

Column A lists the main work packages from the project work breakdown. This list must include all cost items, including software tasks and summarized miscellaneous items. If more detail is required, this can be provided on back-up sheets.

Column B gives the cost code for every item. This makes it easier to refer back to the original estimates and budgets and to audit the data presented.

In column C the original budgets for the work packages are shown, and these add up to the total original project budget at the foot of the column. This is the cost budget originally authorized and approved, which should be equal to the original cost estimates. Consideration must be given to the inclusion or otherwise of escalation and other below-the-line estimates, and it may be necessary to add explanatory notes in the accompanying report text.

As the project proceeds, it can be expected that a number of variations or modifications will arise that are agreed with the client, and for which the client will pay. These must

Project cost report summary   Page   of

Project title: Project number: Report date:

A Item	B Cost code	C Original budget	D Authorized budget changes	E Authorized current budget	F ACWP	G BCWP (assessed)	H CPI	J Forecast costs remaining (E-G)/H	K Forecast costs at completion F+J	L Forecast variance at completion E-K

A tabular project report that uses earned value analysis to forecast costs remaining to completion.

Figure 13.5   **A tabulated project cost report**

obviously increase both the project revenue and the budget. Budget increments from this cause are listed in column D. These, when added to the original budget for each project section, give the current revised authorized budgets, in column E (the current budget).

In any project of significant size there are usually variations under consideration or awaiting approval that could ultimately affect the budget (and progress assessment). Until such variations have been agreed with the client it is obviously not possible to take the additional revenue for granted. It may, nevertheless, be of considerable interest to know the value of any such proposals which happen to be 'in the pipeline' at the report date. Although not shown in the example of Figure 13.5, a column can be included in the report layout, if desired, to give this advance information.

Column F lists the costs actually recorded as at the report date. These comprise the ACWP and include the following:

- all labor-hours booked to the project (on timesheets or job tickets) converted at standard cost or other appropriate rates into the project control currency;
- overheads and administrative costs;
- payments for directly relevant insurance premiums, licences, legal fees, and consultants' fees;
- payments made to, or legitimately claimed by, subcontractors;
- the cost of all materials committed, which includes the cost of all materials and equipment already used or delivered, plus the value of all other materials and equipment for which orders have been placed at the report date. In all cases freight, packing, insurance, agents' fees, and duties paid or committed must be included;
- any other costs incurred or committed up to the report date than can be directly attributed to the project.

Column G is obtained as a result of earned value analysis using the methods described earlier in this chapter. It shows the assessed earned value of all project work performed at the report date.

In column H the cost performance index has been calculated from the data in columns F and G. If the CPI is shown on an item-by-item basis, as here, any variation between the different work packages might be useful management information.

Column J forecasts the costs remaining to completion, obtained by factoring estimates for work remaining by the cost performance index.

Column K indicates the best prediction possible of the final, total project costs at completion. As time passes, the forecast element of this figure will become less, the proportion of actual costs will become greater, and the final prediction will grow more accurate.

The final column, L, highlights any variances between the authorized budgets and the predicted final costs.

POST MORTEM

When the project is finished and the final costs become known, an investigation can be conducted to compare the actual expenditure with the original estimates. Such post-mortem examinations are obviously far too late to be of benefit to the completed project, but they can be helpful in pointing out mistakes to be avoided when estimating or conducting future projects.

14

Project Closure and Post-Project Activities

Project management activities do not usually end abruptly when all the tasks on the plan have been performed successfully. A number of loose but important ends need to be tied up in a process which some people call 'closeout'.

REASONS FOR CLOSING A PROJECT

The most usual reason for closing any project is that the project has been finished and handed over to the project investor or owner—we hope with all the objectives fulfilled. But projects do not always end successfully and there are a number of reasons why projects are occasionally interrupted or abandoned before their intended finish date. Here are a few of the many possible reasons for stopping work on a project before it has been carried through to meet its planned objectives:

- The project contractor has run out of funds and gone into liquidation, leaving the owner to find a new contractor.
- The project owner has permanently run out of funds, killing the project.
- The project owner wishes to make fundamental changes, causing the project to be scrapped and restarted.
- Changed economic or political conditions mean that the project will no longer be financially viable for the owner in the foreseeable future (for example, a fall in the world price for a commodity).
- The customer asks for the project to be 'put on hold' (delayed indefinitely) pending a possible improvement in market conditions or to await the results of a reappraisal.
- Government policy changes (possible for many reasons) result in the termination of some government contracts. Defense contracts for weapons systems, ships, and aircraft are always subject to such risks and there have been many examples of cancelled projects in the aviation industry.
- An Act of God (flood, tempest, earthquake, volcanic eruption, and so on) has intervened, causing further work on the project to be suspended or abandoned.
- Hostile activities in an internal or international conflict make further work on the project impossible.

Whatever the reason for closing a project, the administrative procedures are usually important for a number of reasons that will become apparent as this chapter progresses.

FORMAL PROJECT CLOSURE ANNOUNCEMENT

Just as it was necessary to issue a formal document of authority to open a project and allow expenditure to begin, so the successful end of a project, or its significant interruption or termination, must be marked by a formal announcement that stops further expenditure and sets the formal closure procedures in motion.

Cost Cut-Off

The most significant reason for issuing a formal project closure statement is to forbid further expenditure against the main project cost accounts. This is particularly important if hard-won profits at the end of a successful project are not to be eroded by an insidious continuation of timesheet bookings to the project simply because the account still happens to be open.

It is well known that the recording of labor-hours on timesheets is open to abuse. There is always a tendency for the less scrupulous staff to try and 'lose' unaccountable or wasted time by booking it on their timesheets to large projects where, it is hoped, it will go unnoticed. Good supervision will minimize this risk, but an instruction to the computer to reject all further timesheet entries against the project number is more effective.

Company accountants may wish to hold a project account open for their own use beyond the official project closure date to collect a few 'tail-end' costs. Although labor time bookings are banned after the closure date, there are usually cost items such as late invoices from suppliers and subcontractors to be accounted for. On a large project some final suppliers' invoices can arrive several months after project closure. They can represent considerable sums, but they should not affect the calculated profit significantly because (unless there has been exceptionally loose control of subcontracts and miscellaneous works) these costs should have been known and accrued in the accounts when they were committed (that is, when the purchase orders or subcontracts were issued).

Project Closure Document

The formal closure notice need only be a very simple form, but it should contain the following information:

- project title;
- project number;
- the effective closure date;
- reason for closure;
- any special instructions;
- signature authorizing the closure;
- distribution, which should at least include all those who received the authorization notice when the project was opened.

An example of a fairly comprehensive closure notice for a small aircraft conversion project is given in Figure 14.1.

Notice of project closure

The following project will be closed to time bookings and all expenses with effect from the date given below

Client: **BB Luxury Airlines Inc.**   Project number: **YY1340/25**

Project title: **YY1340 cabin upgrade for BBLA**   Closure date: **30 Apr 2010**

The following budgets are hereby authorized for the closedown activities marked in the checklist below

Department	Labor hours by standard cost staff grade						$
	1	2	3	4	5	6	
Design engineering	10			20	40		7 000
Project support office				10			500
Purchasing			15				800
Installation and commissioning							None
Flight testing	5		5				3 250
Computing				3			150
Records and archives			10		80		10 900
TOTALS	15		30	33	120		22 600

Special instructions:
Take special care with document filing and keep special tooling. Customer indicates a possible further order for 5 more aircraft to this special build standard within 2 years.

CHECKLIST OF PROJECT CLOSURE ACTIVITIES

Project case history	**PM to write, keep it brief**
Project specification	**File revised specification indefinitely**
Project variations	**List and check that the file is complete**
Drawing list	**Keep 10 years in engineering files**
Design calculations	**Keep indefinitely in engineering files**
Our drawings	**Check they are as-built and keep indefinitely**
Client's drawings	**Not applicable to this project**
Purchase control schedules	**Keep 10 years in engineering files**
Suppliers' drawings	**Keep 10 years**
Purchase orders	**Keep 10 years**
Inspection reports	**Keep indefinitely**
Test certificates	**Keep indefinitely**
Operating/maintenance instructions	**Keep indefinitely**
Spares lists	**Keep records for supply to customer if req'd**
Maintenance contracts	**Not applicable—customer's responsibility**
Subcontract documents	**Keep 10 years**
Correspondence files	**Keep 10 years**
Final cost records	**Keep 10 years in general reference files**
Photographs	**Edit. Discuss with publicity dept and client**
Critical path networks	**Destroy after 1 year and erase computer files**
Management information system	**Delete project from MIS at year end**

Prepared by: Project manager: Approved by:
Christina Burns   Lisa Su   *Bradley Rubinstein*

Figure 14.1   **Project closure notice with checklist**

Authorizing Unfunded Post Project Expenditure

Although a guillotine must be imposed on time bookings at project closure, it must be recognized that large projects often leave a backwash of documentation work in their wake. Some of these activities are summarized in this chapter. They may require considerable effort, although much of this can be assigned to clerical and fairly junior engineering staff. Just how well such tasks are performed depends to a large extent upon how much money the contractor is prepared to spend on them. Best practice is to keep all documentation as up to date as possible during the active course of the project, so that updating and filing or archiving at the end of the project requires as little effort as possible.

In most organizations, final project documentation and closedown procedures must be treated as an overhead expense. There are a few project contractors who are more fortunate in having budgets and funding contractually agreed with their customers for these post project tasks, but those projects tend to be confined to projects carried out by professional engineering companies in industries such as mining and petrochemicals. The organization that spends billions of dollars designing and developing a new passenger airplane is unlikely to be so fortunate, yet here is a case when the post-project activities are vital because every aspect of the aircraft's design and development history must be recorded with critical care.

Whether treated as an overhead cost or as a directly recoverable expense, post-project work should be regarded as a work package in its own right, separately identifiable from the main project. The most prudent approach is to close the main project, and then open a new 'closure project' with specified budgets and clear instructions to ensure that vital shutdown activities are performed on time, without fail, but at minimum cost. Giving the closedown work its own special project name and number means that it should be relatively easy to monitor and control. One safeguard is to limit authorization to a few named individuals, so that only timesheet bookings by staff with the specified names or staff numbers will be accepted by the computer for bookings against the closure project account.

The project closure form illustrated in Figure 14.1 acts as an authorization document for a limited amount of expenditure on the post-project work package. Clearly this example would need modification in practice to suit each contractor's own project circumstances and management systems. It does, however, demonstrate a method that can help to ensure the orderly closedown of a project. The version in Figure 14.1 states the budgets allowed. It also includes a checklist of all the final project activities, together with some management directives regarding the disposal of documents.

POST-PROJECT SERVICES TO THE CUSTOMER

Most sales contracts include terms granting some kind of redress to the customer should the goods supplied prove to be faulty. That, of course, is of little comfort to the buyer of an aircraft that subsequently 'goes in' with all souls on board as a result of a design or manufacturing fault. Fortunately, however, most claims on manufacturers' financial or technical resources after product delivery are far less severe or tragic.

A company that manufactures aircraft will have to provide advice and formal written instructions to all its customers, and to those who purchase or lease its products at second or third hand, so that the aircraft can be correctly serviced and maintained. This means that the manufacturer must always have available a library of maintenance instruction manuals, recommended spares lists, and similar documents including records for the servicing and maintenance of the airframe, the engines, the landing gear and tires, the avionics, and all other important components.

Flight training manuals and the provision of flight simulators will probably be required so that aircrews can be trained not only when the aircraft in question are brand new, but for the whole of their serviceable life.

Post-project services also, unfortunately, involved sometimes when it is necessary for an aviation company to give information to accident investigation authorities. In those cases it might be necessary to track back to documents such as design calculations, and the whole history or development of an aircraft including any modifications or manufacturing concessions concerning a particular airplane. This subject of traceability was described in Chapter 11 in the context of managing modifications and changes, and it is when the initial development project is closed down that particular attention must be given to the archiving of all these important documents.

FINAL PROJECT COST RECORDS

Final cost accounting information provides an important databank from which comparative cost estimates can be made for future projects. This is especially true of the labor-hour records. Costs for materials and purchased equipment and the monetary conversion of labor-hours into wages plus overheads are not quite so useful because these records become invalidated by cost inflation as time passes.

Those needing to retrieve information from any of these records will find their task made immeasurably easier if all the data have been filed under a logical and standard cost-coding system which has been rigidly applied across all projects. The best cost coding systems tie in with the standard system of coding for work breakdown structures.

DISPOSAL OF SURPLUS MATERIAL STOCKS

Surplus materials and components often remain upon completion of a project. Sensible consideration must be given to the most cost effective method of their disposal.

Some specialized components may be saleable to customers as part of a recommended holding of spare parts. Other items may be returned to common stock, sold, or (if necessary) scrapped.

Redundant stocks must not be allowed to accumulate because they represent a useless investment in money and space. Space available in manufacturing stores and in general warehouses can become eroded if disposal of post-project materials and components is not managed with determination. It might be argued that quantities of very tiny, low-cost items take up little space and represent insignificant investment ('worth keeping because they might come in useful one day') but even these can cost time and money to store. Remember, also, the unfunded effort required to log and count these useless stocks at each annual stocktaking.

If project materials and components are never going to be used, their value can be expected to dwindle steadily towards their scrap value as they deteriorate or become obsolete. Get rid of them.

AS-BUILT CONDITION OF A PROJECT THAT IS INTERRUPTED BEFORE COMPLETION

This chapter began by listing a few reasons why a project might be closed or put on hold before its successful completion. An as-built record will be particularly important, yet most difficult to achieve, if there is any expectation that the customer will resurrect a cancelled project at a later date. Interrupted projects pose great difficulties, especially if work in progress has reached the stage when materials have been bought or some components are in various stages of manufacture.

A London engineering company was working on a large engineering project for an external customer that was suspended late in its engineering design phase because a change in world economic and market conditions rendered the customer's original business case for the project invalid. However there was a possibility that, if the world economy and market conditions should improve in the future, the project could be restarted from where it had been stopped. Closing and archiving this project became a project in itself, taking many months, employing professional engineers as well as clerks and costing millions of pounds. Although the actual costs of recording the as-built condition of this project were recovered from the customer on a cost-plus basis, the project contractor incurred considerable subsequent cost and space problems in storing the vast quantities of drawings and other engineering data. Incidentally, that project was not restarted and never will be.

Project interruptions usually prove very expensive for the contractor. Even if all the sunk costs are recovered from the customer, it is not easy to estimate the considerable costs of 'mothballing' the project against the day when it might be restarted. Questions might arise about where responsibility lies for storage of partially completed drawings and hardware. Some very difficult contractual negotiations might be needed before a solution is found that is fair to both parties.

MANAGING FILES AND ARCHIVES

The amount of work needed at the end of a project to closedown all the files and store the information safely will be indirectly proportional to the care and attention given to files during the active life of the project. A contractor that has been careless in document control during project execution will pay a higher price for this neglect at the end of the project when the time comes to put adequate records in storage in a form from which any items can easily be retrieved on demand.

Storage

It is very easy to build up substantial files in a very short space of time. These can occupy large areas of expensive office floor. In recent years various technologies have helped to overcome this problem, first through the use of microfilm and, later, through digital storage on a range of media. It seems, however, that paper will never be absent from the office. If bulky documents are a problem, the following options can be considered:

1. Hire off-site space for the storage of non-active files, possibly in a secure repository managed by one of the specialist archive companies. This method has the drawback

that the files can easily be forgotten, the only reminder of their existence being the regular monthly invoices for space rental.

2. Label each file prominently with a review date, at which time the file must be considered for microfilming or scanning before being destroyed.

3. Invest in space-saving filing equipment. Lateral filing cabinets use less space than drawer-type filing cabinets. Motorized rotary files can be purchased which extend upwards into ceiling voids. Anyone who has ridden in a paternoster form of elevator will recognize the principle.

If any method other than hard copy is used (which really means either microfilm or digital storage) adequate safeguards need to be taken to ensure compatibility with existing and future equipment.

Indexing And Retrieval

Finding any document in a large file repository, regardless of the storage medium used, demands that all records are carefully indexed. It should be possible, for instance, to be able to search for an individual letter from a client either by reference to its subject, or by its date, or by both of these. If the storage medium is digital, searching to retrieve information should be easier using keywords.

Security

Records are usually at risk from fire, flood, accidental erasure, or other loss and it is always good sense to consider maintaining a security copy (on the basis that tragedy is unlikely to strike in two places simultaneously). If, however, there should be a fire which consumes the original files, the backup copy will be of less practical use without an index of its contents. An up-to-date copy of the index for the main files must therefore form part of the security files.

The security of computer files is obviously important, but this is a subject that should be familiar to any competent person responsible for computing activities in a company. That person will ensure that regular backup copies are made and held offline in data safes or other secure areas.

Information held in computer files has to be remembered at project closure time. Unwanted files should be erased. While a few unwanted items left on disks may not present a problem, a forgotten set of project management files held on a hard disk (possibly including a large network analysis exercise, drawing schedules, and purchase schedules) is a needless waste of memory. Any such files that are not required as part of an online database should be erased or transferred to some more suitable offline storage a part of the project closure procedure.

RECORDING THE PROJECT MANAGEMENT EXPERIENCES

Case History Or Project Diary

If sufficient time and money can be spared for the purpose, it is useful for the project manager to write a brief case history or diary of the project. This document does not have to be a literary masterpiece. It could be written in the form of a simple chronological list, but it should record every significant event, and list all serious problems that had to be overcome during the project, together with their solutions.

When filed with other key documents (such as the project specification, risk register, minutes of meetings, drawing lists, purchase schedules, change records, and so on) a case history becomes a valuable asset in the future and will be essential if legal or other questions arise about the project. Reference to past case histories may also help when formulating the strategy for new projects. Also, reading about past mistakes can help new managers to avoid repeating them in the future. 'Lessons learned' should, therefore, feature as a main heading in the project diary.

The project diary is a document that can be written by spending a few moments each day as the project journeys through its life cycle.

Compiling Or Updating Checklists

We have stressed the value of checklists throughout this book in the context of a number of project management functions. Every checklist is a repository of experience from past projects. Now the project that we are closing down is about to become another 'past project' that should leave its own legacy in our fund of project management experience. We therefore have to consider whether or not we have gained any new experiences from this most recent project that should be used to augment or correct our existing checklists, or which could provide the basis for compiling one or more new lists.

AVIATION PROJECT MANAGEMENT: A RECAPITULATION

In Chapter 1, we identified four different categories of projects and discussed the life cycle of a typical project. Many project life cycles end with a period when the benefits of the project are realized. For the project contractor, those benefits arrive when the project outcome is sold and passed on to the customer, but in major aircraft development projects it can be as long as 20 years before the aircraft company recovers all its original investment in design and manufacturing costs.

Chapter 2 stressed the need to ensure that anyone embarking on a new project is clear on what the project is about, what their involvement will be (in other words the scope of the project), and on the goals or benefits that the project is intended to deliver. Thus we arrive at the project specification, which must (for investment projects) link into a business plan. Writing this book has been a project, and we have treated, scheduled, and managed it as such. Thus we had to practise what we preach and begin by defining our project. Our initial project specification was documented in a contract made jointly between ourselves and our 'customer', Ashgate Publishing Company.

Chapters 3 and 4 took the preliminary phases of project management farther by estimating the costs and assessing any risks that might pose a threat to successful project completion.

Chapter 5 described the all-important subject of project organization. Recognizing that many project managers are appointed to an existing organization, and can take no part in choosing the organization for their project, we offered some advice to those senior managers who can exercise that power of choice. Summing up, the project organization can be a functional matrix, in which the project manager might be given little power or complete project authority, or the organization can be an autonomous team in which the project manager has supreme power. In general, a matrix is favored for a company that carries out a number of projects simultaneously, and this organization can lend stability to the company's organization. On the other hand, for a single project where high motivation and short communication channels are needed to get the job done, a dedicated team or even a task force is indicated.

In Chapter 6 we gave examples of various work breakdown structures, stressing the need for breaking any large project down into work packages that can be assigned to individual senior supervisors or managers. We noted that for very simple projects a list of tasks would suffice for the work breakdown, but in general a logically structured, hierarchical arrangement is to be preferred that is overlaid with a sensible coding system. The WBS for our book project was determined early in our work by listing all our chapter titles, and the chapter numbers gave us our simple but adequate coding system.

Chapters 7 and 8 were devoted to planning the project timescale and, where the company directly employs project workers or other resources, to scheduling the project resources. We stressed the need to use critical path analysis in preference to simple Gantt charts, because then the slack for every task can be calculated to give the best possible indication of its priority.

The important subject of mobilizing everyone to begin work on the new project was described in Chapter 9, and this was followed in Chapter 10 by the important but often neglected topic of purchasing the materials and components needed to build the project. We noted that the cost of all purchased materials and services can sometimes be as high as 80 per cent of total project expenditure, so that budgeting and controlling purchasing costs is crucial to project cost control, and getting the materials to the project on time is essential to project progress.

Changes to the project specification can delay a project and cause work done to be scrapped and restarted. Generally speaking, the later in the project that a given change occurs, the worse the effect will be. We gave advice on managing project changes, and on the related topics of production permits and concessions, in Chapter 11. Here we also gave emphasis to the particular need in aviation and defense projects for all significant design and modification steps to be documented faithfully in case future airline users or crash investigators needed to track back through the build of a particular aircraft so as to be able to fit the correct replacement parts during maintenance or take steps following an accident or malfunction to trace all similar aircraft and ground them until discovered faults can be rectified.

Although Chapter 12 is called 'Managing Costs', it really deals with the cost accounting procedures of recording what has been spent at any given time on a project and comparing the results with budgets. Earned value analysis and cost reporting measures described in Chapter 13 are simply a refinement of the methods described in Chapter 12. None of these measures is cost control and they actually add costs to a project without adding value. Cost control can only be exercised by taking action, not by taking measurements. That action means following all the project management steps that we recommend. If a project manager can control progress, avoid unnecessary changes and exercise good control over purchasing, the project should finish on time and within budget.

Finally we have arrived at this Chapter 14, in which we have described some of the formalities necessary when a project is closed down.

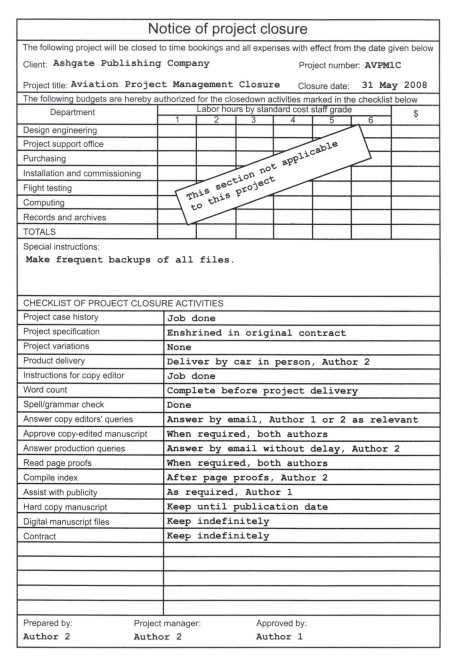

Figure 14.2   Project closure checklist for this book

Coincidentally it is time for use to closedown our writing project and hand over the finished manuscript to our 'customer', Ashgate Publishing. However, as with any typical aviation project, a number of post-project activities remain, and we have (perhaps a little tongue-in-cheek) produced our own project closure notice in which these late tasks are shown. We modeled our closure notice (shown in Figure 14.2) on the format of the version originally shown in Figure 14.1.

Bibliography

Burke, R. (1999), *Project Management: Planning and Control*, 3rd edn, Chichester, Wiley.

Buchanan, D.A. and Huczyinski, A. (2003), *Organizational Behaviour: An Introductory Text*, 5th edn, Hemel Hempstead, FT Prentice-Hall.

Buttrick, R. (2005), *The Project Workout*. 3rd edn, London, FT Prentice Hall.

Chapman, C.B. and Ward, S.A. (2002), *Project Risk Management: Processes, Techniques and Insights*, Chichester, Wiley.

Devaux, S.A. (1999), *Total Project Control: a Manager's Guide to Integrated Planning, Measuring and Tracking*, New York, Wiley (This book is recommended for its common sense approach and especially clear descriptions of the precedence network system).

Fleming, Q.W. and Koppelman, J.M. (2000), *Earned Value Project Management*, 2nd edn, Newtown Square, PA, Project Management Institute.

Gattorna, J.L., (ed.) (2003), *Gower Handbook of Supply Chain Management*, 5th edn, Aldershot, Gower.

Gray, B., Gray, C.F. and Larson, E.W. (2005), *Project Management: The Managerial Process*, 3rd edn, Singapore, McGraw-Hill.

Harrison, F. and Lock, D. (2004), *Advanced Project Management: A Structured Approach*, 4th edn, Aldershot, Gower.

International Chamber of Commerce (2000), *Incoterms 2000*, ICC publication No, 560, Paris, ICC Publishing SA.

Kerzner, H. (2006), *Project Management: A Systems Approach to Planning, Scheduling and Controlling*, 9th edn, New York, Wiley.

Lock, D. (2007), *Project Management*, 9th edn, Aldershot, Gower.

Meredith, J.R. and Mantel, S.J. Jnr. (2003), *Project Management: A Managerial Approach*, 5th edn, New York, Wiley.

Nicholas, J.M. (2004), *Project Management for Business and Engineering*, 2nd edn, Burlington, MA, Elsevier, Butterworth-Heinemann.

PMI (2004), *A Guide to the Project Management Body of Knowledge (PMBOK® Guide)*, 3rd edn, Newtown Square, PA, Project Management Institute.

Rosenau, M.D. Jr. (2005), *Successful Project Management: A Step-by-Step Approach with Practical Examples*, 4th edn, New York, Wiley.

Viccars, P. (2001), *Aviation Insurance: A Plane Man's Guide*, London, Witherby.

Ward, G. (2008), *Project Manager's Guide to Purchasing*, Aldershot, Gower.

Webb, A. (2000), *Project Management for Successful Product Innovation*, Aldershot, Gower.

Webb, A. (2003), *Using Earned Value: A Project Manager's Guide*, Aldershot, Gower.

Webb, A. (2003), *The Project Manager's Guide to Handling Risk*, Aldershot, Gower.

Index